NATAL CHARTING

A complete guide to the technical
foundations of natal astrology.

GW00675088

NATAL CHARTING

How To Master the Techniques of Birth Chart Construction

by

John Filbey D.F. Astrol.S.

THE AQUARIAN PRESS
Wellingborough, Northamptonshire

First published 1981
Fourth Impression 1984

British Library Cataloguing in Publication Data

Filbey, John
   Natal charting.
   1. Horoscopes
   I. Title
   133.5'42   BF1728.A2

   ISBN 0-85030-246-3

Printed and bound in Great Britain

CONTENTS

ACKNOWLEDGEMENTS

I wish to acknowledge, with thanks, the permission given by W. Foulsham and Company to reproduce various pages from their *Raphael's Ephemeris 1980* and from their *Tables of Houses for Northern Latitudes.*

I also acknowledge, with thanks, the permission given by the Director of Publishing, Her Majesty's Stationery Office, to reproduce World Standard Times from the *1980 Nautical Almanac.*

To the Council of The Faculty of Astrological Studies, I extend my thanks for granting permission to use their birth chart forms.

Special thanks are due to P. M. Filbey B.Sc. for his invaluable assistance in compiling the astronomical information, drawing the diagrams, and advising on the presentation of the various calculation tables.

I am also indebted to my wife for her patient efforts in reading the manuscript and for making several constructive suggestions.

Any errors which occur, and I hope they will be few, are solely my responsibility, and I apologize for these in advance.

INTRODUCTION

The purpose of this book is an endeavour to present in a simple manner the fundamental principles underlying the theory and practice of natal chart calculations. The work has been designed to assist those who wish to acquire a reasonable proficiency in calculating natal charts, and also an understanding of the various factors associated with the technical side of astrology.

One does not need to understand the astronomical framework, or the mathematical concepts upon which an astrological chart is constructed. However, it is much more satisfying to know the reasons for the various calculations than to work blindly by 'rule of thumb'.

Unless the natal chart is accurate, all subsequent work involving interpretation and analysis is a wasted effort, because incorrect conclusions will be drawn from the chart, and this in turn will, justifiably, attract criticism—not only of the practitioner, but also of astrology in general. Astrology is a subject which lends itself to all forms of bizarre statements, ideas and opinions, but we can at least ensure that our charts are correct.

Those who study astrology for any length of time will discover that it embodies universal truths, and that it demonstrates that man and nature are subject to celestial influences and to the various cosmic patterns. The principles set out in this book are the first, and essential, step towards that realization.

Astronomy is excellent; but it must come up into life to have its full value, and not remain there in globes and spaces.

Emerson.

The stars, that Nature hung in heaven, and filled their lamps with everlasting oil, to give due light to the misled and lonely traveller.

Milton.

Thence oblique
Brancheth the circle where the planets roll,
To pour their wished influence on the world.

Dante.

1
THE BIRTH CHART: MAP OF THE HEAVENS

Definition

The birth chart, sometimes referred to as the natus, the horoscope, the nativity or the geniture, is a chart or diagram computed for a precise time and place.

This chart is based on astronomical data and shows the position of the Sun, Moon and planets at a specified moment in time as viewed from a definite locality on Earth.

In the computation of a chart two things, apart from the date of birth, are essential. (1) the time of birth, (2) the place of birth. Neither is of much use without the other. Although the planets will be in the same zodiacal signs on a given day for all places on Earth, their mundane positions (house positions) will be different according to the time of day and the place on Earth from which they are viewed.

At noon in London, the Sun will be close to the upper meridian, while at New York it will be just above the horizon (rising). For example, in a place 90° east longitude, the Sun will be setting, and so on round the globe. Hence the importance of knowing the *when* (time) and the *where* (place) that a birth or event occurred. With these two co-ordinates of time and place, a chart can be set up, and this chart will show the 'sky patterns' existing at a particular time and place.

The Scope of the Chart

Astrology is both an art and a science. It is an *art* insofar as the interpretation of the astrological factors demand a wide experience of
astrological symbolism and its relationship to every area of human
experience. The chart indicates the *potentialities* of the individual—which
may manifest in a variety of ways, subject to heredity and environmental
factors.

One cannot forecast the future from the study of an astrological chart.
No reputable astrologer would attempt to predict precisely events and
conditions; what he can do is to determine the periods during a lifetime
when agreeable or discordant conditions are likely to prevail. From his
judgement of the natal chart, he can obtain a very clear indication of the
basic personality traits, and this enables him to discern how a particular
individual will react to a definite set of circumstances. The interpretation of
charts is not something which can be acquired 'overnight', but is a
sustained discipline requiring not only perseverance but also a degree of
intuition, coupled with the ability to assess the astrological factors in a
realistic and empirical manner.

Astrology is a *science* because the interpretation and delineation of its
symbolism is related to astronomical factors and mathematical concepts.
The natal chart is based on an astronomical framework: planets, signs and
houses; and however bizarre the theory of celestial influences may appear
to some, there can be no disputing the scientific basis of the natal chart.

No matter what aspect of astrology you may find interesting, mundane,
psychological, vocational or comparison of charts, the basis rests on a
properly calculated chart. If the chart is incorrectly calculated, then all
subsequent work relating to analysis and assessment is wasted effort. As in
most things, practice gives confidence, and although initially the
computation of a chart may appear difficult, it is in actual fact, a simple task
if dealt with in a methodical manner.

Astrological Arithmetic

The handling of the figure work in natal charting should present no
difficulties if one thinks of what the chart actually represents. Basically, we
are charting astronomical positions for a given time and place and, if we
relate our results to the knowledge we have acquired regarding elementary
astronomy, we will know whether the chart is correct within a reasonable
margin.

For instance, if we chart for a noon birth, we know the Sun must be close
to the midheaven (in the south in the northern hemisphere, in the north in
the southern hemisphere), and if we find that it is elsewhere when we have
completed our charting, then we know that there is an error due to
miscalculation. Likewise, if we find Mercury more than 27 degrees from
the Sun, we know we have erred in extracting its position from the
ephemeris.

Astrological arithmetic, insofar as natal charting is concerned, consists of simple addition and subtraction: one does not need to understand advanced mathematics in order to compute an astrological chart. Certainly, the more advanced techniques of astrology, such as certain forms of progressions, need an understanding of the geometry of the sphere, but for natal charting, the arithmetic is basic.

Fortunately, the astrologer is assisted in his calculations by the use of mathematical tables (such as Tables of Houses), which are ready-made reference tables enabling him to extract the information that he requires regarding the ascending sign and house cusps. The astronomical ephemeris lists all the planetary data that are required to locate the planets and their longitudes.

Charting

Essential Information
In order to set up a chart, certain information is essential, and the more precise this information is, the more accurate the chart will be. A chart can be calculated with inexact data but the interpretation of the astrological factors and particularly the progressions (assessment of future trends) will not be so detailed as with a precisely timed chart. The essential information required can be analyzed under three main headings:

1. *Birth time.* This is probably the most important factor, for it is only by knowing the time of birth that the exact relationship existing between the great circles in the heavens (Ecliptic and House Division) and a location on Earth can be determined.
2. *Date of Birth.* The planets are in constant motion and are changing their respective positions daily, particularly the Moon, which moves rapidly through the zodiacal signs in a short space of time. Each day, the planets form different configurations (aspects) with one another and, although the slower-moving planets remain in one particular sign for many months and sometimes for years, they all have their significance in the overall relationship existing on a particular day.
3. *Birth Place.* Due to the Earth's rotation, all signs of the Zodiac 'pass over the Ascendant', once in 24 hours (except in polar latitudes) and the sign rising and culminating will depend on the latitude of birth. The twelve mundane houses which indicate the mode of expression according to the sign on the cusp, and the planets located within the house, are based upon definite mathematical formulae which indicate how the horizon 'cuts' the Ecliptic, and this intersection of horizon and Ecliptic varies according to the terrestrial latitude of the birth place. The nearer the pole, either north or south, a place may be, the more obliquely are the Equator and Ecliptic cut by the horizon. Hence the need to have separate Tables of Houses for every circle of latitude. However, unless absolute precision is required, a table for a particular

latitude can be used for places on or near that latitude. The London Table of Houses can be used for places between 50-53 degrees north latitude, and those for Liverpool for latitudes between 53-55 degrees north.

So, the three main essentials for natal charting are *time, date* and *place,* and with this information, a chart can be calculated for any place on Earth.

Time of Birth

Regarding the time of birth, you may ask when is the actual time of birth determined? Is it the first cry? Or is it when the cord is severed? Normally it is when the child cries and takes its first independent breath. The chart struck for this moment will be the birth chart and will show the potentialities which may manifest during the life, subject to heredity and the environmental factors.

However, insofar as character analysis is concerned, a slight discrepancy in the recorded time of birth is unimportant, but in the analysis of progressions and the timing of events and conditions, it *is* important, for a few minutes difference in the time of birth will 'throw out' the progressions and their timing to a greater or lesser degree, depending on the margin of error in the recorded time.

Preparing for Chart Calculation

The essential information of time, date and place needs careful verification, and much time and labour can be saved if a few preliminary enquiries are made regarding the authenticity of the birth data.

Firstly, the time must be clearly stated. Is it clock time, Standard Time, Summer Time or what? The average person is not much concerned with the different types of time. To him, the time is as indicated by a clock or timepiece. So normally, if a person quotes a time, it can be assumed that it was the time as indicated by the clock at that particular birth place. Occasionally, people try to be helpful and state the time in a form which they think will help the astrologer. For instance, they may quote the Greenwich time during a period when Daylight Saving Time is in operation, without stating that they have deducted the one hour or so, thereby misinforming the astrologer, who naturally will assume that the time given is the clock time of birth and will deduct another hour from the time given which, in turn, results in an incorrect chart.

Vague statements are also made regarding birth times, such as, 'I was born at tea time', or 'when father returned home from work'. These statements convey very little and, although they may indicate the approximate time of the day when birth occurred, they are of little use for setting up an accurate chart. It is therefore important to obtain the clock time of birth and to make all the necessary adjustments concerning time conversion from this initial data.

The date of birth normally presents no difficulties; most people know their date of birth, even if they do not know the exact time. The only exception to this may be in the case of elderly persons born in countries which were using the Old Style Calendar (see 'Calendar'), and, unless they state quite clearly that the date they are giving is the New Style date, then a conversion from the Old Style to the New Style calendar must be made.

The place of birth is very important and the terrestrial latitude and longitude of the birth place must be obtained from a good gazetteer. Note also that many countries and areas have changed their names during this century, particularly the African countries, and therefore a good reference work is essential for the date and place in question.

The first important task of chart calculation, therefore, is *to obtain, check, and verify the essential data, (time, date and place)*. It is far better to spend time and effort in obtaining this information as precisely as possible, because unless this information is accurate, the natal chart calculations will be wrong and all subsequent work connected with the chart will be in error.

We discussed in broad outlines the definition and scope of a birth chart and the essential information required in order to calculate the chart for a particular time and place. We will now consider the astronomical factors relating to chart calculation. It is not essential that the astronomical basis of astrology is thoroughly understood. A motorist does not need to know how a car engine works in order to drive a car, but he is a better motorist and can avoid many frustrating situations if he has some knowledge of car mechanics. Likewise, the astrological student will be a more knowledgeable person and understand the reasons for his calculations if he has a working knowledge of the astronomical factors upon which the astrological calculations are based.

2.
THE ASTRONOMICAL BASIS (1)
CIRCLES AND PROJECTIONS

The Celestial Sphere

Viewed from the Earth, the sky resembles a vast inverted bowl, and the stars and other heavenly bodies appear to be on the inside of a large sphere with the Earth at the centre. Within this large imaginary globe (the Celestial Sphere) the Earth rotates upon its axis from west to east, and to an observer on Earth, the Celestial Sphere appears to move westward. This apparent movement westward causes the Sun and other bodies to appear to rise east of, and to set west of, the observer's meridian (the imaginary semi-circle that passes through the north and south points of the horizon and the point directly overhead, the zenith, and which divides the sky into eastern and western hemispheres).

Astronomical Co-ordinates

The co-ordinates used in positional astronomy are similar to geographical co-ordinates in as much that the terms poles, horizon, Equator and meridian are used. The great circle which divides the Earth into two hemispheres (north and south) is the *Equator* and measurement along this circle is termed *longitude,* whilst measurement either north or south of the Equator is termed *latitude.*

These two co-ordinates enable any place on Earth to be located. The zero point for measuring longitude is the Greenwich meridian, the measurement being from 0 degrees-180 degrees east or west, whilst latitude is measured from 0 degrees-90 degrees either north or south of the Equator.

Similarly, any object in the heavens can be located if its co-ordinates on the Celestial Sphere are known. The celestial equivalents of terrestrial longitude and latitude are termed *Right Ascension* and *Declination* respectively, and these co-ordinates enable astronomers to,'fix' a celestial body or point. The frame of reference for astronomical measurements is the *Celestial Equator* which is the Earth's Equator projected onto the Celestial Sphere. This Celestial Equator has as its poles the *Celestial Poles,* which are the poles of rotation of the Celestial Sphere and are directly overhead at the terrestrial poles. In the northern hemisphere, it appears as though the heavens are rotating around a single point which is the *North Celestial Pole,* and the Earth's rotational axis extended into space points towards the Pole Star (Polaris).

An observer's view of the heavens is governed by his movements along the Earth's surface and the latitude from which the observations are made. The *altitude* (the angular distance above the horizon) of the north pole is equal to the observer's latitude. At the north pole of the Earth, the Celestial Pole is directly overhead, and all the visible stars will appear to circle around the Celestial Pole and remain above the horizon. As one proceeds south, the Celestial Pole is no longer overhead, but moves closer to the horizon, and at the terrestrial Equator, where the Celestial Equator extends from the east point through the zenith to the west point, the Celestial Poles

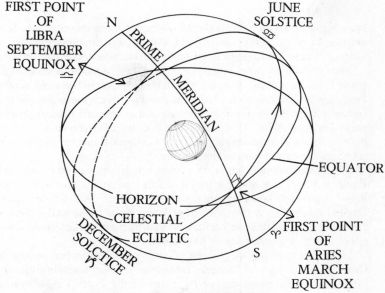

Figure 1. The Celestial Sphere.

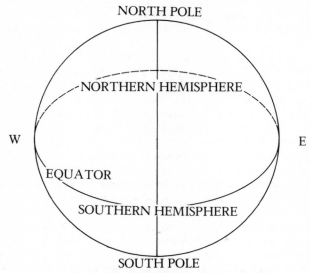

Figure 2. Hemispheres of the Earth.

The great circle of the Equator is midway between the two poles and divides the earth into the Northern and Southern Hemispheres. The Celestial Equator is the Earth's equator projected onto the celestial sphere and its intersections with the Ecliptic (Sun's apparent path) denote the Equinoctial points, First Point of Aries and the First Point of Libra.

are on the north and south points of the horizon. In other words, the latitude of the observer determines the amount of elevation that the Celestial Poles and Equator have above the horizon.

The Celestial Equator (otherwise termed the *Equinoctial*) has as its zero point *'The First Point of Aries'* (Vernal Equinox). In the same way that longitude on Earth is measured from the Greenwich meridian, measurements of Right Ascension along the Celestial Equator are made from a fixed point 0 degrees Aries. This point is like a 'Celestial Greenwich', and is the *point of intersection* at any moment of the celestial Equator and the *Ecliptic* (the Sun's apparent path in the heavens).

The measurement of Right Ascension which is made eastward from the Equinox (First Point of Aries) is in hours and minutes of time, each hour of Right Ascension being equivalent to 15 degrees (360 divided by 24). Declination, which is the other co-ordinate of the Equatorial system and corresponds to latitude on Earth, is measured from the Celestial Equator, either north or south, from 0-90 degrees.

The Ecliptic, which we will discuss in greater detail when we consider Celestial Longitude and Latitude, represents the Sun's yearly path, or, in other words, the projection of the plane of the Earth's orbit onto the Celestial Sphere. The Ecliptic, so named, because eclipses can only occur

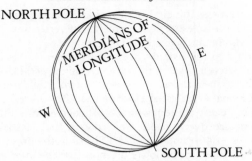

Figure 3. Meridians of Longitude.

The Greenwich meridian marks the zero point (0°) longitude, and it is from this zero meridian that longitude is reckoned up to 180° east and west. Each degree of longitude is equivalent to 4 minutes of time (15° = 1 hour), and, as the Earth rotates 360° in 24 hours, each hour corresponds to 15° of distance. Places east of Greenwich will have a time that is 'fast', while those west of Greenwich will have a time that is 'slow' as compared with Greenwich Mean Time. When it is noon G.M.T., the time in a place 15° east will be 1 p.m., while in a place 15° west, the time will be 11 a.m. A place 120° west will have a time that is 8 hours slow compared with Greenwich ($\frac{120}{15}$), and so on around the globe.

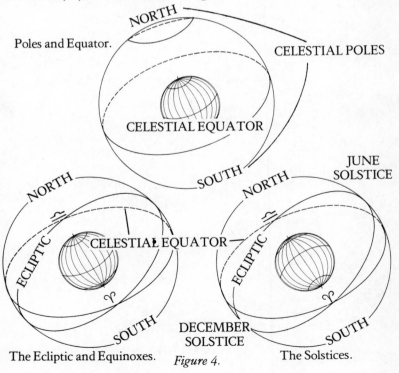

Figure 4.

when the Moon crosses this circle, is a very important great circle, and its intersection with the Celestial Equator marks the zero point (First Point of Aries) for measurements of Celestial Longitude.

When we refer to the *horizon,* we usually mean the visible horizon, which is a small circle formed by the apparent joining of Earth and sky, and which is parallel to the *Rational Horizon.* The two should not be confused for it is the Rational or Celestial Horizon (which is a great circle on the Celestial Sphere), every point of which is 90 degrees from the observer's zenith (the point directly overhead), which divides the Celestial Sphere into two hemispheres—upper and lower. All bodies in the upper hemisphere are visible, while those in the lower are not. It is the intersection of the eastern point of the horizon with the Ecliptic that determines the degree rising (Ascendant) for a particular time and place. All great circles passing through the observer's zenith are perpendicular to the Celestial or Rational Horizon and are termed *vertical circles.*

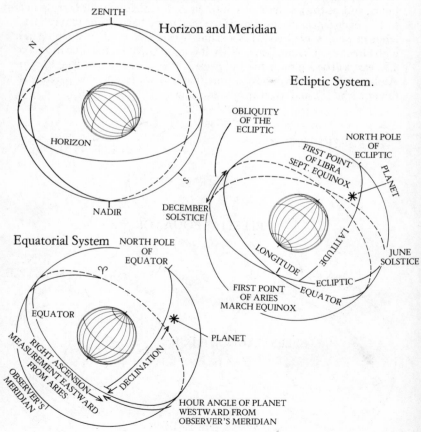

Figure 5.

The Prime Vertical is that vertical circle which passes through the east and west points of the horizon, the zenith and nadir (the point directly opposite the zenith). All other vertical circles, which also pass through the zenith and nadir, do not pass through the east and west points of the horizon. The plane of the Prime Vertical corresponds to the points of intersection of the horizon and Equator.

To an observer on Earth, the great circle on the Earth's surface which runs perpendicular to the Equator and passes through the north and south poles is the *meridian* and represents his north-south line. For the purposes of astronomical position and time measurement, the meridian is projected onto the Celestial Sphere and termed *the Celestial Meridian*. This great circle corresponds to the observer's meridian of longitude on Earth. As the Earth rotates, the observer and his Celestial Meridian are carried toward the east, resulting in the stars appearing to shift westward and cross or transit the Celestial Meridian. Meridian transits are important as they form the basis for the measurement of time which we shall discuss later on.

In astrological charting, we are not directly concerned with the Equatorial co-ordinates of Right Ascension and Declination, but with the Ecliptic co-ordinates—*Celestial Longitude* and *Latitude*. Celestial Longitude is the angular distance along the Ecliptic and is measured eastward from the First Point of Aries in degrees and minutes of arc. Celestial Latitude is the angular distance between the Ecliptic and a celestial body measured in degrees and minutes either north or south of the Ecliptic. Remember not to confuse it with terrestrial latitude, which is of course measured from the Earth's Equator.

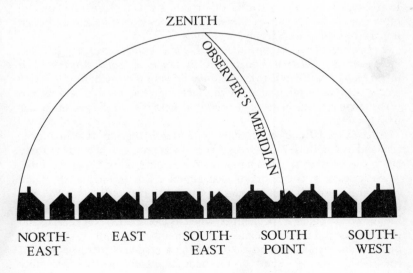

Figure 6. The Observer's Meridian.

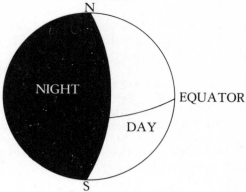

Figure 7.   The Equinoxes.

When the Sun in its apparent path crosses the Celestial Equator at the March and September Equinox, its declination is zero and it is vertically overhead at the Equator. Day and night have equal duration at all places on Earth.

The Ecliptic

The Sun's Path

To an observer on Earth, the Sun appears to rise in the east, crosses the meridian at or about noon when it has reached its greatest altitude, and then declines and sets in the west. In its daily motion across the sky, the Sun keeps to a well-defined path against a background of apparently fixed stars. In reality, of course, it is the Earth's rotation which causes the Sun and other celestial bodies to rise and set, but to an observer it appears as though it is the heavens which revolve around us.

This apparent path of the Sun is the *Ecliptic,* which is a great circle that intersects the Celestial Equator at an angle of 23½ degrees. The inclination of the Ecliptic to the Celestial Equator is termed 'the *Obliquity of the Ecliptic*' and is due to the fact that the Earth's axis is not perpendicular to the plane of its orbit, but departs from the perpendicular by 23½ degrees.

At the Vernal Equinox, on or about 21 March, the Sun's Declination is zero and its longitude is 0 degrees Aries. As it continues its yearly journey along the Ecliptic, its Declination increases until on or about 21 June, when it reaches its maximum Declination 23½ degrees north of the celestial Equator. It then appears to stand still, hence the term *Solstice,* before gradually decreasing in Declination until it reaches the Autumnal Equinox on or about 23 September, when its Declination is again zero and its longitude is 0 degrees Libra. At the September Equinox, it crosses the Equator and its Declination is south, which gradually increases until it reaches 23½ degrees south on or about 22 December—the December Solstice, when its longitude is 0 degrees Capricorn. From this date onward, the Declination decreases until the Sun once more returns to 0 degrees Aries, the Vernal Equinox.

The terms Summer and Winter Solstices are confusing. In the southern hemisphere, the seasons are the reverse to those in the northern hemisphere. When it is Spring or Summer in the northern hemisphere, it is Autumn or Winter in the southern hemisphere, likewise Autumn and Winter in the northern hemisphere correspond to Spring and Summer in the southern hemisphere. Simplicity is required to describe these terms, and it is easier to refer to them as the June or December Solstice, or if we are referring to the Equinoxes, the March or September Equinox.

At the time of the Solstices, on or about 21 June and 22 December, the maximum and minimum periods of daylight are experienced. In the northern hemisphere, long days in June and short days in December; in the southern hemisphere, the position is the reverse—long days in December, short days in June. Within the polar circle (66½°), day and night progressively lengthen until the periods of night and day reach their maximum duration.

Owing to the Obliquity of the Ecliptic, the Sun is above the horizon for different periods of time at different seasons. The tilt of the Earth's axis determines whether the Sun's rays strike at a low angle or more directly. At the June Solstice in London, the more direct rays produce about three times as much heat as the more slanting rays experienced at the December Solstice. The angle of the Sun above the horizon and the length of daylight determine the heat received by any region, hence the differences in seasons in various parts of the world. Within 23½° of the poles, the Sun will remain above the horizon 24 hours a day during some part of the summer, and all places within the Polar Circle experience the phenomena of the 'Midnight Sun'.

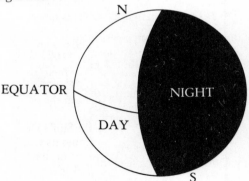

Figure 8. The Solstices.

On or about 21 June and 22 December, the maximum and minimum periods of daylight are experienced: in the northern hemisphere long days in June, short days in December; in the southern hemisphere the position is reversed: short days in June and long days in December. Within the polar circle, day and night progressively lengthen until, at the poles, the periods of night and day reach their maximum duration.

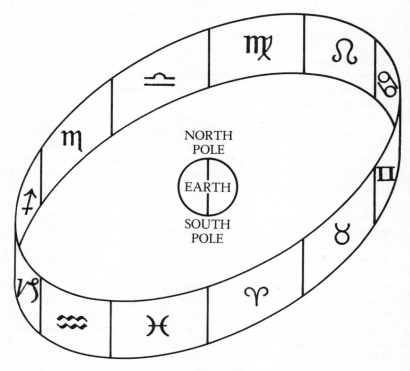

Figure 9. The Zodiac (Circle of Animals).

Within 23½° of the Equator, the Sun is overhead at noon at some time during the summer. In the intermediate latitudes between the Equator and the Poles, the highest point reached by the Sun in summer will be 90° minus the latitude of the place, plus 23½°. Conversely, in midwinter, the low point of the Sun at noon will be 90° minus the latitude, minus 23½°.

When the Sun in its apparent annual path crosses the Celestial Equator at the March and September Equinox, its Declination is zero and it is vertically overhead at the Equator, and day and night have equal duration at all places on earth. As the Sun rises north and south of east at different times of the year, it will during the course of the year rise exactly due east and set due west at least twice, and this occurs at the time of the Equinox (March and September) when its longitude is 0° Aries and Libra respectively.

The Zodiac

On either side of the Ecliptic and extending for approximately 8-9 degrees north and south is a band or belt termed the Zodiac (Circle of Animals), within which the Sun, Moon and planets always remain, except Pluto whose inclination to the Ecliptic is 17 degrees as measured in Celestial Latitude.

This imaginary band is divided into twelve signs of thirty degrees each bearing the names of the constellations, although owing to *Precession,* the signs and constellations no longer coincide. Sun sign astrology columns which appear in daily papers and women's magazines are based solely upon the Sun's zodiacal position and, as the Sun appears to enter a different sign each month, those born in a certain month are attributed with similar characteristics. This popular astrology does little harm, provided the readers are aware that the so-called 'horoscope' given for each sign is no more than a very broad generalization and should be viewed accordingly. It should not be treated seriously, for as we shall see when we commence natal charting, there is much more to astrology than just the sign which contains the Sun.

Precession of the Equinoxes

Precession is caused by the slow movement of the Earth's axis which results in the Celestial Poles and the Equator appearing to move against the background of the stars. This gradual shift of the Equinoctial Points along the Ecliptic is a westward movement at the rate of 50 seconds per year and, in the course of 25,800 years, the Earth completes one precessional cycle. The intersection of the Celestial Equator and the Ecliptic denote the Equinoctial Points, and Precession results in the Sun crossing the Equator in Spring approximately 20 minutes earlier each year, and 50 seconds of arc further westward along the Ecliptic.

This *'Moving Zodiac'* is known as the *Tropical Zodiac* and the passage of the Sun through the Vernal Equinox (First Point of Aries) marks the commencement of the *Tropical Year* (seasonal year), the length of which is 365 days 5 hours 48 minutes and 46 seconds in mean solar time. The *Sidereal Year,* which is the true year, is the time taken by the Earth to complete a revolution round the Sun, or in other words, it is the period of time in which the Sun will return exactly to the same position relative to the background of the constellations as seen from the Earth. Owing to the fact that the First Point of Aries is not 'fixed', due to precessional movement, the Sidereal Year is 20 minutes longer than the Tropical Year, i.e. 365 days 6 hours 9 minutes 9 seconds in mean solar time. It is the Tropical Zodiac which is used by most students of astrology, although there is a school of thought which considers the *Sidereal or Fixed Zodiac* to be more appropriate. The opinions of the Siderealists deserve respect, particularly when one considers the vast amount of research and investigation that has been done by several notable researchers concerning the Zodiac.

Tropical or Sidereal Zodiac

When comparing the relative merits of one system with another, it is first necessary to understand what each represents. The term 'Zodiacs' is misleading and confusing, for there is only one circle of the Zodiac, and whether we call it 'Tropical' or 'Sidereal' will depend solely on the point from which it is measured. The Tropical Cycle is the cycle of the seasons, corresponding to the Sun's yearly return each March to the Vernal Equinox—The First Point of Aries; and the solar monthly progress is measured through the signs along the Ecliptic in degrees of longitude. The Sidereal Cycle is that of the retrogression of the Vernal Point through the twelve zodiacal constellations (at present from Pisces to Aquarius) during an era of some 25,800 years. It is measured from a fixed reference point on the same ecliptic circle which locates the fixed star Spica (Alpha Virginis) permanently in 29 degrees Virgo.

Critics of astrology argue that astrology must be a pseudo-science because its advocates (or at least those who use the Tropical Zodiac) fail to take into account the phenomenon of precession. The argument is that astrology is not based on fact because the Vernal Equinox no longer corresponds with the constellation Aries, but has moved in relation to the stars. Consequently, the division of the Zodiac no longer coincides with the constellations, and although the Sun 'enters' Aries at the Vernal Equinox, it is in fact in the constellation Pisces. Whether this criticism has validity or not depends on which cycle is considered the more important. If the yearly solar cycle, which is seasonal, is considered to have greater significance, then the Tropical or Moving Zodiac is more important. Likewise, the Sidereal (starry) or Fixed Zodiac merits consideration if precession of the Equinoctial Points is regarded as being significant.

The Vernal Point is important astronomically as well as astrologically, for it is from this point that astronomers check movements and determine positions on the celestial Sphere. In contrast to the Tropical Zodiac, the Sidereal Zodiac of the constellations is non-moving and non-precessional, being permanently aligned to the fixed stars. According to modern researchers, notably Cyril Fagan and Garth Allen (whose contributions to astrological science merit the highest commendations), the 'Zodiac of antiquity' was the Zodiac of the constellations and was used particularly by the Babylonian astronomer-astrologers.

As a result of the extensive researches into the history of astronomy and into the archaeology of the Tigris-Euphrates valley civilizations, it was concluded that it was the Zodiac of the constellations that was used. These researches tended to confirm that the Babylonians and the Egyptians measured their longitudes from 'markers' in the heavens. These fiducials were the Pleiades in 5° Taurus, Aldebaran in 15° Taurus, Regulus in 5° Leo, Spica in 29° Virgo and Antares in 15° Scorpio. As 'watchers of the heavens', the Babylonians were observational astronomers, and in the course of time were able to adapt and refine their knowledge of celestial motions and phenomena. The Babylonian astronomical knowledge and

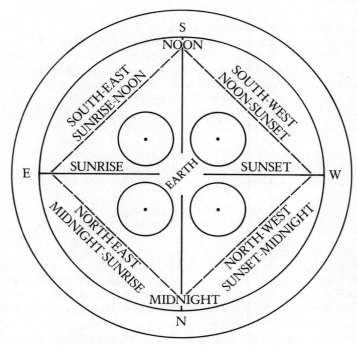

Figure 10.   The Sun's Position in the 4 Quadrants.

the associated traditions formed the basis upon which early Greek astronomy was founded. Hipparchus, who established astronomy on a sound geometrical basis, confirmed from his observations that the position of the Equinox was the initial point for measurements both in Right Ascension and longitude.

The year A.D. 221 was, according to Fagan, the 'zero' year when 'both Zodiacs' coincided, i.e. the Vernal Point had retrogressed to the exact conjunction with its sidereal counterpart. However, owing to the continual shift of the Vernal Point in relation to the fixed stars, the difference between 0° Aries Tropical and 0° Aries Sidereal is now approximately 24 degrees. This difference, termed the 'Ayanamsa' by the Sidereal advocates, has to be subtracted from all Tropical Longitudes in order to convert to Sidereal Longitudes. In subtracting this difference, the precession which has accrued since A.D. 221 is expunged from the tropical longitudes. Tables to facilitate the conversion are given in publications dealing with Sidereal astrology. The Sidereal techniques offer an interesting field of research, but for those 'new' to astrology, the Tropical system should be considered and used before attempting the Sidereal calculations, which although not difficult, can in some cases, be rather complex.

The Sun's Position

Position in the Zodiac and in the Chart
During the course of each year the Sun 'enters' each sign of the Zodiac on or about the date listed below. Also, its position in the chart depends on the time of day that the birth or event occurred. If, after the chart calculations have been completed, the Sun is found in a sign or a quadrant other than those indicated below, there is an error, and the calculations need re-checking.

Zodiacal Positions

20 March	Aries	22 September	Libra
19 April	Taurus	23 October	Scorpio
20 May	Gemini	22 November	Sagittarius
21 June	Cancer	21 December	Capricorn
22 July	Leo	20 January	Aquarius
22 August	Virgo	19 February	Pisces

Quadrant Position
The Sun's position in the chart depends on the time of day for which the chart is calculated. At sunrise, it will be close to the Ascendant; from sunrise to noon it will be in the south-east until it culminates at noon. Having culminated, the Sun will decline and set in the west and during this time, it will be in the south-west.

The twelve signs of the Zodiac all 'pass' over the Ascendant every 24 hours, the average time for one sign to ascend being two hours, although this varies depending on the latitude of birth. This factor of 'long and short ascension' will be discussed in greater detail when we commence chart calculations.

As the Sun remains in one sign of the Zodiac for about one month, and its longitude increases by an average of one degree per day, it is obvious that the sign and degree which contains the Sun will be in the appropriate quadrant depending upon the time of day. For example, if the date was 21 June, the Sun has just entered Cancer and it will remain in this sign until it enters Leo on or about 22 July. However, each day the Sun will rise and, in the course of 24 hours, will move through each of the four quadrants. If the birth occurred at sunrise, the Sun will be close to the Ascendant and the rising sign will be Cancer; at sunset, the sign containing the Sun will be on the Descendant (the opposite point to the Ascendant), and therefore the opposite sign to Cancer (= Capricorn) will be rising on the Ascendant.

So we have the Sun in its yearly journey moving through all twelve signs, and in its daily journey passing through all four quadrants or twelve houses. At noon, the sign containing the Sun will be on the meridian (culminating) and at midnight, it will be at the opposite point (the lower meridian). In the southern hemisphere, the Sun culminates in the north as opposed to the south in the northern hemisphere.

3.
THE ASTRONOMICAL BASIS (2)
THE SOLAR SYSTEM AND
THE PLANETS

The Solar System

The Solar System is the planetary system which contains not only the Sun, Moon and planets including the Earth, but also other bodies, such as the satellites of the planets, asteroids (a belt of small planets found between the orbits of Mars and Jupiter), comets and meteoroids.

The Sun is the focal point of the Solar System, and it is around the Sun that the planets orbit. The scale of the Solar System is vast but, despite the enormous distance, the planets move in regular orbits, and each planet has a pull of gravity which varies according to its mass and size. The attraction that one planet has for another, causes irregularities in motion and is termed 'perturbation'.

The planets can be considered to be divided into two groups: the terrestrial or earth-like planets, and the Jupiter-like planets. The terrestrial planets include Mercury, Venus, Earth and Mars. The Jupiter or Jovian planets are Jupiter, Saturn, Uranus and Neptune. Pluto, although earth-like in size, is the most remote planet in the Solar System. The physical and orbital characteristics of the terrestrial planets are opposite to those of the Jovian planets. The former group of planets rotate slowly compared with the Jovian planets and are near to the Sun. They are rocky and earth-like, whereas the Jovian planets are large and composed of gaseous elements, except Pluto which is rocky. All the planets revolve in elliptical orbits, and their distances from the Sun are continuously changing. Mercury, Venus, Earth and Mars move round the Sun fairly quickly, but the outer planets (Jupiter, Saturn, Uranus, Neptune and Pluto) take considerably longer.

The Sun

The Sun is at the centre of the Solar System and is the source of heat and light for the Earth. It is an enormous sphere of incandescent gas with a diameter of 864,000 miles; it is 93 million miles from the Earth and its volume is over 1 million times that of the Earth.

Even though the Sun is the most important body in the Solar System and life as we know it could not exist without it, nevertheless it is merely one star among thousands of millions and is nothing out of the ordinary. To us on Earth, however, it is all-important as a life-giving force. It is continuously emitting radiation, but only a mere fraction of the total energy emitted by the Sun is received by the Earth. However, even a slight change in the radiation output would significantly alter the Earth's climate.

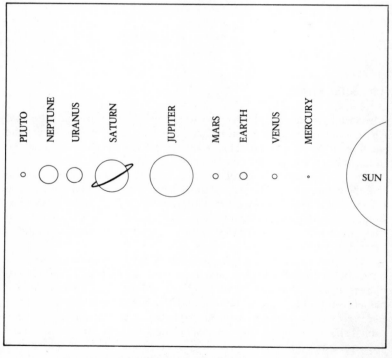

Figure 12(a).   The Solar System.

Planet	Mercury	Venus	Earth	Mars	Jupiter	Saturn	Uranus	Neptune	Pluto
Distance (mean) from Sun (millions of miles)	36	67.2	93	141.6	484.3	886.1	1783	2793	3660
Period of revolution about Sun (sidereal)	87.9 days	224.7 days	365.25 days	686.98 days	11.86 years	29.46 years	84.01 years	164.79 years	247.70 years
Diameter (miles)	3000	7700	7927	4219	88700	75100	29300	31200	3700
Period of rotation about axis (sidereal)	58.5 days	243 days	23 Hrs 56 Min	24 Hrs 37 Min	9 Hrs 51 Min	10 Hrs 14 Min	10 Hrs 48 Min	14 Hrs	6 days 9 Hrs
Inclination of orbit to Ecliptic	7° 0'	3° 24'	0° 0'	1° 51'	1° 18'	2° 29'	0° 46'	1° 46'	17° 10'
Eccentricity of orbit	0.206	0.007	0.017	0.093	0.048	0.056	0.047	0.009	0.246
Mass (Earth = 1)	0.05	0.81	1.00	0.11	318	95	15	17	?
Density (Water = 1)	5.4	4.99	5.52	4.12	1.3	0.7	1.65	2.0	?

Figure 12(b). The Solar System: Planetary Data.

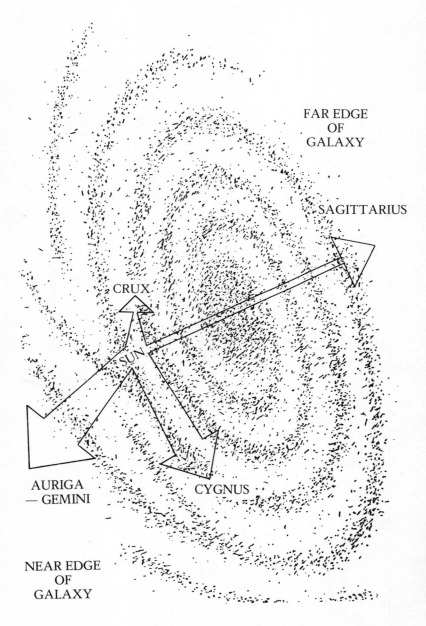

Figure 11. Our Galaxy.

The visible surface of the Sun is called the photosphere, and it is here that the energy which originates deep within the Sun bursts forth. Immediately above the photosphere is a layer of gas a few hundred miles thick known as the reversing layer, and above this layer is a further layer of gas called the chromosphere, so called because it is red in colour, although it can only be seen during a total eclipse, or with special instruments. The Sun is mainly composed of hydrogen and, from our knowledge of the gas laws of physics and of how gases behave under high pressures and temperatures, we can therefore determine the nature of the Sun's interior. At the Sun's core which has a temperature of millions of degrees, a continuous process of conversion is taking place. The Sun is converting its hydrogen to helium, and this nuclear reaction causes some of the hydrogen to change into radiant energy at the rate of 4 million tons per second.

Eventually, in about 8000 million years, the Sun will have exhausted the available hydrogen fuel and will swell outward engulfing all the inner planets including the Earth. The Sun has a magnetic field, and solar activity is connected with this field and with its differential rotation (which is a rotation period that varies with latitude, the period at the Equator being shorter than at other latitudes).

The rotation of the Sun enables the passage of sunspots to be detected. These important features on the surface of the Sun take the form of a very dark central section (the umbra) surrounded by a lighter grey area (the penumbra). The umbra appears almost black but this is because it is being seen against the intensely bright background of the rest of the surface.

Sunspots are only temporary features, lasting for periods of between one day and a few months. Most last a few weeks, and appear singly or in groups, and are of differing sizes, varying from tiny pores a few hundred miles across to giant spots up to 50,000 miles in diameter. If a sunspot is observed over a period of several days, it will be seen to move across the Sun's disc, due to the rotation of the Sun, the mean period being 27 days. As the Sun consists of gas, it does not rotate as a solid body but rotates differentially. These sunspots are closely associated with the Sun's magnetic field, being centres of magnetic activity. They give the false impression of being holes in the Sun's surface, but they are merely cooler regions of the surface. The number of sunspots visible at any one time varies, developing to a maximum number in an average period of eleven years.

In the vicinity of sunspots, there is often an area of the photosphere that is hotter and brighter than general, and this area is known as a plage. At the active plage areas, solar prominences are observable, which are great tongues of solar matter rushing thousands of miles into space.

The Sun is an active, roaring, violent body continuously emitting energy and the solar flares (lasting from a few seconds to a few minutes) demonstrate this violence. These solar flares cause radio disruption and can also affect the Earth's magnetic field. Streaming out from the Sun are rapidly moving particles (electrons and protons) and this stream is known as the Solar Wind. At the time of a total eclipse of the Sun, when the bright photosphere is covered by the Moon, the corona (a faint halo of gas surrounding the Sun) is visible, and the coronal streamers extend several solar diameters. The increase in magnetic storms at the time of maximum sunspots seems to indicate that there is a relationship with solar events and terrestrial happenings. Interference with short wave radio reception is a most marked occurrence at the time of solar activity.

So the Sun, even though it may be insignificant when compared with the millions of other stars, is to us the most important body in the Universe without which we could not exist.

Astrologically, the Sun represents power, vitality, the life-giving energy and denotes all manner of creativity.

The Moon

The Moon is the nearest natural object in space, being only 240,000 miles away, which, astronomically speaking, is an extremely short distance.

The Moon shines by reflecting sunlight and its most obvious characteristic is the fact that it shows phases as it revolves around the Earth. As the Moon moves round in its orbit, it goes from New (thin crescent) until it eventually becomes Full and reaches the opposite part of the sky from the Sun. After Full Moon, it gradually begins to wane,

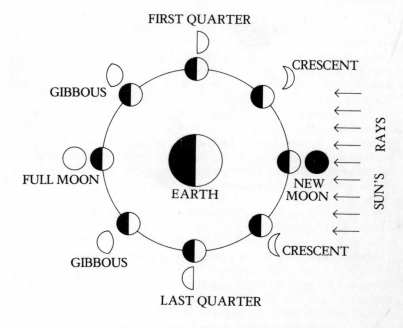

Figure 13. The Phases of the Moon.

steadily turning less and less of its illuminated side toward the Earth, until it becomes New again, and the cycle is begun all over again. The time interval between two successive New Moons is called the Moon's synodic period, and is equal to 29½ days, so that First Quarter occurs about 7½ days after New Moon, Full Moon about 14½ days after New Moon, and Last Quarter about 22 days after New Moon.

The Moon's path through the sky during the month is tilted at an angle of 5° 8' to that of the Sun, so the Moon will closely follow the path traced out by the Sun during one month. The result of this is, that sometimes the Moon will appear high in the sky, sometimes low down, and at other times at an intermediate altitude.

The mean daily motion of the Moon in its orbit is 13° 12', but this varies somewhat, and the interval between two quarter phases can be as little as six days or as great as nine days. Because this motion is eastward, the Moon rises later each day, by an average of fifty minutes. The difference between the times of rising on any two successive days is called the *retardation* for those days. This retardation depends upon the angle that the Moon's orbit makes with the horizon. The Moon at any given phase will transit the meridian at different altitudes, depending upon the time of year.

As the Moon rises later each day, it will appear at different times of the day or night at different phases. So a Full Moon rises at sunset at all times of the year—but as the Moon wanes it rises, culminates and sets later until at the last quarter, it rises around midnight (although it will rise as early as 10 p.m. if at maximum north Declination and as late as 2 a.m. if at maximum south Declination). As it continues to approach the new phase, it will rise with the Sun, but will be invisible. Likewise, a waxing Moon is only visible in the afternoon, evening or early part of the night.

The Moon's orbit is inclined to the Ecliptic by an angle of 5° and the two points of intersection between the orbit of the Moon and the plane of the Ecliptic are the *nodes*. The line connecting these two points is referred to as the Nodal Line, and this Nodal Line shifts westward along the Ecliptic, completing a retrograde revolution in a period of 18.6 years. When the Moon moving northward crosses the plane of the Earth's orbit, it is at the ascending node, and when moving southward it is at the descending node. If the plane of the Moon's orbit coincided exactly with the Ecliptic, an eclipse of the Sun would occur once every 29½ days, and an eclipse of the Moon would occur about fourteen days later at each Full Moon. However, owing to the inclination of the Moon's orbit to the Ecliptic an eclipse can only take place when new or full Moon occurs with the Moon near a node of its orbit.

Astrologically, the Moon is a very important body, and is associated with instinctive behaviour, personal traits and habits. Owing to its rapid motion, it 'moves' through each zodiacal sign in about 2½ days and can form several aspects with the various planets in a short space of time. Modern research is tending to confirm that some of the 'old wives' tales' concerning the Moon's influence on mentality, childbirth and vegetation, may after all, have some foundation in fact. Despite the Moon's eccentricities of motion, it may be that the 'inconstant mistress' is more reliable and trustworthy than we imagine.

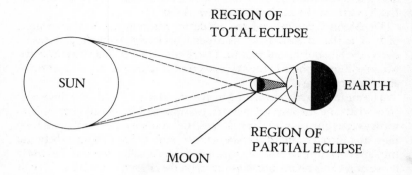

Figure 14.   Solar Eclipse.

Solar and Lunar Eclipses

The two Figures (14 and 15) illustrate how solar and lunar eclipses occur. The Sun, Earth, Moon and the distances between them are not to scale because the diameter of the Sun is 400 times greater than that of the Moon. The Sun and Moon appear to be about the same size in the sky, and this means that, if the Moon passes in front of the Sun, it blocks off the latter completely. Such an occurrence is known as a *solar eclipse.*

The path of the Moon around the Earth is tilted at an angle of 5 ° 8′ to the Ecliptic, and for this reason, eclipses do not occur once every month, but only when one of the Moon's two *nodes* coincides with a New Moon (the nodes, as we have seen, are the two points where the Moon's orbit intersect the Ecliptic). Eclipses, therefore occur at six-monthly intervals. Because the distance from the Earth to the Moon is not constant but varies by about 10 per cent, the Moon's umbra (full shadow) does not always reach the Earth's surface and, in this case, we get an *annular eclipse,* when a ring of the Sun is left around the Moon. Even in a total eclipse, the cone of shadow is never more than 170 miles wide at the Earth's surface. This cone sweeps out a band as the Moon moves through space and as the Earth rotates. A total eclipse can be seen from a very limited part of the Earth's surface but, on the other hand, a *partial eclipse* is visible from a much wider area (several thousands of miles either side of the track of totality). When the Sun is totally eclipsed, the sky and countryside become dark, a few of the brighter stars become visible and so does the Sun's atmosphere (the corona).

When the Moon passes into the Earth's shadow a *lunar eclipse* occurs. As with solar eclipses, lunar eclipses occur at six-monthly intervals when one of the Moon's nodes coincides with the Full Moon. Unlike solar eclipses, lunar eclipses are visible over the whole night hemisphere of the Earth when they occur, and, furthermore, the cross-sectional diameter of the Earth's full-shadow (the umbra) is greater than the diameter of the Moon. This means that the Moon can be totally eclipsed for a considerable length of time, up to two hours in fact, as against the seven or eight minutes maximum for a total solar eclipse.

If only a part of the Moon passes into the Earth's umbra, the Moon is partially eclipsed, while if it misses the umbra altogether but passes through the penumbra, it is penumbrally eclipsed and appears slightly dulled. In a total lunar eclipse the Moon is sometimes still visible, shining with a faint coppery glow because the light from the Sun is refracted into the umbra by the Earth's atmosphere. In other eclipses the Moon's light is completely obliterated.

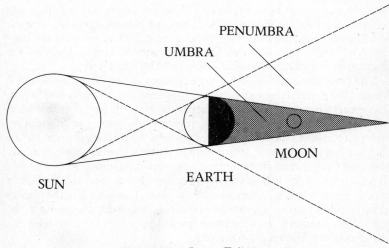

Figure 15. Lunar Eclipse.

The Planets

Introduction

The Sun has a family of nine planets in orbit around it, of which the Earth is one. These planets are Mercury, Venus, Earth, Mars, Jupiter, Saturn, Uranus, Neptune and Pluto in order of increasing distance from the Sun. Their orbits all lie in nearly the same plane, so that they are confined to the narrow band of the sky we call the Zodiac, against which they appear to move.

The two planets Mercury and Venus, which are nearer the Sun than Earth, are known as *inferior* planets, while those whose orbits lie outside that of the Earth are known as *superior* planets (Mars, Jupiter, Saturn, Uranus, Neptune and Pluto). The two inferior planets can never be opposite the Sun in the sky, but can only appear on either side of it alternatively as a 'morning or evening star'. The superior planets on the other hand, can 'take up any position' relative to the Sun.

During the course of one year, the planets pass from conjunction (when they are passed by the Sun), through morning quadrature (90° from the Sun), opposition (exactly opposite the Sun), evening quadrature (90° from the Sun) and back to conjunction again. The further a planet is from the Sun, the more slowly it will move and the less it will appear to have moved against the stars in one year. Because they are in orbit around the Sun, planets will come to opposition later each year.

Planets normally appear to move eastward against the stars as they orbit the Sun; near opposition, this motion is reversed and the planet moves westward a short distance. A planet moving westward in this way is said to be in *retrograde* motion. The nearer a planet is to the Sun, the greater is the retrograde motion. Only five planets (Mercury, Venus, Mars, Jupiter and Saturn) are visible to the eye. The outermost planets, Uranus, Neptune and Pluto are too faint to be seen without optical aid. For this reason, only the five bright planets were known in ancient times. Uranus was discovered in 1781, Neptune in 1846 and Pluto in 1930.

The time taken for one orbit of the planets varies: Mercury 88 days, Venus 243 days, Mars nearly 2 years, Jupiter nearly 12 years, and Saturn 29½ years. Because of these differing periods of revolution, the planets can make any number of different configurations with respect to one another and with respect to the background of the stars. So there can be one, two or three or (very rarely) four or five planets visible above the horizon at any one time. Conjunctions between two or more planets sometimes occur, but they do not pass one behind the other because they do not orbit the Sun in exactly the same plane. Every month the Moon passes each of the planets in turn and, because it appears as a relatively large body compared to the size of the planets, it sometimes passes in front of a planet; this phenomenon is known as *occultation.*

A planet can be distinguished from a star by the fact that a star twinkles (particularly when near the horizon), but a planet does not. Stars generate their own luminosity, while planets reflect the light of the Sun.

Mercury

This is the nearest planet to the Sun, orbiting it at a mean distance of 36 million miles. Its orbital period is 88 days, so a conjunction with the Sun occurs once every 44 days. Even when furthest from the Sun (i.e. *maximum elongation*), the angle between Mercury and the Sun is never greater than 27 degrees. Mercury moves in a highly eccentric orbit, and this means that at some maximum elongations, its distance from the Sun does not exceed 18°. So even at the best of times, Mercury is a difficult object to see, and may require optical aid to render it visible. In the British Isles it is never visible in a dark sky, only in a twilit one, and then only low down near the horizon. Mercury is a very small planet, its diameter is about 3000 miles, so it is not much larger than the Moon. It has practically no atmosphere and, because it is so near to the Sun, its surface temperature is very high, around 400° Centigrade.

Astrologically, Mercury represents all forms of communications, linkages, and factual knowledge.

Venus

This is the next planet out from the Sun, being at a distance of 67 million miles from it. Its orbital period is 225 days but, because its orbit is much closer to that of the Earth's than Mercury's, intervals between successive conjunctions (inferior) are much longer than this (around one year seven months).

Because Mercury and Venus are both inferior planets, they appear to move around the Sun (as seen from the Earth) in the same way, and both appear alternately as evening and morning 'stars'.

At its brightest, Venus is brighter than any object in the sky except the Sun and Moon. It appears as a brilliant white star-like object and can be seen in broad daylight. As the inferior planets move around the Sun, they move from inferior conjunction (that is between the Sun and the Earth), through morning elongation (maximum distance west of the Sun) to the superior conjunction (when on the far side of the Sun) and evening elongation (maximum distance east of the Sun), and finally back to inferior conjunction again.

The total time taken for a complete cycle is called the *synodic* period. For Mercury this is 3½ months, and for Venus 1 year 7 months. When Venus is at morning or evening elongation, its greatest distance from the Sun is about 47 degrees, so that unlike Mercury, it is visible in a dark sky. The diameter of Venus is 7700 miles and its mass is not much less than that of the Earth, but its temperature is about 400° Centigrade.

Astrologically, Venus represents the principles of harmony, unity and co-operation at all levels.

Mars

Mars is the first of the *superior* planets (those whose orbits lie outside that of the Earth's). It is only about half the diameter of the Earth, and it takes 687 days, or nearly two years to orbit the Sun once, at a mean distance of 142 million miles.

Being a superior planet, it can be opposite the Sun in the sky, and such oppositions occur once every 2 years 2 months. Its orbit, however, is highly eccentric like that of Mercury, and therefore its distance from the Earth varies from opposition to opposition.

When at its nearest to the Sun, Mars is said to be at *perihelion;* and when furthest from the Sun it is at *aphelion.* The axis of Mars is inclined at an angle of 25 degrees to the perpendicular of the plane of its orbit, and so the planet experiences seasons like the Earth. Because the Martian axis always points in the same direction in space, we can see different poles at different oppositions. The rotation period of Mars is 24 hours 37 minutes. Owing to its mineral composition, it has a reddish appearance, and it is subject to violent dust storms.

Mars has two satellites or moons named Deimos and Phobos (Terror and Fear). Deimos orbits Mars once in 30 hours, and Phobos in just 7½ hours. The latter satellite presents an interesting phenomena in that to an observer on Mars, Phobos would rise in the west and set in the east three times a day.

Astrologically, Mars represents the principles of energy and initiative.

Jupiter

This is the largest planet in the solar system with a diameter of 88,000 miles, or about eleven times that of the Earth. It orbits the Sun at a mean distance of 483 million miles and takes 11.86 years to complete one orbit of the Sun.

Viewed through a telescope, Jupiter is whitish in colour and is crossed by a number of darker belts. It is unlike the inner planets in that it consists largely of gas (at least in its outer layers) and the different dark belts and bright zones rotate at different speeds. The gas which makes up most of the mass of the planet is hydrogen. An interesting feature of this planet is the Giant Red Spot which astronomers consider is a type of atmospheric phenomenon, and which changes colour through different shades of pink and red.

This giant planet has at least thirteen satellites and four of these are visible in any small telescope, because they are bright and large, with diameters ranging between 1800 and 3200 miles. These four satellites, termed the Galilean Moons, were discovered by Galileo in 1610 with the newly invented telescope. The other satellites are much fainter and may be minor planets attracted by Jupiter's massive gravitational pull.

Jupiter was once thought to act in the same way as a star, giving off light and heat, although rather feebly. It is now known that this is not possible, for a true star shines and is powered by nuclear reactions in its core, and the mass of Jupiter, high though it is, is not great enough to cause the enormous pressures and temperatures which are required for the hydrogen-into-helium nuclear reaction to proceed.

With a rotation period of once in just under 10 hours, Jupiter has the fastest rotation of all the planets. This rapid rotation causes Jupiter to be slightly flattened at its poles.

Astrologically, Jupiter represents the principle of expansion in all forms.

Saturn

This is the next of the giant planets, orbiting the Sun at a distance of 886 million miles, in a period of 29½ years. It is not much smaller than Jupiter, having a mean diameter of 75,000 miles. The most striking feature of

Saturn is its rings, which are composed of millions of particles which revolve in the plane of the planet's Equator. Saturn rotates once in 10 hours 14 minutes, and this rapid rotation has caused appreciable flattening at the poles, and bulging at the equator, in the proportion of 1 to 10 (so it is more oblate than Jupiter). Saturn is very similar to Jupiter in its constitution, for both are largely composed of hydrogen, and it is the least dense of all the planets, its mean density being only 0.71 that of water.

When Galileo first observed Saturn in 1610, he was not able to see the rings properly because the optics of his telescope were rather poor. The rings were first seen as such by the Dutch astronomer Huygens in 1655, who described them as 'a flat ring, which nowhere touches the body of the planet and is inclined to the ecliptic'. There are four rings, all concentric with the planet and with one another. The outer ring, which is dull white, has a width of 10,000 miles; then there is a gap of 3000 miles known as Cassini's division, named after its discoverer. Inside the bright middle ring is a faint ring through which starlight can be observed. The fourth ring nearest to Saturn can only be seen with a large telescope.

As the planet revolves once around the Sun in 29½ years, the rings face the Earth every 15 years, and are seen 'open' and 'edge-on' every 7½ years. When the rings are 'edge-on', they become invisible except in the largest telescopes. At the present time (1980/81), they are invisible in small telescopes.

Saturn is known to have eleven satellites all of which orbit beyond the ring system. The largest of these satellites is Titan and, with a diameter of 3600 miles, is the biggest moon in the Solar system.

Astrologically, Saturn represents the principles of contraction and limitation.

Uranus

Until 1781, Saturn was the outermost planet known to exist. In that year, Herschel was carrying out a survey of the sky (making star counts in selected areas of the sky) when he noted on 13 March, that there was a small, bright, disc like object among the stars, which had not been seen before. Further observations enabled its orbit to be calculated and it was found to be a new planet, moving far beyond the orbit of Saturn.

Uranus has a revolution period about the Sun of 84 years, and its mean distance from the Sun is 1783 million miles. Its diameter has been measured as 29,000 miles (or just under four times that of the Earth). An interesting feature of the planet is its extremely high axial inclination, 98° to the perpendicular of the plane of its orbit. This means that the north and south poles alternately point almost straight toward the Earth at the solstices, and the Equator at the equinoxes.

Without optical aid, Uranus is practically invisible, being on the threshold of vision, hence, until the invention of the telescope it remained undiscovered. It appears as a small disc, but no markings are visible upon its surface except with a large telescope and then only with difficulty. The markings which can be observed on the disc take the form of faint greyish belts parallel to the equator like those of Jupiter and Saturn, and which are darker than the rest of the surface which is of a greenish tint. Uranus rotates relatively rapidly with a period of 10¾ hours, and this has caused appreciable flattening at the poles, as with Jupiter and Saturn. The exact constitution of Uranus is not known, but it probably has a solid core and an atmosphere of hydrogen and helium with clouds of methane; any ammonia must be in the frozen state because of the very low temperature of the atmosphere (around minus 190° centigrade).

It has five satellites, with diameters between 200 and 700 miles, and revolution periods of between 1½ and 13½ days. Two of the satellites were found by Herschel in 1787. Observations in March 1977 suggest that Uranus may have a system of rings similar to those of Saturn, but which are too faint to be visible from Earth.

Astrologically, Uranus represents the new and unexpected, and is associated with changes and disruptions.

Neptune

After Uranus had been observed for a few decades, it became clear that it was not moving in its predicted path, but was acting as if another, yet undiscovered planet was affecting it gravitationally (perturbation). The mass and position of this unknown planet was predicted by Adams in England and Leverrier in France, and Leverrier's calculations were sent to the Berlin Observatory in September 1846, where on the 23rd of that month, the astronomers d'Arrest and Galle found the new planet, less than one degree away from its predicted position. The planet was named Neptune and is further out than Uranus. It orbits the Sun at a mean distance of 2793 million miles in a revolution period of 165 years. At the time of its discovery, it was in the constellation Capricornus and it will not return to this point until the year 2011.

The diameter of Neptune was originally thought to be about 28,000 miles, making it slightly smaller than Uranus, but more recent measurements (1969) gave it a value of 31,000 miles.

The exact constitution of Neptune is unknown, but it probably has a solid core, and is known to have an atmosphere of hydrogen, helium and methane. Markings on the disc are difficult to resolve even with a large telescope, but have been observed from time to time. Temperatures in the atmosphere are around minus 220° centigrade. The overall colour of the planet is bluish-white and it appears to be very similar to Uranus. Neptune and Uranus together with Jupiter and Saturn make up the four 'gas giants'—large planets of relatively low density with an appreciable proportion of their masses contained in their atmospheres.

Neptune has two satellites, Triton and Nereid. Triton is one of the largest moons in the Solar system and was discovered by Lassell in 1846, a few weeks after the discovery of Neptune. Nereid is much smaller (200 miles) and was found by Kuiper in 1949; it orbits Neptune once in 362 days, while Triton goes round once in 6 days. The discovery of Neptune was a brilliant confirmation of Newton's laws concerning the mass and motion of the planets.

Astrologically, Neptune represents abstractions, unreality, isolation and withdrawal.

Pluto

As with Uranus, Neptune was also found to be wandering from its predicted orbit and this led astronomers to suggest that there must be a ninth planet beyond it. The astronomer Lowell (who also observed 'canals' on Mars) carried out computations in order to determine the mass and position of an unknown planet which was thought to be responsible for the irregularities in the orbits of Uranus and Neptune. An extensive photographic programme by Tombaugh of the Lowell Observatory at Flagstaff, Arizona, led to the discovery of this highly eccentric planet which moves in an orbit greatly inclined to the Ecliptic (about 17 degrees). Pluto was discovered in 1930 (fourteen years after Lowell's death). Its mean distance from the Sun is 3660 million miles and its orbital revolution period is 248 years.

Owing to its highly eccentric orbit, which is greater than that of any other planet, Pluto at perihelion is within the orbit of Neptune, and perihelion will occur in 1989. However, owing to its unusually high inclination to the plane of the Ecliptic, there is little likelihood of a collision with Neptune.

No surface markings are visible on Pluto since it is difficult to see it as a disc even with the largest telescopes; however, a rotation period of 6 days 9 hours has been derived from observations of the fluctuations in brightness of the planet. Unlike the four previous planets, Pluto is solid throughout. From the surface of the planet, the Sun would appear as only a very brilliant star and would give no more illumination than the Full Moon on Earth.

The surface is also extremely cold, around minus 230° centigrade (or only about 40-50 degrees above absolute zero). It is unlikely that Pluto has any atmosphere, because its low surface gravity is unable to hold onto any gaseous hydrogen or helium and the extremely low temperatures mean that compounds such as water, carbon dioxide, ammonia and even methane are all in the frozen state upon its surface.

The size of Pluto is not known with any certainty. Estimates vary from a diameter of 2000 to one of 6000 miles. The mass of the planet is about 1/10th that of the Earth but, again, this value is uncertain. Moreover, this mass is nowhere near great enough to produce the perturbations upon Neptune, which led to the discovery of Pluto. One explanation maintains that the estimated size and mass of the planet are far too low, and that the surface is covered with ice which causes the planet to shine like a dark mirror, so that all which is seen of Pluto is the reflection of the Sun in the ice, with the rest of the planet invisible. On this theory, Pluto could be considerably larger than the Earth. Another theory holds that a tenth planet exists beyond Pluto with a mass which is sufficient to produce the observed perturbations upon Neptune. Any search for an 'additional'

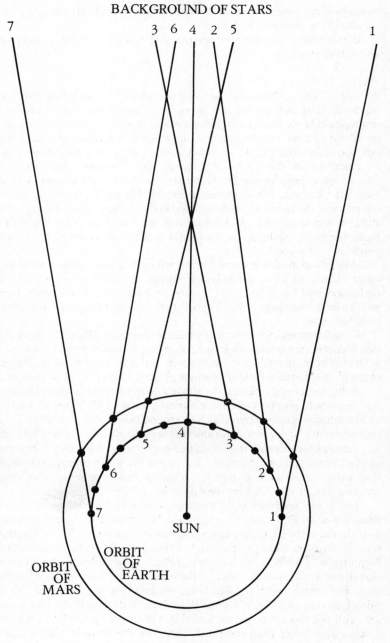

Figure 16. Retrograde Motion.

planet would be extremely difficult and would require very large telescopes.

In 1978 it was found that Pluto possesses a satellite which is almost as large as the planet itself (although its mass is much less than Pluto's), so that Pluto is in effect a double planet. This accounts in some way for the observed perturbations upon Neptune, and it is quite possible that additional planets beyond Pluto do exist.

Astrologically, Pluto is an extremely interesting planet, and is representative of the principles of regeneration, commencements and closures and finality.

Retrogression

If the motion of a superior planet (one outside the Earth's orbit) is observed, it will not always move eastward against the background of the stars, but will move westward for a time around opposition.

This occurs because the Earth, completing one circuit of the Sun in a shorter time than the superior planet, overtakes it when passing it at opposition; this phenomenon is known as retrogression. This apparent 'moving backwards' is the result of a planet dropping behind the Earth. An inferior planet is seen to move in a retrograde direction while it is overtaking the Earth. In the Ephemeris, retrograde motion is denoted by the glyph ℞.

In Figure 16, the Earth, when at position 1, sees Mars at 1 against the background of the stars and it is moving eastward against them. This eastward motion becomes slower as both planets move from 1 through 2 and 3. Between 3 and 4, Mars appears to stop (the point where it does this is called a stationary point) and then starts moving westward, attaining its maximum westward speed at opposition (4). Between 4 and 5, Mars again appears to stop, and thereafter resumes its normal eastward motion. The more distant a planet is from the Sun, the less it retrogresses.

Astrologically, this phenomenon has been given undue importance, and many absurd statements have been, and are, made concerning the influence of retrograde planets.

4
TIME (1)
THE CALENDAR

Introduction

Time is an elusive entity. We do not know what *time is,* but we do know what *time it is.* Sophisticated measuring devices enable us to ascertain the exact time at any instant to within a fraction of a second, but we still cannot define it. We cannot change time; it is time that allows us to see changes. Time and the awareness of time enable us to relate the concepts of past, present and future; to recollect the past, observe the present and endeavour to visualize the future.

To early man, the passage of time was related to his primitive existence —his life span in a hostile environment, the changing seasons, and probably his observations of the changing heavens. The movements of the Sun and Moon and the slow gradual shift of the various constellations, became the basis for reckoning the passage of time. The Earth's annual journey around the Sun, and the Moon's monthly orbit, as it fluctuated from New to Full, denoted a sequence and pattern of time which could be measured and eventually adopted for the needs of the community.

Timekeeping is based on our knowledge of how the Earth and celestial bodies move in relation to each other. From the primitive astronomical reckonings of early man we have acquired a basis for the measurement of time and this in turn has contributed to the development of modern science. Basically, however, it is the 'awareness of time' that is the important factor, for without it, there would be little or no association regarding the past, present and future.

The Calendar

To the people of antiquity, the heavens must have presented a picture of the mysterious and the supernatural. To early man, the apparent movement of the Sun and Moon coupled with the other heavenly bodies were forces which needed interpretation and understanding, particularly when certain celestial phenomena appeared to correlate with mundane happenings. The fear of the unknown and the associated superstitious beliefs resulted in early man developing a mythology of the heavens. The various sky patterns which he observed during the course of time were imagined to be animals, gods and goddesses, heroes and demons. These sky patterns (constellations) could be identified and related to the ancient folk-lore of the tribe or community. Watching the heavens, initially for portents and omens increased his knowledge, and that which had been regarded as inexplicable and mysterious was gradually accepted and adapted for more practical purposes. All civilizations, however remote or isolated, had myths which were similar in nature and this mythology which played an important part in rituals and associated activities depended upon observational astronomy. These observations formed the basis for an astronomy and its symbolic counterpart (astrology) which enabled a system of time reckoning and a chronology to be formulated.

During the last few decades, the researches and investigations concerning the megalithic ruins which stretch from North to South America, and from Carnac in Brittany to the Scottish islands, indicate that prehistoric man possessed a knowledge of celestial alignments, and was capable of erecting vast astronomical structures with remarkable precision. The science of archaeo-astronomy is in its infancy, but as this fascinating science develops, its discoveries will confirm that early man's knowledge of the heavens and of the celestial motions of the Sun and Moon was far greater and more sophisticated than we have hitherto imagined.

The observations of the heavens over a vast period of time enabled the early civilizations to compile a form of calendar which was lunar-based, the reckoning being from New Moon to New Moon. As astronomical knowledge increased, the observers realized that the Sun, Moon and planets moved in a predetermined cycle and kept to a well-defined path in the sky. The Sun in its daily motion from east to west marked out the periods of night and day, while the Moon in her monthly course fluctuated from New to Full. All these phenomena were observed and by the time of recorded history, the length of the solar year had been determined as 365.25 days.

The ancient civilizations of Babylonia, Egypt, India and China had a highly developed system of time-recording and their calendars were based on the lunar and/or solar cycles. The Egyptians knew of the 365.25 day year, their computations being based on the heliacal rising of Sirius, which appears as the brightest star in the heavens. With the conquests of Alexander the Great, the astronomy and astrology of Egypt, Babylonia and India were acquired by Greece and the lunar-solar year was adopted by the

Greeks, replacing their former lunar year. The spread of this ancient knowledge continued, and the advances made by the Babylonians became the basis for the Greek astronomy.

However, the constant wars of conquest which preceded the Christian Era did little to encourage calendar reform. It was not until 45 B.C. that any serious attempt was made to correlate the various calendars of the known world. The Julian calendar (named after Julius Caesar who initiated the reforms) is now known as the Old Style Calendar, and it remained in existence until A.D. 1582 when it was replaced by the Gregorian or New Style Calendar. The Julian calendar incorporated several reforms including the introduction of the leap year, abolishing the lunar year, fixing the length of the mean solar year at 365.25 days, redistributing the days of the month, and returning the Equinox to March. This Old Style calendar continued in use until 1577 when corrections were made which resulted in the New Style or Gregorian Calendar coming into effect five years later in 1582, and it is this calendar which is now used.

The New Style calendar was introduced because it had become apparent to astronomers that the Old Style calendar based on the Julian Year of 365.25 days was not entirely compatible with the Tropical Year; the Julian year of 365.25 days was in effect eleven minutes in advance of the Tropical Year, and this advance over the centuries, had by the late sixteenth century amounted to ten days. If this discrepancy was not corrected then the error would continue to accumulate, so that Christmas, Easter and other festivals would occur at different seasons.

The New Style calendar was authorized for general use by Pope Gregory as from 15 October 1582 New Style. Ten days were 'removed', so making 5 October Old Style, 15 October New Style. This New Style calendar differed from the Old Julian calendar in its method of marking off leap years. Every fourth year was to be a leap year but the century years were not to be leap years unless they were exactly divisible by 400. Therefore the years 1200, 1600 and 2000 are leap years, but 1700, 1800, 1900 are not.

Despite the introduction of this New Style calendar in 1582, it was not universally accepted, and many countries continued using the Old Style calendar for many centuries afterwards. The Catholic countries readily adopted the New Style calendar; Italy, France, Spain and Portugal changed over in 1582. The German Catholic states, Prussia, Switzerland, Holland and Flanders in 1583; Poland in 1586, Hungary in 1587, the German and Netherland Protestant states and Denmark in 1700. In Sweden the change was gradual and achieved by omitting eleven leap days during the period 1700-1740. Great Britain and her colonies including the North American colonies changed to the New calendar in 1752. Certain European states did not change until the early part of the twentieth century; Bulgaria changed in 1915, Turkey and Soviet Russia in 1918, Yugoslavia and Rumania in 1919, and Greece in 1916. Japan adopted the New Calendar in 1872 and China in 1912.

It is therefore very important, that when dates are quoted, we are aware of which calendar was in use in a particular country. To use an Old Style date for a birth in this century would result in an error of thirteen days. Shakespeare's birth date is reputed to be 23 April, but this is Old Style reckoning. The date by New Style calendar is the 3 May (plus ten days). To change Old Style (O.S.) dates into New Style (N.S.): add to Old Style the following number of days.

	Century	Days			Century	Days
0-99	1st	−1		1000-99	11th	+ 6
100-99	2nd	−1		1100-99	12th	+ 7
200-99	3rd	0		1200-99	13th	+ 7
300-99	4th	+ 1		1300-99	14th	+ 8
400-99	5th	+ 1		1400-99	15th	+ 9
500-99	6th	+ 2		1500-99	16th	+ 10
600-99	7th	+ 3		1600-99	17th	+ 11
700-99	8th	+ 4		1700-99	18th	+ 11
800-99	9th	+ 4		1800-99	19th	+ 12
900-99	10th	+ 5		1900-99	20th	+ 13

Example: 1 January 1923 O.S. is equivalent to 14 January N.S. (Add thirteen days for twentieth century.)

5.
TIME (2) SIDEREAL TIME, SOLAR TIME AND TIME CONVERSION

Basis of Time Measurement

The rotation of the Earth upon its axis with reference to the apparent angular motion of the heavenly bodies is the basis of time measurement, and a day can be defined as the interval between two successive transits of the same object over a particular meridian. In the case of the Sun, it is known as a *Solar Day*, or if a star or the First Point of Aries, it is a *Sidereal Day*.

A great circle (the observer's Celestial Meridian) passing through the north and south points of the horizon and the point directly overhead (zenith) coincides with the observer's *Meridian of Longitude*. The moment at which a celestial body or point is on the meridian of the observer is known as the *culmination, transit* or *meridian passage* of that body or point.

Methods of Time-keeping

There are two methods of time-keeping based upon the rotation of the Earth;

1. *Solar Time,* which is kept with reference to the Sun.
2. *Sidereal Time,* which is measured with reference to the stars.

These two methods of time-keeping, although based upon the rotation of the Earth, differ in that a Solar Day and a Sidereal Day are of unequal length.

Variations of Time

The time required by the Sun to make two consecutive meridian transits is known as an *Apparent Solar Day,* but as this varies with the time of year, it is necessary to define the *Mean Solar Day* as the average solar day. The variations in the length of the day are due to two causes: (a) the Sun does not move along the Ecliptic at a uniform rate due to the varying distance of the Earth from the Sun during the year, (b) the Sun moves in the Ecliptic and not along the Celestial Equator. Its Celestial Longitude (measurement along the Ecliptic) is in general different from its Right Ascension (measurement along the Celestial Equator). Revolution causes the Sun to appear about one degree of arc to the east each day, and therefore the Earth must turn an additional degree of arc or four minutes of time to bring the Sun to the meridian the following day.

To overcome the variations of the *Apparent or True Sun's* motion, a fictitious *Mean Sun* is used which moves eastward along the Celestial Equator at a uniform speed equal to the average rate of the True Sun along the Ecliptic. The time between two successive lower transits of the *Mean Sun* is defined as a *Mean Solar* or *Civil Day,* which is approximately four minutes longer than a Sidereal Day.

The Equation of Time

The time shown by a Sun dial is known as Apparent or True Solar Time, and this differs from Mean Solar Time by an amount known as the Equation of Time. Owing to the non-uniform motion of the Earth relative to the Sun due to the elliptical nature of the Earth's orbit, and because the real Sun moves along the Ecliptic whereas the Mean Sun moves along the Celestial Equator, Apparent Solar time and Mean Time differ from each other. This difference (the Equation of Time) varies throughout the year. The angular speed of the Earth in its orbit is not constant, being greatest in early January when the Earth is nearest to the Sun. At the Equinoxes, the Apparent Solar day is shorter than average, whereas at the Solstices it is longer. During certain times of the year, the True Sun is ahead of the Mean Sun, and conversely, at other times of the year, the Mean Sun is ahead of the True Sun.

From about 25 December until 15 April, and from mid-June to late August, the True Sun is ahead of the Mean Sun. Between mid-April and mid-June, and from late August to about 25 December, the Mean Sun is ahead of the True Sun. In February, the Equation of Time has a maximum value of minus fourteen minutes, while in early November its value is plus sixteen minutes. The speed of the True Sun coincides with that of the Mean Sun on four dates in the year, namely, on or about 15 April, 14

June, 1 September and 25 December. The value of the Equation of Time at these dates, is of course, zero. On these dates, the time as indicated by a Sun dial will correspond with Mean Time (clock time); True Noon and Mean Noon coincide.

The early navigators had little difficulty in determining their latitude because, by observing the Sun at noon when it is on the meridian, they could calculate their latitude from the observed altitude of the Sun which, subtracted from $90°$, gave its zenith distance; by adding or subtracting the Sun's Declination, depending on the date of the observation, they could find their latitude. The finding of longitude was, however, a different matter, and it was not until the invention of the marine chronometer by Harrison in the eighteenth century that longitude could be accurately determined.

As the Sun always culminates at 12 noon Apparent Time, longitude in hours and minutes can be found by noting the Greenwich Time of the solar noon and applying the Equation of Time and converting the result into degrees.

In astrological charting we do not need to concern ourselves with the Equation of Time as we are using Mean Time and Sidereal Time.

Sidereal Time (Star Time)

This is reckoned by the transit of the First Point of Aries, and the Sidereal Day is the time interval between two successive transits of this point.

Sidereal Time measures the rotation of the earth relative to the First Point of Aries (Vernal Equinox) and is identical with the *Right Ascension of the Meridian.*

During the course of a Sidereal Day, the Earth rotates on its axis in a period of 23 hours, 56 minutes 04 seconds of Mean Time (Civil Time), and for an observer located at a particular longitude, the Sidereal Day is equivalent to the apparent rotation period of the Celestial Sphere. This rotation period can be determined by measuring the interval between two successive upper transits of the First Point of Aries or of a given star across the meridian.

Sidereal Time at any instant is the *Hour Angle of the Vernal Equinox* expressed in time, or in other words, the angle between an observer's meridian and a body or point measured westward from the meridian in a direction parallel to the Celestial Equator.

Sometime during the course of 24 hours, the First Point of Aries will be on the meridian, and the time of day when this occurs will depend upon the longitude of the observer and the time of year. When the First Point of Aries is on the meridian, its hour angle is zero and the Sidereal Time zero hours. The constant rotation of the Celestial Sphere increases this angle, and at, say, $45°$, 3 hours have elapsed, and the Sidereal Time is 3 hours. At $90°$, it will be 6 hours, and so on until after 24 hours, the First Point of Aries once again returns to the meridian.

Sidereal Time is *always local,* it cannot be otherwise. The difference between *Local Sidereal Time* (L.S.T.) and *Greenwich Sidereal Time* (G.S.T.) corresponds to the longitude of the observer expressed in time, 1 hour being equivalent to 15°, since the Earth rotates through 15° per hour. Places on the same meridian always have the same *Local Sidereal Time*. Sidereal Time at Greenwich is local for the Greenwich meridian and for all places on that meridian irrespective of latitude. Other places on earth, not on the Greenwich meridian, would have a Local Sidereal Time differing from the Greenwich Sidereal Time, and this difference would depend on the longitude of the place east or west of Greenwich.

In determining the Local Sidereal Time for a given time and place, we can ascertain the culminating degree of the Ecliptic, either from a Table of Houses or from Tables of Right Ascension (Sidereal Time and Right Ascension being synonymous). Reference to Tables of Houses for the latitude of birth and noting the appropriate Local Sidereal Time will give the Rising Degree (Ascendant) and the other factors related to *House Division* (mundane position).

Correction Mean to Sidereal Time

A Mean Solar Day is equivalent to 24 hours 3 minutes 56.56 seconds of Sidereal Time, and therefore the calculation of Sidereal Time from a given Mean Solar Time requires a correction at the rate of 9.86 seconds per hour. For normal purposes, this can be treated as 10 seconds per hour, but where precision is required, the exact factor should be used. This correction is often referred to as the *acceleration on the interval,* but as in all things, simplicity should be the aim, and it is easier and less confusing to call it *the Mean Time correction.*

A Tropical Year of 365.2422 Mean Solar Days is equivalent to 366.2422 Sidereal Days. An astronomical clock will indicate 24 hours in 23 hours 56 minutes 4.09 seconds of ordinary clock or Mean Time. The fact that a Tropical Year contains 366.2422 Sidereal Days and 365.2422 Mean Solar Days results in the Sidereal clock registering 1 hour 0 minutes 9.8565 seconds in one hour of Mean Time. In other words, the Sidereal clock gains 9.8565 sidereal seconds on the Mean Time clock in one hour of Mean Time. This quantity of 9.8565 seconds is the acceleration of the Sidereal clock per Mean Time hour. Therefore, any interval of Mean Time will necessitate an addition of 3 minutes 56.56 seconds per 24 Mean Time hours, in order to convert it to the equivalent interval of Sidereal Time, and conversely, any interval of Sidereal Time requires to be diminished by 3 minutes 55.91 seconds per 24 Sidereal hours to convert it to the equivalent interval of Mean Time.

Mean Time Correction

Example No. 1
Find the correction to be applied to convert 5 hours 10 minutes Mean Time to Sidereal Time.

Working
From Tables:

		M	S		M	S
5 hours	=	0	49.28			
10′	=		1.64	=	0	50.92

Using calculator:

5.166 hours × 9.86″		=		50.94
		=	0	51

It is not necessary to be so precise for ordinary natal charting, as the difference between Mean Time and Sidereal Time can never be greater than 2 minutes in 12 hours or just under 4 minutes in 24 hours.

Example No. 2
Find the correction to be applied to convert 11 hours 17 minutes Mean Time to Sidereal Time.

Working
From Tables:

		M	S		M	S
11 hours	=	1	48.42			
17′	=		2.79	=	1	51

Using calculator:

11.283 × 9.86″	=	1	51

Greenwich Sidereal Time

In our discussions on time and time conversion we noted that Sidereal Time at any instant is the Hour Angle of the Vernal Equinox expressed in time, and is identical with the Right Ascension of the Meridian.

The Sidereal Time for each day of the year at noon is listed in the ephemeris for the Greenwich meridian. If we refer to *Raphael's Ephemeris* for 1 January 1980, we can see that the Sidereal Time (S.T.) was 18 hours(H) 41 minutes(M) 13 seconds(S). This entry is for noon on that day, and if we require to know the Sidereal Time at, say, 3 p.m. on that day in London, we add 3 hours, plus the correction for Mean to Sidereal Time (9.86 seconds per hour) to obtain the Sidereal Time at 3 p.m. In this case it would be 21 hours 41 minutes 42 seconds.

For a place other than the Greenwich meridian, the Sidereal Time would be different, depending upon the longitude of the place, either east or west from Greenwich. The entry for 1 January tells us that it is 18 hours 41 minutes 13 seconds, since the First Point of Aries was on the meridian at London, and it will be about 5 hours 19 minutes Sidereal Time later, when it once again returns to the Greenwich meridian.

The average increase of Sidereal Time over Mean Solar Time is 3 minutes 56 seconds per day, hence the necessity to correct Mean Time hours by 9.86 seconds per hour. Even though the Sidereal Time as shown in the ephemeris for noon increases by 3 minutes 56 seconds per day, the

Earth has in a period of 24 hours clock time, turned a full 24 hours plus the additional 3 minutes 56 seconds.

When the birth place is not on the Greenwich meridian, a further correction is necessary in order to obtain the *Local Sidereal Time* at birth. This correction is termed the *Longitude Equivalent* in time and consists of converting the longitude of the birth place into time at the rate of 15 degrees per hour ($\frac{360}{15}$). If the birth place is east of Greenwich this longitude correction is *added,* and if the birth place is west of Greenwich, the correction is *deducted.* The result is the Local Sidereal Time at birth.

For absolute precision a further correction of 9.86 seconds per hour of longitude should be made by adding for west longitude and deducting for east longitude. In the same manner that we corrected for Mean to Sidereal Time, so we correct for longitude (space). However, unless the birth data are precise, this correction can be ignored. Calculation tables to facilitate the conversion from Mean to Sidereal Time, and for finding the longitude equivalent in time, are listed under 'Calculation Tables'.

The Local Sidereal Time of Birth

The Sidereal Time given in the ephemeris is for noon, for the Greenwich meridian and all places on that meridian irrespective of latitude.

If we require to know the Sidereal Time other than that at noon and for a place other than on the Greenwich meridian, a simple calculation will enable us to find it. On any particular day, according to the time of year, the Sidereal Time at noon will be anything from 0 hours to 23 hours 56 minutes, increasing by just under 4 minutes per day. As Sidereal Time is the Hour Angle of the Vernal Equinox expressed in time, the constant rotation of the celestial sphere increases this angle and in the course of 24 hours, the First Point of Aries will return to the meridian, and the Sidereal Time will be 0 hours.

To determine the Local Sidereal Time of birth we take the Sidereal Time at Noon on the day of birth, add or deduct the interval of time depending on whether the birth time was a.m. or p.m., apply the necessary correction for Mean Solar Time, and if appropriate, apply the longitude equivalent in time. The result is the Local Sidereal Time of birth which enables us to determine the rising degree and sign, and the cusps of the houses for a particular time and place.

Sidereal Time, as we have seen is *always* local; the Sidereal Time listed in the ephemeris is local for the Greenwich meridian and all places on that meridian. Places not on the Greenwich meridian have different Local Sidereal Times depending on the longitude of the place either east or west from Greenwich.

Example:
6 January 1980, 7.15 p.m. G.M.T. the Sidereal Time at London is:

	H	M	S			H	M	S
	19	00	56					
+	7	15	00	Interval				
+		1	11	Correction	=	2	17	07

At New York: Long. 73° 57' west

	H	M	S			H	M	S
	19	00	56					
+	7	15	00					
+		1	11					
	2	17	07					
Less	4	55	48	Long. Equiv. west	=	21	21	19

At Munich: Long. 11° 33' east

	H	M	S			H	M	S
	19	00	56					
+	7	15	00					
+		1	11					
	2	17	07					
Add		46	12	Long. Equiv. east	=	3	03	19

The rising degree and sign are found from the appropriate Tables of Houses for the particular latitude of birth.

Example No. 1
Required to find the Local Sidereal Time (L.S.T.) for a birth at 5.15 p.m. G.M.T. 1 January 1980 at London.

		H	M	S
Working				
Sidereal time at noon 1 January:		18	41	13
Time after noon: 5.15	*add*	5	15	00
Correction mean to Sidereal Time				
(5.25 × 9.86):	*add:*			52
Local S.T. at London 5.15 p.m. G.M.T.	=	23	57	05

From the Tables of Houses for London the Ascendant to the nearest degree is 26° Cancer, and the M.C. is 29° Pisces.

Example No. 2
Required to find the L.S.T. for a birth at 2.30 a.m. G.M.T. 2 January 1980 at London.

		H	M	S
Working				
Sidereal Time at noon 2 January:		18	45	10
Time before noon: 12.00				
less: 2.30	*less:*	9	30	00
See Tables (Interval of Time to Noon)		9	15	10
Correction 9.30 (9.5 × 9.86 secs):	*less:*		1	34
Local S.T. at London 2.30 a.m.	=	9	13	36

From the Tables of Houses for London the Ascendant to the nearest degree is 4° Scorpio, and the M.C. is 16° Leo.

Example No. 3
Required to find the L.S.T. for a birth at 5.00 p.m. Eastern Standard Time, New York, 1 January.

Working		H	M	S
Birth time as given: E.S.T.		5	00	00
Convert to G.M.T. (New York 5 hours slow)				
therefore *add* 5 hours:		5	00	00
Greenwich Mean Time (p.m.):		10	00	00
Sidereal Time at noon 1 January:		18	41	13
Greenwich Time 10 hours after noon:	*add:*	10	00	00
Correction Mean to Sidereal Time				
10 × 9.86 secs:	*add:*		1	38
*Sidereal Time at Greenwich:		28	42	51
Longitude equivalent (73° 57')				
= 73.95 over 15 = 4 hrs 55' 48"				
West longitude — *deduct:*	*less:*	4	55	48
Local S.T. at New York:		23	47	03

From Tables of Houses for New York, Ascendant 16° Cancer, M.C. 26° Pisces.

* The S.T. at Greenwich is 4 hours 42 mins 51 secs, but for ease of subtraction we show 28 hours 42 mins 51 secs.

Example No. 4
Required to find the L.S.T. for a birth at 11.00 p.m. Eastern Standard Time, New York, 1 January 1980.

Working		H	M	S
Birth time as given (p.m.): E.S.T.		11	00	00
Convert to G.M.T. (*add* 5 hours):		5	00	00
G.M.T. (note change of date 2 January) a.m.:		4	00	00
Sidereal Time at noon *2 January:*		18	45	10
Interval of time to noon 12.00				
less 4.00	*less:*	8	00	00
		10	45	10
Correction Mean to Sidereal Time				
8 × 9.86":	*less:*		1	19
		10	43	51
Longitude equivalent west				
73° 57' (73.95 over 15)	*less:*	4	55	48
Local Sidereal Time New York:		5	48	03

From Tables of Houses for New York, Ascendant 27° Virgo, M.C. 27° Gemini.

Local Time

The term Local Time generally means the time in use in a particular locality, normally the *Standard Time* which has been adopted for a certain zone or area, whereas Local (Mean Solar) time is the mean solar time for a definite meridian. Local Mean Solar Time differs by 4 minutes for every 1 degree of longitude, but Standard Time is Zone Time and is the Local Mean Time of a certain standard meridian of a Standard Time Zone.

For example, New York uses the standard meridian 75° West, and all clocks are 5 hours slow on Greenwich. New York, however, is not exactly on the 75th meridian but is 73° 57' west of Greenwich, so that this longitude when expressed in time is 73° 57' over 15 which equals 4 hours 55 minutes 48 seconds. When it is noon G.M.T. in London, the New York clocks show 7 a.m. Eastern Standard Time (which is 5 hours slow based on the 75th meridian), but the local (Mean Solar) Time of New York is 12.00 less 4 hours 55 minutes 48 seconds, which equals 7 hours 4' 12" a.m. Local (Mean Solar) Time. Unless information is given to the contrary, it can be assumed that the term Local Time when given for chart calculations, is the clock time of the particular locality.

Edinburgh, which 3° 11' west longitude, uses the Standard Time common to Great Britain, normally G.M.T., but the Local (Mean Solar) Time according to the meridian of Edinburgh is 12 minutes 44 seconds slow on Greenwich, and although the Edinburgh clocks show G.M.T. its local time always differs by 12' 44". When it is noon G.M.T. it is 11.47.16 a.m. Local Time at Edinburgh.

If we were calculating a chart for Edinburgh for a given clock time of, say, 2 p.m. and assuming no Summer Time was in operation, this would be G.M.T. and the planets' places would be calculated for this time. However, to find the Ascendant and the various house cusps, we would deduct the longitude equivalent (12 minutes 44 seconds) from the Greenwich Sidereal Time at birth in order to obtain the Local Sidereal Time at birth.

Longitude Equivalent

In discussing the Local Sidereal Time at birth, we mentioned the Longitude Equivalent in time and as this is an important part of natal charting, examples will be given of this conversion.

All places on Earth can be identified by reference to their latitude and longitude. Latitude is measured from the Equator 0-90° either north or south and longitude is measured from the Greenwich meridian 0-180° either east or west. Each degree of longitude is equivalent to 4 minutes of time (15° per hour) and, therefore, to find the longitude equivalent in time of any place, we merely convert the longitude into time by dividing the degrees and minutes of longitude by 15. If the place is east of Greenwich, we add this time to the Greenwich time, or if the place is west, we deduct it, and the result is the Local Mean Time of the place. The Mean Time at any place (Local Mean Time) is the hour angle of the Mean Sun measured from the meridian of that place. Greenwich Mean time is the Local Mean time kept on the meridian of Greenwich. At all places east of Greenwich, the Mean Sun transits the meridian earlier than at Greenwich, and at places west of Greenwich the transit occurs later, hence the addition for east longitudes and the deduction for west longitudes.

Example No. 1
Required to find the longitude equivalent in time for a place 120° 45' east.

Working

						H	M
120.45	=	$\dfrac{120.75}{15}$	=	8.05	=	8	3

If the time at Greenwich was Noon, then the *Local Mean Solar Time* at 120° 45' east is 12.00 + 8 hours 3 minutes = 8   3

In other words when it is noon at Greenwich it is 8 hours 3 minutes p.m. in terms of the Mean Sun.

If the longitude was 120° 45' west then the Local Mean Solar Time would be 12.00 less 8.3 which = 3 hours 57 minutes a.m.

Example No. 2
Required to find the longitude equivalent in time for a place 45° 30' east.

Working

						H	M
45.30	=	$\dfrac{45.5}{15}$	=	3.03	=	3	2

If the Greenwich Time was 10.00 a.m. then the Local Mean Solar Time in 45° 30' east would be 10.00 + 3.2 = 1 hour 2 minutes p.m.

The finding of the longitude equivalent in time is a simple matter, and tables are included with this work to facilitate the necessary conversions.

Example No. 3

On 1 January 1980 in longitude 96° 15' west, the Greenwich Mean Time was 6 hours 15 minutes a.m. Find the Local Mean Time for this longitude.

Working		H	M	
G.M.T. 1 January:		6	15	a.m.

Longitude in time

$$96.15 = \frac{96.25}{15} \qquad = \quad 6 \quad 25 \quad Deduct \text{ west}$$

		H	M	
Therefore, *add* 12 hours to		12	00	
facilitate deduction:	+	6	15	
		18	15	
Less Longitude in time:	=	6	25	
Local Mean Time:	=	11	50	p.m.

Note change of date:
The Local Mean Time is 11.50 p.m. on 31 December 1979.

Example No. 4

On the 1 January, the G.M.T. of a particular place was 10.30 a.m. and the Local Mean Time was 2.30 p.m. Find the longitude.

Working	H	M	
Local Mean Time 1 January:	2	30	p.m.
G.M.T.:	10	30	a.m.

Difference in time:	12.00			
less:	10.30			
	1.30			
add:	2.30	=	4	00

4 hours × 15 = 60

Therefore, the longitude was 60 degrees east, as the difference was 4 hours greater than the quoted G.M.T. (10.30 a.m.).

The International Date Line

The Earth turns on its axis once every 24 hours. So the Sun will transit the meridians of different places at different times. By international agreement, the meridian passing through Greenwich was chosen as the 0° meridian. Therefore, when it is noon at Greenwich, it will be midnight at 180° longitude. But at longitude 195° East (that is 165° West) the time is not 1 hour ahead of midnight but a full 23 hours behind it. This is because the date must change somewhere on the Earth, and by convention, the meridian of longitude 180° East from Greenwich was chosen for this purpose.

This meridian is known as the International Date Line, and crossing it from west to east, one loses a full day; crossing it from east to west, one gains a full day. Each side of the Date Line has a different day. To the west it is a day later; to the east a day earlier. The Date Line is drawn so that it

	EAST												GREENWICH NOON	WEST											
	FAST ON GREENWICH													SLOW ON GREENWICH											
	P.M.													A.M.											
Degs. of Long.	180	165	150	135	120	105	90	75	60	45	30	15	0	15	30	45	60	75	90	105	120	135	150	165	180
Long. Equiv. Hours	12	11	10	9	8	7	6	5	4	3	2	1	0	1	2	3	4	5	6	7	8	9	10	11	12
Standard Time	Mid-Night	11	10	9	8	7	6	5	4	3	2	1	Noon	1	2	3	4	5	6	7	8	9	10	11	Mid-Night

Figure 17(a).　Standard Times.

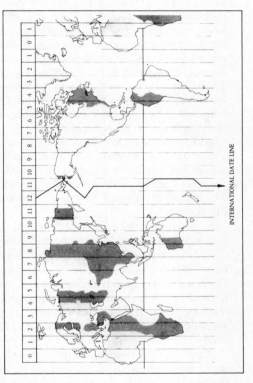

Figure 17(b).　International Date Line.

follows a zig-zag path either side of the 180th meridian, thus avoiding the tip of Asia and certain of the Pacific Islands.

Standard Time

Prior to the adoption of *Standard Time Zones,* much confusion existed regarding the recording of time in particular localities. Some places used Solar Time or True Sun Time as indicated by a Sun dial; other places used Mean Time as indicated by their longitude. With the rapid expansion of transport during the last century, and particularly the railway services in large countries such as the United States and Canada, the question of time became a paramount issue. The railways had to operate over vast distances and to specified time schedules, and it was essential that a standard time system be adopted. At a convention held in 1883, the General Railway Time Committee agreed to adopt the Greenwich meridian as the origin of world time and to establish time zones with intervals of 15 degrees longitude (1 hour). The new time was introduced in Canada and the United States at noon on 18 November 1883.

Although the large railway systems adopted Standard Time, it was, in some cases, many years later that Standard Time as such became the recognized system for a certain locality. Consequently, in the early days, the term 'railway time' referred to the official time used by the railways which may or may not have coincided with the time used by the local inhabitants.

In North America, several Standard Time Zones are in operation ranging from Atlantic Time (eastern seaboard) to Pacific Time on the west coast, and these standards, based upon a central meridian, are from 3 to 8 hours behind the time recorded at Greenwich. Likewise, places east of Greenwich have Standard Times which are in advance by several hours depending upon the longitude which has been adopted as the central meridian. Central Europe, for example, uses the longitude 15 degrees east as the central meridian and all clocks show 1 hour in advance of Greenwich time.

Standard Time is now used throughout the world but caution is needed when ascertaining the standard of a particular area as many changes have been made since the inception of Standard Time. Also, many countries have altered or revised their original time zones. A good reference work should always be consulted for the *date and year* in question, or enquiries should be made at the appropriate embassy or to the representative. The clock time of birth is normally the standard in operation, but this is subject to variations during certain times of the year owing to the introduction of *Daylight Saving Time (Summer Time)* which was first used during the First World War. In order to arrive at the Greenwich time of birth, the Standard Time has to be *added* for *west* longitude and *deducted* for *east* longitude, and if Daylight Saving Time was in operation, this must be *deducted* from the time given. Time to an astrologer is of the utmost importance, and it is essential that the various 'kinds of time' are fully understood.

Daylight Saving Time/Summer Time/War Time

These terms are identical and relate to advancing the clock for certain periods during the year. The amount of the advance is normally one hour but there are variations regarding the amount, particularly during war time. The clocks are put forward in the early Spring and put back again in the Autumn, but some countries use permanent 'Summer Time' all year round. Again, a good reference work needs to be consulted for the date and year required. War Time was the term used in the United States and North America generally during World War I and II. During the Second World War, all time zones in the U.S.A. were advanced 1 hour from 2 February 1942 to 30 September 1945. When this 'artificial' time is in operation, the amount of the advance must be *deducted* from the clock time given in order to arrive at the Standard time of the country or state.

Universal Time

This term is synonymous with Greenwich Mean Time and is used in scientific notation, astronomical data etc. It is reckoned from 0-24 hours (e.g. 21.00 hours = 9 p.m.).

Ephemeris Time

Up to and including the year 1959, Raphael's Ephemeris was based on Greenwich Mean Time. From 1960, it has been calculated in Ephemeris Time. Ephemeris Time is a system with a constant rate defined by reference to the motions of the Sun, Moon and planets. Greenwich Time is defined by the rotation of the Earth, and as the rotation of the Earth is not constant, time systems based on the Earth's rotation are not constant. Owing to the irregularity of the Earth's rotation, it does not provide a satisfactory basis for astronomical time systems, and for tables compiled from the gravitation theories of the Sun, Moon and planets. The value of Ephemeris Time changes annually and is listed in the Ephemeris (at present, 1980, it is approximately + 51 seconds). To all intents and purposes, it can be disregarded but for absolute precision, the Greenwich Mean Time should be converted to Ephemeris Time before finding the Sun's, or Moon's, position from the tables.

Example: If the Moon's position is required for 10.30 a.m. G.M.T. on 1 January 1980, it will be necessary to calculate for 10.31 a.m. (51 seconds later rounded up to the nearest minute). The times of Phenomena given in the Ephemeris are in Ephemeris Time, and in this case 51″ or 1′ must be deducted to give the Greenwich Time.

British Summer Time

British Summer Time became effective at 2 a.m. G.M.T. on *21 May 1916* and continued until 3 a.m. British Summer Time (2 a.m. G.M.T.) on *1 October 1916.*

The Summer Time Act was introduced into the British House of Commons on 8 and 9 May 1916 and became law on 17 May effective from 21 May. The principal reason for its introduction was the need for economy during the First World War. This measure stipulated that the clock should be advanced one hour during the Summer months. This artificial time has been in operation each year since 1916, but the amount of the advance and its duration has varied, particularly during the Second World War years when Double British Summer time (+ 2 hours) was used.

An experiment with *British Standard Time* was introduced on *18 February 1968 and continued until 31 October 1971*, in which all clocks were advanced one hour ahead of G.M.T. Therefore, all clock times quoted for this period should have one hour *deducted* to arrive at the G.M.T. In 1972 British Summer Time was re-introduced, whereby all clocks are advanced one hour from March to October and this practice has continued each year. (See Table for dates and duration.)

Greenwich Time and Standard Time

The Standard Time of a particular country is the time that has been adopted for a certain zone or area, and is based on a certain central meridian. In North America, the Standard Time Zones range from 3 hours to 8 hours and as the longitude is west, these standard times are slow on Greenwich. Likewise, places which are east of Greenwich have Standard Times which are in advance (fast) on Greenwich Time. When using a Greenwich based ephemeris such as Raphael's, the clock time given must be converted to the equivalent Greenwich Time because the data in the ephemeris are calculated for Greenwich Times. In actual fact, the times in the ephemeris are for Ephemeris Time, but for ordinary purposes can be considered as for Greenwich Time. We need the Greenwich Time of birth in order to calculate the planets' places (longitudes) as distinct from the Local Sidereal Time, which we use for determining the Ascendant, Midheaven and house cusps. So it is *Greenwich Time for planets,* and *Local Sidereal Time for Houses.*

Example No. 1
Required to find the Greenwich Time of birth for the following data.
2 January 1980 10.30 a.m. Eastern Standard Time New York.

Working

H	M		
10	30	a.m.	= Clock time E.S.T.
5	00		= Standard Time (5 hours slow)

Therefore the time at New York is behind Greenwich, so we add the Standard Time difference which gives:

	10	30	
+	5	00	= 3.30 p.m. at Greenwich.

If the New York clocks were registering noon, it would be 5.00 p.m. in London (Greenwich). At midnight in London, the New York clocks would show

```
    12   00
—    5   00        = 7.00 p.m.
```

Example No. 2
Find the Greenwich Time when the clock time in San Francisco shows 7.00 p.m. Pacific Standard Time, on 2 January.

Working

H	M		
7	00	p.m.	= Pacific Standard Time
8	00		= Standard Time (8 hours slow)

Therefore the time in San Francisco is behind that at Greenwich so we *add* the Standard Time difference which gives:

```
     7   00
+    8   00   = 15    = 3.00 a.m. on 3 January
```

Note that in this case, the date has changed and the time at Greenwich is in the early hours of the morning on the next day (3 January). When it is noon in San Francisco, the time in London is 8.00 p.m. the same day.

Example No. 3
Find the Greenwich Time when the clock time in Hong Kong shows 2.00 a.m. 2 January.

Working

H	M		
2	00	a.m.	= Clock Time Standard meridian 120.00° east
8	00		= Standard Time (8 hours fast)

Therefore, the time in Hong Kong is 8 hours in advance of Greenwich, so we *deduct* 8 hours which gives:

```
     2   00
—    8   00        = 6.00 p.m. on 1 January.
```

Example No. 4
Find the Standard Time at Sydney, New South Wales, Australia, when the Greenwich Time is 6.00 p.m. 1 January.

Working

H	M		
6	00	p.m.	= Greenwich Time
10	00		= Standard meridian 150° east

Therefore, the time in Sydney is 10 hours fast on Greenwich so we add the Standard Time difference (10 hours) which gives:

```
      6    00
 +   10    00   =   16
                less 12   = 4.00 a.m. the next day (2 January)
```

Example No. 5
Find the Standard Time at Salt Lake City when the Greenwich Time is 1.00 a.m. 2 January.

Working

H	M		
1	00	a.m.	= Greenwich Time
7	00		= Standard meridian $\frac{105.00}{15}$ west

Therefore, the Standard Time at Salt Lake City is 7 hours slow on Greenwich, so we deduct the Standard Time difference (7 hours) which gives:

```
     1    00
    12    00   add for ease of subtraction

    13    00
     7    00   less      = 6.00 p.m. on the previous day,
                           1 January
```

Example No. 6
The clock time in Tokyo, Japan shows 5.00 p.m. What is the Greenwich Mean Time?

Working

H	M		
5	00	p.m.	= Clock Time Tokyo
9	00		= Standard Time based on 135.00°
			east = $\frac{135}{15}$ = 9 hours

Therefore the time in Tokyo is 9 hours in advance of Greenwich, so we deduct the Standard Time difference (9 hours) which gives:

```
     5    00
    12    00   add

    17    00
     9    00   minus     = 8.00 a.m. = Greenwich Time the
                           same day.
```

Example No. 7
What is the Greenwich Time and date when the clocks in Tokyo show 3.00 a.m. 2 January?

Working

H	M		
3	00	a.m.	= Clock Time Tokyo
9	00		= Standard Time (east long. deduct)

Therefore the clock time minus the Standard Time difference =

3	00	
12	00	*add*
15	00	
9	00	*minus* = 6.00 p.m. G.M.T. 1 January

Example No. 8
The Clock Time at Kingston, Jamaica shows 11.15 p.m. on the 1st January. What is the Greenwich Time?

Working

H	M	
11	15	= Clock Time Kingston
5	00	= Standard Time based on 75° west

$$= \frac{75}{15} = 5 \text{ hours}$$

Therefore the Standard Time difference is added to the Clock Time as we are dealing with west longitude which gives:

11	15	
5	00	*add*
16	15	= 4.15 a.m. 2 January = Greenwich Time and date.

Finding the Greenwich Time and date when Daylight Saving Time/Summer Time is in operation

Example No. 1
Birth data: 1.00 a.m. 23 May 1916, London.
British Summer Time was in operation from 21 May 1916 (see Tables), therefore 1 hour must be *deducted* from time given, which gives the birth time as midnight 22/23 May G.M.T.

Example No. 2
Birth data: 1.00 a.m. 23 May 1941, London.
Double British Summer Time was in operation in 1941 from the 4

May-10 August, therefore *2 hours* must be deducted from the time given, which gives the birth time as 11.00 p.m. 22 May 1941. Note change of date. The Greenwich Time and date = 11.00 p.m. 22 May 1941.

Example No. 3
Birth data: 4.00 p.m. 1 January 1970, London.
British Standard Time was in operation from *18 February 1968-31 October 1971,* therefore, *all clock times given have to be reduced by 1 hour.* 4.00 p.m. less 1 = 3.00 p.m. G.M.T. 1 January 1970.

Example No. 4
Birth data: Midnight 31 December/1 January 1969/70, London.
British Standard Time in operation, therefore *deduct* 1 hour which gives Greenwich Time and date of birth as 11.00 p.m. 31 December 1969.

In North America generally, during World War I and II, War Time was in operation whereby all time zones were advanced 1 hour. Details concerning time changes in the United States and North America are contained in the excellent publications by Doris Chase Doane (see references).

Example No. 5
Birth data: 10.15 p.m. clock time, 1 January 1943 New York. The Greenwich Time of birth is found as follows:

H	M		
10	15	p.m.	= Clock Time = War Time
1	00	*minus*	= War Time advance
9	15	p.m.	
		E.S.T.	= Standard Time New York
5	00	*add*	= Standard Time based on 75 ° west
14	15		= 2.15 a.m. 2 January 1943 = Greenwich Time and date.

Whenever War Time or Daylight Saving Time/Summer Time is in operation, the amount of the advance (normally one hour) must be *deducted* from the given clock time in order to obtain the Standard Time of the place. Unless the various time conversions are carried out correctly, the chart will be in error by an hour or so and all subsequent work connected with the chart will be wasted.

6.

THE EPHEMERIS

An ephemeris is a publication which contains all the essential astronomical information necessary for the calculation of astrological charts. Several types of ephemerides are available, ranging from those published for each year to extensive series which cover many years ahead. A well-known and very reliable ephemeris is *Raphael's Astronomical Ephemeris* which is published annually. For well over a century, this ephemeris has maintained a remarkably high standard and is recommended for all astrological calculations. Certain of the astronomical information in the ephemeris is based upon the Astronomical Ephemeris, a government publication.

The astrological ephemeris is an indispensable publication for the calculation of charts and other forms of astrological computing. Copies of Raphael's ephemerides can be obtained for any year from the 1860s onwards. Over the years, the format has been slightly altered and additional information has been included with slight variations in the listing of data. Prior to 1934, Pluto's positions were not listed, since this planet was only discovered in 1930. For the years prior to 1934 Pluto's positions (1840-1960) can be found in the publication *The Influence of the Planet Pluto* by Elbert Benjamine, published by the Aries Press.

Raphael's Ephemeris is a noon ephemeris, which means that the positions listed, unless otherwise stated, are for noon on a particular day. Some ephemerides such as *Die Deutsche* are calculated for 0 hours, that is, the commencement of the day.

Up to and including the year 1959, *Raphael's Ephemeris* was calculated for noon G.M.T., but since 1960 it has been calculated in Ephemeris Time (see previous chapter). As the value of Ephemeris Time varies annually

(1980 + 51 seconds), the G.M.T. requires the addition of the Ephemeris Time value before using the information that is contained in the ephemeris. However, unless the time of the birth or event is absolutely precise, the conversion from G.M.T. to Ephemeris Time can be ignored and the data in the ephemeris can be treated as for Greenwich Mean Time.

Symbols

At first glance, the ephemeris may appear to be a mass of symbols and figures—almost incomprehensible. However, with a little practice, the reading of an ephemeris is a simple matter. Firstly, the symbols listed at the top of the monthly pages refer to the Sun, Moon and the planets.

Sun	☉	Mars	♂	Uranus	♅
Moon	☽	Jupiter	♃	Neptune	♆
Mercury	☿	Saturn	♄	Pluto	♇
Venus	♀				

Reference to page 2 and 3 of the ephemeris for January 1980 shows the planetary symbols and underneath each symbol is the word Long. which is the abbreviation for longitude, and in each column, we have the degree and minute of the particular sign of the Zodiac that each planet occupies at noon on a certain day. The signs of the Zodiac are listed for the first day of the month and again for the last day. When a planet changes sign, the symbol for the sign is shown against the day when the change occurred. In ascertaining a planet's longitude for times other than noon, care is needed to note the sign occupied and not merely take the sign shown at the top of the page for the 1st day of the month.

The signs of the Zodiac are:

Aries	♈	Libra	♎
Taurus	♉	Scorpio	♏
Gemini	♊	Sagittarius	♐
Cancer	♋	Capricorn	♑
Leo	♌	Aquarius	♒
Virgo	♍	Pisces	♓

The symbol ℞ which appears in the planetary positions column (page 3) indicates that the planet has turned *retrograde* on that particular day. An explanation of retrograde motion is given on page 43. 'D' indicates *Direct*, that is a planet is going from ℞ (retrograde) to forward motion. The far right hand column (page 3) shows the Lunar Aspects (the aspects formed by the Moon on a particular day). In the lower half of the page, the Mutual Aspects are those formed between the planets on a particular day. The symbols shown in the Lunar and Mutual Aspects column refer to the type of aspect formed; different aspects representing the distance in degrees that the Moon or planets are from each other. Aspects and their significance are discussed on page 129, but the following table shows the aspects used in astrology. In the interpretation of charts, considerable attention is given to aspects as they are very important factors.

Types of Aspects

Although many of the aspects are classified as minor, astrological research is tending to confirm that some of the so-called minor aspects have great value, and are more important than has previously been thought.

Type	Symbol	Degrees apart	Classification
Conjunction	☌	0	Major
Occultation	⚈	0	Major
Semi-Sextile	⚺	30	Minor
Semi-Quintile	⊥	36	Minor
Semi-Square	∠	45	Major
Sextile	✳	60	Major
Quintile	Q	72	Minor
Square	□	90	Major
Trine	△	120	Major
Sesquiquadrate	⊡	135	Minor
Bi-Quintile	±	144	Minor
Quincunx	�	150	Minor
Opposition	☍	180	Major
P (Parallel in declination)	——	0	Variable

Planetary Positions

The Sun

The planets' positions as listed in the ephemeris are given in Celestial Longitude (measurement along the Ecliptic eastward from the First Point of Aries) and, unless absolute precision is required, can be regarded as for noon G.M.T. On page 2, 1 January 1980, the Sun's longitude is given as 10 degrees 13 minutes 25 seconds Capricorn. In calculating a planet's position for a time other than noon, the odd seconds can be ignored, in this case we treat the longitude as 10 degrees 13 minutes. This procedure applies for times of birth or events which are not precisely recorded; for times that are exact then the chart should be calculated accurately.

Charts for Solar Returns, which will be discussed later on, must have the Sun's position calculated to seconds. In taking out the Sun's position from the ephemeris the sign should be noted, as this changes each month on or about the 21st/22nd. On 1 January, the Sun is in Capricorn but on the 21st, it is shown as 0 degrees 36 minutes 4 seconds of Aquarius. Sometime between 20 and 21 of January, it has 'entered' Aquarius; the exact time of its entry can be found from the table in the ephemeris on page 39. In this

particular case, it entered Aquarius at 9.50 p.m., which is Ephemeris
Time, but we will assume is G.M.T. If we wished to check this time, the
following calculation enables us to do so.

		°	′	″	
Sun's position Noon 21 January	=	0	36	4	Aquarius
Sun's position Noon 20 January	=	29	34	59	Capricorn
Motion in 24 hours:		1	1	5	

9.50 = 0.4097 Day × 1.018°

= 0.417 = 25′ 1″, which added to
the noon position on

20 January:	29	34	59	Capricorn
		25	1	
=	0	0	0	Aquarius

In the column next to the Sun's longitude there appears the heading
'Sun Dec.' (Declination), and this relates to the distance that the Sun has
above or below the Equator. The measurement is in degrees and minutes
either north or south of the Equator. The position of the Earth relative to
the Sun determines the Sun's Declination. From the ephemeris we note
that the Sun's Declination on 1 January is 23° 3′ S, which tells us that the
Sun is 23° 3′ south of the Equator. At the end of the month, it is 17° 32′,
so it is decreasing and will continue to do so until about 20 March, when it
will then have zero declination as it crosses the Equator going from south to
north at the Vernal Equinox. Its declination will then be north and
increasing until it reaches its maximum declination 23° 26′ at the June
Solstice on or about 21 June.

The Moon
Whereas the Sun's motion is on average about one degree per day, the
Moon's motion is about 13 degrees, and its moves rapidly through all
twelve signs of the Zodiac in about 27½ days. On average, it passes
through each sign in 2½ days. When the Moon changes signs, the sign is
listed in the ephemeris but only if the change occurred before noon. As
with the Sun, the actual time of entering a sign is shown on page 39. In
calculating the Moon's position for a specific time, we note its motion from
noon to noon, or from noon to midnight or from midnight to noon,
depending on the time for which the chart is required. The longitude of the
Moon need only be calculated in degrees and minutes; odd seconds can be
ignored.

The easiest way to obtain the daily motions of the planets is to refer to the
table on pages 26 and 27 of the ephemeris which gives the motions of the
Sun, Moon and the faster moving planets. The slower-moving planets are

not given in the table, but simple proportion will give their longitudes for a given time. The column headed 'Moon Lat.' (Latitude) page 2, refers to the Moon's position in terms of Celestial Latitude, which is the measurement in degrees and minutes of arc north or south of the Ecliptic. The Sun has no latitude being always on the Ecliptic, its apparent path. Relative to the plane of the Ecliptic, the Moon's orbit is tilted, the mean tilt being 5° 8' (see astronomical chapters). The ephemeris shows the Moon's latitude for each day, and this indicates how its orbit is tilted relative to the plane of the Ecliptic. In astrological charting, latitude is not normally used.

The Moon's Declination shown in the ephemeris for both noon and midnight increases or decreases either north or south during each month. On 1 January, the Moon's Declination is 18° 59' north and it reaches its maximum Declination 19° 9' north on 2 January. Thereafter, its Declination decreases until on 9 January it is zero, and it is then that the Moon is on the Equator. From the 9th onwards, the Declination increases until it again reaches the maximum south declination on 16 January.

The maximum Declination of the Moon varies from month to month and from year to year. During a period of 19 years, this variation is from about 28½° to about 18°, and this phenomenon is termed the 'regression of the nodes', which is a retrograde motion along the Ecliptic. The ascending node is where the Moon crosses the Ecliptic from south to north, and the descending node is where the Moon crosses going from north to south. Astronomically, the line joining these two points is referred to as the Nodal Line, which is the line of intersection of the plane of the Earth's path and that of the Moon's path.

Planets

The longitude of each planet from Mercury to Pluto is listed on page 3 of the ephemeris, and as with the Sun and Moon, the daily motions of the faster moving planets can be obtained from pages 26 and 27. The slow moving planets are not listed, but owing to their relatively slow motion their positions are easily calculated. In the lower half of pages 2 and 3, the latitude and Declination of all the planets are given—for every other day for the slower moving planets, and for each day for the faster moving planets.

Lunar Aspects

The table on page 3 lists all the aspects (angular distance between the Moon and a planet as measured in Celestial Longitude). The aspects as shown in the table are exact on the day shown, but astrologers allow certain 'orbs' of so many degrees either more or less than the degree of exactitude. For example, if two planets (and here we include the Sun and Moon) were 112° or 128° apart (that is, plus or minus 8°), it would be considered a trine aspect (120°). In the table however, the aspect is listed for the day that it is exact.

Mutual Aspects

This table (lower right corner page 3) lists all the aspects between the planets excluding the Moon. Again, this is a useful table to use for checking the chart after it has been erected. In this table, if a planet makes more than one aspect on a particular day, the planet's symbol is not repeated, but each aspect is separated by a comma. e.g. 15 January, Sun sesquiduadrate Jupiter, sextile Uranus.

Lunations

The Moon's phases—New, First Quarter, Full, and Last Quarter—are shown at the top and bottom of each page. The time of occurrence is given as well as the Zodiacal sign and longitude in degrees and minutes. The lunations are considered important in Mundane Astrology, and this information is useful for setting up charts connected with this particular branch of astrology.

A Complete Aspectarian

On pages 30-37 of the ephemeris is a section which lists all the aspects formed between the Sun, Moon and the planets during the year. This table gives the date, time of day and the aspect formed. The letters B, G, b, g, etc. refer to the nature of the aspect and are based on the traditional meanings assigned to the various aspects. B for example means bad, G means good, small b: fairly bad, small g: fairly good.

Modern astrology does not accept many of the traditional and somewhat archaic meanings associated with aspects, and the terms good and bad should not be taken too seriously. Certainly, some aspects appear to be connected with difficult and tension-producing situations and conditions, whilst others appear to correlate with easy and favourable forms of expression. The square aspect (90°) and the opposition (180°) are more indicative of tension and obstacles which may have to be overcome. Again, it depends on the nature of the planets involved. A Mars/Saturn contact is more 'tension producing' than say a Moon/Venus square or opposition. However, this table is extremely useful, particularly, when progressions have to be listed. Progressions (not dealt with in this book) refer to 'progressing' the chart so many days after birth according to the person's age and assessing the likely trends which may manifest according to the configuration between the natal chart and the progressed positions.

Distances apart of all conjunctions and oppositions

This table (page 38-39) lists all the conjunctions and oppositions occurring during the year. It gives the date, time and—in the fourth column—the distance apart of the two planets in degrees and minutes of declination. The times given are for the Greenwich meridian, and for meridians other than Greenwich, where G.M.T. is not used, a conversion has to be made into the time of the country concerned. The Local Mean Solar Time of the aspect can be obtained by using the longitude equivalent (terrestrial longitude divided by 15) and adding or deducting this equivalent depending on whether the place is east or west of Greenwich. Declination is the measurement either north or south of the Celestial Equator, and when two planets are within an orb of about 1½° of the same degree, either on the same or opposite side of the Equator, they have a Parallel of Declination.

On 21 January, the Moon is opposition Saturn with a Declination of only 8 minutes apart, a very close contact. On the other hand, on 10 January the Moon is conjunction Pluto with a wide Declination of 12° 7'. The closer the contact, the more powerful the aspect. In the table, certain conjunctions are shown 'blacked out', and this indicates an occultation, which is caused by the Moon being in the same degrees of longitude and Declination as a planet, and the Moon will, for a short time, 'eclipse or hide' that planet.

Daily Motions of the Planets

As the ephemeris is calculated for noon, birth times other than noon, need to have the planetary longitudes calculated for the time of birth or event. The table of Daily Motions (pages 26-28) shows the distance that a planet has travelled from one noon to the next. The distance which is measured in Celestial Longitude along the Ecliptic varies, and the table shows this variation for each day. For example, on 1 January, the Moon's motion is listed as 12° 58' 11", and on the 2 January as 12° 42' 30". If we wish to find the Moon's longitude at 7.30 p.m. on 1 January, the following calculation will give it:

12.969 (12.58.11) × 7.5 (7 hrs 30') over 24

$$= \frac{12.969 \times 7.5}{24} = 4.053 = 4° \, 3' \, 11''$$

which added to the noon position on 1 January

$$
\begin{array}{rrl}
= & 29° & 43' & 43'' \text{ Gemini} \\
+ & 4° & 3' & 11'' \\
\hline
& 3° & 46' & 54'' \text{ Cancer (Moon's position 7.30 p.m.)}
\end{array}
$$

If we take the noon to midnight motion (12 hours) on 1 January and calculate the position for 7.30 p.m., we find a slight difference in the position as compared with calculating over a 24-hour period. The motion for 24 hours is the average motion; as the Moon is subject to what is known as *acceleration* and *retardation,* its motion is not constant but varies, hence the difference when comparing the 24 hours motion with the 12 hours motion. It is better to use the 12-hourly motion when calculating the Moon's place.

The daily motion listed in the tables is for the Sun, Moon and planets, and relates to their movements from noon to noon. Therefore, for an a.m. birth, the motion to be taken will be from noon on the day previous to birth to noon on the birthday, e.g. birth 8 a.m. 5 January, the Moon's motion on 4 January is 12° 46' 6" and the interval of time to noon is 4 hours. The Moon's motion in 4 hours should be deducted from the noon position (5 January) and this will give the position at 8 a.m. Alternatively, the midnight position on the 4th, plus 8 hours motion, will give the Moon's longitude for the time required.

In this table of daily motions is shown the number of degrees and/or minutes that a planet has moved from noon to noon each day. Owing to retrograde motion, planets appear to 'move backwards', that is, slow down and become stationary and then go retrograde. There will, therefore, be instances where the longitude of a planet can be determined without the need of calculation. An example of this is Mars during January 1980. At the beginning of the month, it is moving slowly, 10 minutes on 1 January, and gradually slowing down, until on 15 January its apparent motion is nil. It is now stationary and about to turn retrograde (R_x) which it does on the 16th. Thereafter, it appears to move backward and by the end of the month its longitude is 13° 50' Virgo.

In calculating the longitude of retrograde planets for a time other than noon, the motion during the interval must be added to the noon position for an a.m. birth, and deducted for a p.m. birth. In other words, the procedure is the reverse to that used for a planet which is in direct motion.

The calculation for finding a planet's Declination is similar to that used in finding the planet's longitude. The Moon's Declination changes fairly quickly, and when the Moon crosses the Equator, it moves fast and covers the greatest distance in Declination. As Declination is the measurement either north or south of the Equator, the Moon's Declination when it is on the Equator is zero. Each month, the Moon crosses the Equator and subsequently it moves north or south of the Equator until it reaches its maximum Declination (greatest angular distance either north or south). The times of maximum Declination, and also when the Moon is on the Equator, are given in the table 'Phenomena' (page 29).

In calculating Declination, especially when the Moon is going from north to south or vice versa, care is needed to note the decrease as it approaches the Equator and the subsequent increase as it moves either north or south. As an example, on 22 January at noon, the Moon's Declination is 1° 3' south decreasing, and on 23 January it is 3° 36' north increasing. Therefore, its motion in 24 hours = 1° 3' + 3° 36' = 4° 39'. If we require to know its Declination at, say, 11.30 p.m. on 22 January, the calculation would be:

4.39 (4.65) × 11.30 (11.5) over 24 $$\frac{4.65 \times 11.5}{24}$$

= 2° 14′ from noon position

Therefore, decrease of	1°	3′	south
plus increase of	1°	11′	north
	2°	14′	

The Moon's Declination at 11.30 p.m. is therefore 1° 11′ north. Taking noon to midnight on the 22nd will give:

	1°	3′	south (noon)
	1°	18′	north (midnight)
	2°	21′	= 12 hours motion

2.21 (2.35) × 11.30 (11.5) over 12 = $$\frac{2.35 \times 11.5}{12}$$

Therefore, decrease of	1°	3′	south
and increase of	1°	12′	north

gives the Moon's Declination at 11.30 p.m. which is 1 minute different from that found using the 24 hour motion.

Phenomena

This section of the ephemeris contains the dates and times of important astronomical phenomena. Although this information is not required for natal charting, it is a useful source for obtaining the times and dates of interesting astronomical data which can be used in astrological research programmes.

In the table 'Phenomena' (page 29) for 2 January 1980, the following entry is shown: 2, 2.00 a.m. Moon Max. Dec. 19° 9′ N. This entry means that the Moon on 2 January at 2.00 a.m. had reached its maximum Declination of 19° 9′ north of the Equator. You will recall that Declination is the angular distance or measurement either north or south of the Celestial Equator, and that each month the Moon crosses the Equator going from south to north or vice versa. On 2 January it had, therefore reached its maximum Declination north, and then with decreasing Declination, it crossed the equator on 9 January at 11.26 a.m. as shown by the entry in the table. By 16 January with increasing south Declination, it reached its maximum south at 0.55 p.m. Thereafter, its Declination decreases and by 22 January, it is on the Equator again, passing into north Declination.

Perihelion and Aphelion

These terms relate to the closest (perihelion) and farthest (aphelion) approach to the Sun in the orbit of a planet. In the case of the Earth, perihelion occurs on 3 January at 2.40 p.m., whilst aphelion occurs six months later on 5 July at 5.17 p.m. As the Earth's orbit is elliptical, the Earth's distance from the Sun varies day by day. In January each year, the Earth reaches its closest point to the Sun; it is then in perihelion. By July of each year, the Earth has reached its farthest point from the Sun, and it is then in aphelion. Periodically, the planets are at perihelion and aphelion, and the times when these occur are listed in the table of Phenomena. On 6 January, Mercury is in aphelion at 7.36 a.m. and on 19 February it is in perihelion. Mercury has, therefore, taken 44 days to go from aphelion to perihelion. The period for Mercury is 88 days between successive perihelion or aphelion points in its orbit. On 3 April, it is in aphelion again, which is the 88-day period from 6 January.

Perigee and Apogee

As the Moon's apparent orbit of the Earth describes an ellipse, the Moon's distance from the Earth varies daily. The point in its orbit at which it is closest to the Earth is known as its perigee, and when it is farthest away it is termed its apogee. On 8 January at 8.07 a.m. the Moon is in apogee and on 20 January at 1.54 a.m. it is in perigee.

Superior and Inferior Conjunctions

These terms relate to conjunctions which occur when a planet is in line with the Sun and the Earth. A superior conjunction occurs when a planet is in line with the Sun and the Earth and is located on the far side of the Sun. An inferior conjunction is one that occurs when the planet is in line with the Sun and the Earth and is on the near side of the Sun (between Sun and Earth). Inferior conjunctions can only occur with Mercury and Venus (the inferior planets), whose orbits lie closer into the Sun than the orbit of the Earth.

Nodes of the Planets

A planet's node is the point where its path around the Sun crosses the Ecliptic either north or south. Celestial Latitude is a measurement either north or south of the Ecliptic, and when a planet is at its node, its latitude is zero, i.e. it is exactly on the Ecliptic. On 14 February 1980 at 3.42 p.m., Mercury is in its ascending node, that is, moving from south latitude to north latitude. The entry in the table of Phenomena can be checked as follows:

From page 4 of the ephemeris for 13 and 15 February, we have Mercury's latitude as 0° 14' south (13th) and 0° 11' north, on the 15th. This tells us that Mercury had zero latitude sometime between these two dates. Therefore, 0° 14' + 0° 11' = 25' motion in 48 hours. In order for Mercury to be on the Ecliptic (zero latitude), it must show a decrease of 14 minutes, from 0° 14' south to zero. The time given in the table is 3.42 p.m. which is 27 hours 42 minutes after noon on the 13th.

So, if 48 hours = 25 minutes, 27 hours 42 minutes will =

$$(25 \text{ mins}) \frac{0.416 \times 27.7}{48} \ (27.42)$$

= 14 minutes

which deducted from the noon position on the 13th gives 0° 0' = Mercury exactly on the Ecliptic.

The ascending (north) node is shown in the ephemeris by the symbol (☊) and the descending (south) node by (☋). The period between two consecutive north or south nodes is equal to the planet's sidereal period.

Greatest Elongation East and West

Elongation is the angle between the Sun and a celestial body when observed from the Earth. The maximum elongation that the inferior planets (Mercury and Venus) can attain is 28° for Mercury and 48° for Venus. All other planets can reach a maximum elongation of 180°. When a planet is located east of the Sun, it is at eastern elongation and as it sets after the Sun, it is termed an 'evening star', whereas a planet located west of the Sun rises before the Sun and has western elongation, and is termed a 'morning star'. Greatest elongation east always follows the planet's superior conjunction with the Sun, whilst greatest elongation west always follows the planet's inferior conjunction with the Sun.

Entry of the Sun, Moon and Planets
into the Zodiacal Signs

This table shows the date and time when the Sun, Moon and planets enter the various signs. The Sun changes signs each month and the Moon every 2½ days on average. This is a useful table for checking calculations that involve planets which are about to leave one sign and enter another. As an example of this, we can consider a birth time of 7.30 a.m. on 6 January. The Moon's longitude will be in the 'tail end' of Leo, and according to the table, it enters Virgo at 7.50 a.m. which is Ephemeris Time, but we will consider it as G.M.T. Calculation gives the following:

Midnight 5th	=	26°	5'	44" Leo
Noon 6th	=	2°	4'	50" Virgo
12 hours' motion		5°	59'	6"

$5°$ $59'$ $6''$ as a decimal $= \dfrac{5.985 \times 7.5}{12}$ (time from midnight)

$= 3° 44' 26''$

which added to the midnight position

$\begin{array}{r} 26° \quad 5' \quad 44'' \\ + \quad 3° \quad 44' \quad 26'' \end{array}$ $= 29° 50' 10''$ Leo.

which is the Moon's position at 7.30 a.m.

At 7.50 a.m. it enters Virgo: $\dfrac{5.985 \times 7.833}{12} = 3.907$

$= 3° 54' 25''$ added to midnight position $=$ (within a second) $0° 0' 0''$ Virgo.

If we require to check the entry of Mercury into Pisces which occurs, according to the tables, at 8.08 a.m. on 7 February, the calculation is as follows:

Mercury's motion in 24 hours from noon on the 6th/7th February $= 1° 45'$.

Noon position 6 February $= 28° 32'$ Aquarius and the distance to go $= 1° 28'$ (0.0 Pisces minus 28.32 Aquarius). Therefore

$\dfrac{1.28 \times 24}{1.45} = 20.7 = 8.07$ a.m.

which is near enough to prove the entry correct.

The entry of the Sun into the Cardinal Signs (Aries, Cancer, Libra and Capricorn) known as the *Solar Ingresses* are considered important in Mundane Astrology, and the dates and times when these ingresses occur are given in the tables. These tables are very useful because they save time and labour in calculating the time of the ingress.

The Local Mean Time of Sunrise and Sunset

This table is useful for finding the time of sunrise and sunset in various latitudes. Not all latitudes are listed in the table, but a simple formula is given whereby the times can be ascertained if required.

Local Time of Phenomena

Raphael's Ephemeris lists the astronomical data in Ephemeris Time (+ 51 seconds 1980) and, if the time of a particular astronomical occurrence is required for a place abroad, then a conversion to the time in operation abroad needs to be made. As an example, the New Moon occurs on 17 January at 9.19 p.m. which is Ephemeris Time. Therefore, the Greenwich Time to the nearest minute will be 9.18 p.m. (-51 seconds rounded up). If we wish to know at what Local Time the New Moon will occur at New York, the following method will give it:

Take the longitude between London and New York, which is 74 degrees west, and convert it into time at the rate of 15° per hour. This gives $\frac{74}{15}$ = 4 hours, 56 minutes from the time at Greenwich (9.18 p.m.), which equals 4 hours 22 minutes p.m. Local Time. However, New York uses Eastern Standard Time which is 5 hours slow on Greenwich, so the New Moon occurs at 9.18 p.m. less 5 hours = 4.18 p.m. Eastern Standard Time, and at 4.22 p.m. Local Mean Time. This difference in time between London and New York (4.56) is termed the *longitude equivalent in time.* In the chapter on the *conversion of time,* many examples are given to illustrate this time conversion.

Tables of Houses

Raphael's Ephemeris contains Tables of Houses for three main cities, London, Liverpool and New York, and these tables cover latitudes between 39-55° north and can be used for calculating southern latitude charts as explained in the chapter dealing with southern latitude calculations. Also available as separate publications are Tables of Houses for Great Britain and Tables of Houses for Northern Latitudes. These tables cover practically all latitudes between 2-59° north and are indispensable for charting within these latitudes.

A Table of Houses is a mathematical table which has been compiled for a specific latitude in order that the rising degree (Ascendant) and the culminating degree (M.C.) can be determined for a definite time and place. There are various systems of House Division which neccesitate different types of tables, principally because of the various differences that occur with the location of the intermediate house cusps. The tables in the ephemeris are based on the system of Placidus (see chapter on House Division) and these are the tables which are used in this work to illustrate chart calculation.

At first glance the tables appear to be a mass of symbols and figures, but they are in fact very simple and easy to use. If we refer to the London tables we see that the layout is as follows:

Sidereal Time H M S	10 Aries ♈	11 Taurus ♉	12 Gemini ♊	Ascen Cancer ♋	2 Leo ♌	3 Virgo ♍
0 0 0	0	9	22	26 36	12	3

If we number these seven columns it will be easier to explain what each represents.

| (1) | (2) | (3) | (4) | (5) | (6) | (7) |

Column (1) The Sidereal Time refers to the *Local* Sidereal Time of birth.

   (2) This is the 10th house cusp or midheaven and the sign and degree shown is the sign and degree (0 Aries) culminating for that particular Sidereal Time.

   (3) This is the cusp of the 11th house—9° Taurus.

   (4) This is the cusp of the 12th house—22° Gemini.

   (5) This is the Ascendant, the sign and degree which is rising at the place (London) for this particular Sidereal Time (26° 36′ Cancer).

   (6) This is the cusp of the 2nd house—12° Leo.

   (7) This is the cusp of the 3rd house—3° Virgo.

We have now listed the sign and degree for six of the mundane houses for a Sidereal Time of 0 hours 0 minutes 0 seconds at London. Only six houses are listed because the other six houses will have the same *degree* but *opposite* sign on their cusps; e.g. the 4th which is opposite the 10th will have 0° Libra, the 5th will have 9° Scorpio, the 6th will have 22° Sagittarius, the 7th will have Capricorn, the 8th will have Aquarius, the 9th will have Pisces, thereby completing the full circle of the twelve houses.

The sign of the Zodiac is shown at the top of the appropriate column but these change according to the Sidereal Time, and care is needed when extracting information from the tables. For example, at a Sidereal Time of 0 hours 22 minutes, Cancer is no longer the ascending sign at London, for Leo has commenced rising. Likewise, the cusp of the 11th house at a Sidereal Time of 1 hour 17 minutes is 0° of Gemini; it has changed from Taurus to Gemini.

With the Placidean system of house division the size of the houses can vary considerably (that is, some houses can contain more than 30°), and a sign which does not 'cut' the cusp of a particular house, but which is contained within the house, is known as an intercepted sign. This distortion with the semi-arc system becomes more pronounced when charts are calculated for high latitudes. When a sign is intercepted in a particular house, the opposite sign will also be intercepted in the opposite house.

When the time of birth is not known to within ten minutes or so, there is little point in listing the exact degree and minutes of the Ascendant. In fact it is misleading to do so, as this implies that the birth time is precise and that the chart has been calculated for an exact time. It is sufficient to list the nearest degree as shown in the tables. If the time of an event or the birth is known precisely, then exact calculations can be made. It is almost certain that when precise calculations are required, the Local Sidereal Time will not correspond with the figures as listed in the appropriate table of houses, and that interpolation will be needed to ascertain the exact degree and minute which is rising and culminating. Several examples of how to find the exact degree which is rising and culminating are given in the calculations section of this book.

Due to the Earth's rotation, all signs rise and set every 24 hours, the average time for the 30° of a sign to rise being about two hours, except at the polar latitudes, where certain signs neither rise nor set. At the Equator, the signs rise 'evenly' but in the intermediate latitudes and, as we approach the poles, the signs do not rise uniformly due to the angle which the Ecliptic makes with the Equator. Signs which take longer than average to ascend are termed signs of 'long ascension', while those that ascend quickly are known as 'signs of short ascension'. At London, for instance, the sign Pisces will rise quickly, in about 52 minutes of Sidereal Time, whereas Virgo the opposite sign takes 2 hours 50 minutes to ascend.

7.
HOUSE DIVISION

Introduction

The universe, even though it is violent, is as far as we know orderly. The celestial bodies keep to their predicted paths and maintain their cyclic motions. These cyclic motions and rhythms and the associated phenomena have over the centuries been found to correlate with mundane events, and with the physical and psychological occurrences common to man. The spirit of the age reflects the prevailing sky patterns to a greater or lesser degree. The basic tenets of astrology do not change, but the interpretation of the cosmic correspondences does alter according to the age and culture to which it is related.

The astrology of pre-history satisfied the needs of early man insofar that he needed gods to worship, and what better symbols than the Sun, Moon and stars, which appeared constant—permanent and unchanging, as they followed their paths across the heavens. The heavens inspired a sense of order in man, and contributed to his need of security, whatever dangers or disasters he may have had to contend with in his struggle for existence. To early man, the question of whether the Sun went round the Earth or the Earth went round the Sun did not arise. No doubt, he assumed that the Sun went round the Earth, but the important thing was that the Sun was the giver of life. Gradually over a period of time, his observations of the Sun and planets enabled him to formulate concepts concerning the correlation between heaven and earth.

In order to relate the sky patterns and predict how these patterns would influence his life, he needed a frame of reference. The obvious example would be the Sun's daily motion as it rose, culminated and set every 24 hours. By dividing the period from dawn to noon, and from noon to sunset, a pattern of time could be established, and this time period could be allocated to certain divisions. These divisions would vary during different times of the year due to the length of time the Sun was above the horizon, but no doubt they formed the basis of what was later to become the so-called mundane houses.

The division of the mundane sphere probably originated during the last centuries B.C. and was an attempt to relate the signs and planets to mundane activities as well as to personal temperament. By the time of the Renaissance (fifteenth century), the astrological mathematicians had invented several systems of dividing the heavens into the twelve 'houses of the horoscope'. These twelve houses, divisions or segments correspond with certain forms of human experience or activity, and although many of the descriptions are archaic, the fundamental basis of house division descriptions is fairly accurate.

Considered mathematically, the purpose of house division is to assign a longitudinal position on the Ecliptic to the cusp (the point of intersection of the semi-circle which forms the boundary of a house, with the Ecliptic) of each of the twelve mundane houses. Due to the Earth's rotation, the signs of the Zodiac on the cusps of the houses change continually, rising, culminating and setting every 24 hours. Therefore, the planets in the signs also change house position, 'passing through' all twelve houses every 24 hours. At the Equator, the signs rise evenly, but at places distant from the Equator, they do not. Some signs rise quickly (short ascension), whilst others rise slowly (long ascension). In the polar regions, certain signs neither rise nor set, and it is in the high latitudes that the houses show a marked distortion. The construction of the various house systems and their associated complexities are discussed in 'Methods of House Division'.

A *birth chart* is a diagram which represents the Ecliptic divided into twelve zodiacal signs of 30° each. The planets are shown according to their longitude in the zodiacal signs, and their house position depends on which sign they occupy and the time of day that the birth or event occurred. In setting up a chart, we are merely charting a specific moment in time for a particular place. Although the planets remain in the various signs for different periods of time, their house position changes every few hours or less depending on the sign rising and the latitude of the place. To ascertain the rising degree (the Ascendant), we need to find the Sidereal Time of the event at the appropriate latitude, and having found this, we can determine the Right Ascension of the meridian which will show the degree of the Ecliptic culminating at the place and time in question.

The intersection of the Ecliptic and the horizon represents the relationship of the Ecliptic to the Earth, and this intersection forms the cusp of the 1st house, the longitude of which, due to the Earth's rotation, varies from 0-360°. In this way, the four angles are determined. However, when we study the mathematics of assigning a Zodiacal degree to each of the intermediate houses, the matter is far from simple.

The houses are a frame of reference whereby the potentialities of an individual as indicated by the signs, planets and their mutual configurations can be related to the events and conditions of life. As mundane position is the only factor which alters in a short space of time, it is important that the house system employed reflects the conditions and events of life as they actually are. The only way that a particular system can be tested is empirically, and no amount of theory or speculation can replace the realistic and practical approach. Astrologers are by no means agreed as to which system, if any, is the correct one, and the subject of house division is one of the most controversial matters, needing detailed research using well attested data. For newcomers to astrology, the tables which are printed in the Ephemeris (Placidus) should be used, and/or the Equal House system, and if he finds these two systems unsatisfactory, then he can proceed to use some other system—and there are plenty to choose from.

Methods of House Division

During the last few centuries, various methods of house division have been devised, and of these probably only six or so warrant serious consideration. The classification of the various systems can be summarized very briefly as:

A   *The Ecliptic Systems*
B   *The Space Systems*
C   *The Time Systems*

In category A, we have the Equal House system, described by Alan Leo (a notable astrologer of the earlier part of the twentieth century) as 'rough and ready', but which was resuscitated about thirty years ago. This system involves no complicated mathematics and is simple to use, and is based on dividing the Ecliptic into twelve equal houses commencing from the Ascendant. For example, if the Ascendant is 10° Aries, then cusp 2 will be 10° Taurus, cusp 3, 10° Gemini, and so on. This system merely reflects the Zodiac onto the mundane sphere, but the 10th house cusp does not necessarily coincide with the midheaven. However, the midheaven is a very significant point and is regarded as such even though it may not be on the 10th cusp. Many astrologers use this system and are convinced of its value, particularly when dealing with 'psychological attributes' as defined by modern concepts concerning human behaviour. Personally, I have not found this system particularly effective; it may be that its value lies with the psychological approach to astrology, as opposed to definite events and conditions.

In the 3rd century A.D. the Porphyry system was devised, and this system is based on trisecting the semi-arcs—the time that a planet, star or degree of the Ecliptic is above the horizon (diurnal semi-arc) or below the horizon (nocturnal semi-arc). With this system, the eastern quadrants of the Ecliptic are each divided into three equal arcs. The cusps of the 11th and 12th houses are found by adding one-third and two-thirds of the diurnal semi-arc respectively to the M.C. For the 2nd and 3rd house cusps, one-third and two-thirds of the nocturnal semi-arc respectively are added to the Ascendant. If, for example, the midheaven is 3° Scorpio and the Ascendant 28° Sagittarius, the following method gives the cusps of the 11th and 12th houses, and the 2nd and 3rd houses. Using the 360° circle we have:

M.C. 3 Scorpio	= 213		
Asc. 28° Sagittarius	= 268		
Difference	55	÷ 3 = 18°	
Asc. 28° Sagittarius	= 268		
I.C. 3° Taurus	= 33		
Difference	125	÷ 3 = 41°	
Cusp 11th = M.C.	+ 18	= 231	= 21° Scorpio
Cusp 12th = Asc.	− 18	= 250	= 10° Sagittarius
Cusp 2nd = Asc.	+ 41	= 309	= 9° Aquarius
Cusp 3rd = I.C.	− 41	= 352	= 22° Pisces

With this system of house division, the great circles forming the boundaries of the house lunes (the portion of the surface of a sphere which is contained within two great semi-circles) meet at the poles of the Ecliptic, and the four angles 1, 10, 7, 4, are cuspal points. The M.C., always a significant point, coincides with the 10th cusp.

In the 1950s, a variation on the Porphyry system was introduced by Colin Evans, and termed the Natural Graduation method. However, this method is subject to criticism in the same manner as Porphyry, because it divides the Ecliptic unequally. Details regarding this method and other systems are given in the work by Colin Evans (*The New Waites Compendium of Natal Astrology,* published in 1953).

When we consider the next category of house division methods —the *Space Systems,* we find that the circle that is divided is not the Ecliptic but some other circle. In the Campanus System, which was invented by Johannes Campanus (a notable mathematician of the thirteenth century), it is the Prime Vertical that is divided into equal arcs of 30° each, the Prime Vertical being the circle perpendicular to the horizon that passes through the east and west points. The basis of this system is the tri-section of a quadrant of the Prime Vertical by great circles mutually intersecting at the north and south points of the horizon, the cusps of the houses being the degrees of the Ecliptic cut by these circles. Passing through the east and west points of the horizon, and the zenith and nadir, the Prime Vertical is divided into four arcs of equal length by the horizon and the meridian. The trisecting of the quadrants form the houses, and the great circles passing through these points and the north and south points of the horizon form the boundaries of the house lunes.

As with the method of Porphyry, the Campanus System retains the four angles as house cusps. Like all house systems, the Campanus method presents difficulties when related to high latitudes, in that the Ecliptic forms an acute angle to the Prime Vertical, resulting in the zodiacal longitudinal position of the house cusps becoming more unequal with respect to the Ecliptic. Whatever the shortcomings the Campanus System may have when related to high latitudes, it is one of the few systems that merits serious consideration. The division using the Prime Vertical appears to be a sensible and practical method for determining the houses.

Johannes Muller, otherwise known as Regiomontanus (1436-1476), was a professor of astronomy at Vienna, and he devised a system which was a modification of the one invented by Campanus. Whereas Campanus used the Prime Vertical as a great circle, Regiomontanus used the celestial Equator, dividing it into equal arcs of 30° and projecting these divisions onto the Ecliptic. With this system, the quadrants of the Celestial Equator are trisected by great circles mutually intersecting at the north and south points of the horizon, the cusps of the houses being the degrees of the Ecliptic cut by these circles. The distortion of the houses produced by this method is not so great as with that of Campanus, and there would appear to be some justification for a system such as this which uses the Celestial Equator and is associated with the Earth's diurnal rotation.

Jean Baptiste Morinus (1583-1656), a French astrologer, devised a system of house division which divides the Equator into equal arcs similar to the method of Regiomontanus, but which unlike Regiomontanus, projects these equal divisions onto the Ecliptic by great circles passing through the Ecliptic poles. With this system of Morinus, the Ascendant is not the zero point, but is defined by adding 90° to the longitude of the M.C. As the Ecliptic poles are fixed points upon the Celestial Sphere, the size of the houses in relationship to the Ecliptic will not vary with latitude owing to the relationship existing between the house boundaries and the Ecliptic. This system is simple in construction but the only association it has with the Ecliptic is that the intersection points of the house cusps are at the poles of the Ecliptic.

The third category of house division systems is the *Time System,* and of the various systems within this classification, the system of Placidus is the one most commonly used. This is the system for which tables are published in *Raphael's Ephemeris.* This method of division was devised by Placidus de Tito, a professor of mathematics, in the seventeenth century. The Placidean system is based on the trisection of the semi-arc of each degree of the Ecliptic. It does not divide time, nor does it divide the space between the horizon and meridian in a simple way. The basis of this system is to take the time for any degree to move from the ascendant to the midheaven and to equally trisect this time to ascertain the time at which this degree will become the cusps of the 12th and 11th houses. Likewise, the semi-nocturnal arc from the I.C. to the Ascendant is trisected, and the times are those at which the same degree will become the cusps of the 2nd and 3rd houses. The following calculation illustrates this method:

At London—Latitude 51° 32′ north

			H	M	Sidereal Time
M.C.	= 4° Scorpio	=	14	7	
I.C.	= 4° Taurus	=	2	7	
Asc.	= 4° Scorpio	=	9	14	

Therefore the semi-diurnal
		H	M	
arc	=	14	7	
	—	9	14	
	=	4	53	÷ 3 = 1 hr 38 mins
and the semi-nocturnal arc	=	9	14	
	—	2	7	
	=	7	7	÷ 3 = 2 hrs 22 mins

4° Scorpio is the midheaven

			H	M
at		=	14	7
11th cusp at	14.7 — 1.38 =		12	29
12th cusp at	12.29 — 1.38 =		10	51
Ascendant at			9	14
2nd cusp at	9.14 — 2.22 =		6	52
3rd cusp at	6.52 — 2.22 =		4	30

The above example shows that, although the time that a degree may spend in a particular quadrant may be unequal, the motion is uniform due to the apparent rotation of the Celestial Sphere. It therefore reaches the points of trisection (I.C.-Asc. and Asc.-M.C.) at precisely one-third of the time which is required to complete the total arc of the particular quadrant. Any degree of the Ecliptic makes a complete revolution in one Sidereal Day, and the time at which it reaches those points on the semi-diurnal and semi-nocturnal arcs which trisect them is the time at which the degree becomes the cusp of the particular house.

As with all methods of house division which use the Ascendant as the zero point, distortion occurs in high latitudes, and at the polar circle latitude (66½°) a degree of the Ecliptic will become circumpolar for the first time. Above the polar circle certain degrees of the Ecliptic will not rise and therefore can never become the Ascendant. Much criticism has been directed against the Placidean system, particularly regarding its use in high latitudes, and statements are made which are misleading concerning the erection of charts by this method in those latitudes. For a detailed discussion on the various house systems and the associated problems connected with them, the student is referred to two excellent publications devoted to the question of house division; *The Elements of House Division* by Ralph William Holden published by L. N. Fowler 1977, and *Tools of*

Astrology: Houses by Dona Marie Lorenz, published by Eomega Grove Press 1973.

The question of house division is a complex one and much argument exists regarding which method should be used, and which method produces the better results. The literature on the subject is sparse, although articles do appear from time to time in various astrological journals where the pros and cons of the various systems are discussed. The methods outlined in this work are only a few of the many systems which exist and, for further information concerning house division, the student should consult the above mentioned works and the chapters in Alan Leo's *Casting the Horoscope.*

8.
PROPORTIONAL LOGARITHMS

Introduction

On the last page of *Raphael's Ephemeris,* there is a table of proportional logarithms, and these tables greatly facilitate the calculation of the planetary positions for times other than noon. These labour-saving tables enable calculations involving proportion to be dealt with speedily and accurately. These tables are not logarithms in the accepted sense but are mathematical compilations using 24 hours (1440 minutes) as the base. By merely adding two logs (logarithms), we can multiply, and by deducting, we can divide. It is not necessary to understand how these tables are compiled in order to use them. All that is required in their use is care in extracting the appropriate log for the value required. Despite the formidable appearance that these tables present, they are extremely easy to use and will present no difficulties even to the least mathematically minded.

The heading at the top of the table shows degrees or hours, and the left hand column shows minutes, so all that one needs to do to obtain the log for a particular degree/hour and minute is to note the entry where the horizontal and vertical columns intersect. For example, the log of 5 ° 30′ is 0.6398. The use of this table will become clear if we deal with some practical examples. As in all calculations, the likelihood of error is reduced if we proceed in an orderly manner and in easy stages. To determine a planet's position for a given time, the following procedure should be adopted:

Step 1 Take out the interval of time between noon and the birth time and find the log corresponding to this interval of time. This log will remain constant and will be used to calculate the positions of all the planets for a particular chart.

Step 2 Take out the daily motion of the planet by referring to pages 26-28 of the ephemeris (bearing in mind that for a.m. births, the motion is that shown for the previous day). e.g. a.m. birth 2 January, take the motion as shown for 1 January. From the Table of Logs take the log of this motion.

Step 3 Add together the logs found in Step 1 and 2, irrespective of whether the interval of time was to or from noon. The sum of these two logs will give the log of the planet's motion in the interval required.

Step 4 To the noon position of the planet add the degree and/or minute as indicated by the log in Step 3 for a p.m. birth or deduct for an a.m. birth, and the result is the planet's position for the time required. If the planet is retrograde, reverse the procedure: add for an a.m. birth and deduct for a p.m. birth.

Calculation of Planetary Positions

The following examples illustrate the use of the table of proportional logarithms and show how easy it is to calculate the positions of planets using this table.

Example No. 1: a.m. Birth
Required to find the Sun's position at 2.00 a.m. G.M.T. 2 January 1980.

Working

	Log
Step 1	
2.00 a.m. = 10 hours before noon (Interval 10):	0.3802
Step 2	
Sun's daily motion 1/2 January	
1° 1′ 8″ (ignore seconds):	= 1.3730 *add*
Step 3	
From table nearest log 1.7604	1.7532
= 25 minutes	

Step 4
Sun's position at noon 2 January:

$$
\begin{array}{lll}
11° & 14′ & 33″ \text{ Capricorn from which deduct} \\
0 & 25 & 00 \\
\hline
10 & 50 & = \text{Sun's position at 2.00 a.m. G.M.T.}
\end{array}
$$

Example No. 2: p.m. Birth
Required to find the Sun's position at 6.15 p.m. G.M.T. 2 January 1980.

Working

Step 1	*Log*
6.15 p.m. = 6.15 after noon:	0.5843

Step 2
Sun's daily motion 2/3 January
1° 1′ 8″ (ignore seconds):   1.3730 *add*

Step 3
From table nearest log 1.9542   1.9573
= 16 minutes

Step 4
Sun's position at noon 2 January:
11° 14′ 33″ plus 16 minutes = 11° 31′.

The Sun's position at 6.15 p.m. on 2 January is 11° 31′ Capricorn.

Example No. 3:
Required to find the Moon's position at 5.45 a.m. G.M.T.
2 January 1980.

Working

Step 1   *Log*
5.45 a.m. = 12.00
less 5.45 = 6.15 (interval to noon):   0.5843

Step 2
Moon's daily Motion 1/2 January
12° 58′:   0.2674 *add*

Step 3
From table nearest log 0.8509   0.8517
= 3° 23′

Step 4
Moon's position at noon 2 January:
 12°   42′   Cancer from which we deduct
  3   23   as it is an a.m. birth

  9   19   Cancer = Moon's position at 5.45 a.m. G.M.T.
             2 January 1980

Using a calculator the result would be:
Moon's position Noon 2 January:	12°	42′
Moon's position Midnight 1/2 January:	6°	15′
Motion in 12 hours:	6°	27′

$$6.27 = \frac{6.45 \times 5.75}{12} \text{ (5.45 a.m.)}$$

= 3.0906 = 3° 5' which added to midnight position 6° 15' =
9° 20' Cancer, which is close enough to the position as found by using
logs.

Example No. 4:
*Find the position of Mercury, Venus and Mars at 3.00 a.m. G.M.T. 2
January 1980.*

Working

Step 1   *Log*
3.00 a.m. = 9 hours interval to noon: 0.4260 constant

Step 2
Mercury's daily motion 1/2 January:
1° 32':   1.1946 *add*

Step 3
From table nearest log 1.6269   1.6206
= 34 minutes

Step 4
Mercury's position at noon 2 January:
    0°   15' Capricorn from which we deduct
    0°   34'

   29°   41' Sagittarius = Mercury's position at 3.00 a.m. G.M.T. 2
                January

Venus

Working

Step 1   *Log*
9 hours interval: 0.4260

Step 2
Venus's motion 1/2 January:
1° 14':   1.2891 *add*

Step 3
From table nearest log 1.7112   1.7151
= 28 minutes

Step 4
Venus's position at noon 2 January:
   13°   15' Aquarius from which we deduct:
    0°   28'

   12°   47' Aquarius = Venus's position at 3.00 a.m. G.M.T.

Mars

Working

Step 1   *Log*
9 hours interval: 0.4260

Step 2
Mars' daily motion 1/2 January:
0° 10':   2.1584 *add*

Step 3
From tables nearest log 2.5563   2.5844
= 4 minutes

Step 4
Mars' position at noon 2 January:
  14°   13' Virgo from which we deduct
   0°   4'

  14°   9' Virgo = Mars' position at 3.00 a.m. G.M.T.

Example No. 5:
Find the Moon's Declination at 4.00 p.m. G.M.T. 6 January.

Working

Step 1   *Log*
4.00 p.m. = 4 hours interval from noon: 0.7781

Step 2
Moon's Declination in 24 hours:
3° 27', north, decreasing: 0.8424 *add*

Step 3
From tables nearest log 1.6143   1.6205
= 35 minutes

Step 4
Moon's position in Declination at noon 6 January:
  10°   55' North decreasing, therefore we *deduct*
   0°   35'

  10°   20' North Declination = Moon's Declination at
                   4.00 p.m. G.M.T. 6 January. If the Declination had been
                   increasing we would have added the amount of 35 minutes
                   to the noon position.

Using calculator:

$$3° \ 27' = \frac{3.45 \times 4}{24} = 0.575 = 0° \ 34' \ 30''$$

which confirms the calculation by logs to the nearest minute.

When planets are retrograde, the motion during the interval of time is added for an a.m. birth and deducted for a p.m. birth.

Example No. 6:
Find the position of Mars at 11.15 p.m. G.M.T. 26 January. Mars is retrograde on this date.

Working

Step 1	*Log*
11.15 p.m. = 11.15 interval after noon:	0.3291

Step 2
Mars' daily motion 26 January:
9 minutes   2.2041 *add*

Step 3
From table nearest log 2.5563   2.5332
= 4 minutes

Step 4
Mars' position at noon 26 January:
  14°   40′ Virgo from which we *deduct*
    0°   4′

  14°   36′ Virgo = Mars' position at 11.15 p.m. G.M.T. 26
              January. Although a p.m. birth we have deducted the
              amount of 4 minutes because the planet is retrograde.

Example No. 7:
Find the position of Mars at 3.30 a.m. G.M.T. 26 January 1980.

Working

Step 1	*Log*
3.30 a.m. = 8.30 interval to noon:	= 0.4508

Step 2
Mars' daily motion 25 January:
8 minutes   2.2553 *add*

Step 3
From table nearest log 2.6812   2.7061
= 3 minutes

Step 4
Mars' position at noon 26 January:
  14°   40′ Virgo to which we *add*
    0°   3′ as the planet is retrograde

  14°   43′ Virgo = Mars' position at 3.30 a.m. G.M.T. 26 January.
              If Mars had not been retrograde, we would have deducted
              the 3 minutes as we are dealing with an a.m. birth.

9.
CHARTING FOR NORTHERN AND SOUTHERN HEMISPHERES

Aids and Equipment

In order to calculate a natal chart, we need certain items of equipment:

1. The birth data: time, date and place.
2. An ephemeris for the year of birth.
3. Tables of Houses for the appropriate latitude.
4. Gazetteer, to ascertain the geographical co-ordinates (latitude and longitude).
5. A Pluto ephemeris (if birth was prior to 1934).
6. Tables and reference works giving Standard Times, Daylight Saving Time/Summer Time.
7. Tables for the conversion of Mean to Sidereal Time and for finding the longitude equivalent in time.
8. Stationery, chart forms, miscellaneous calculating aids.
9. A calculating machine with a sexagesimal function. This is not an essential tool, but if many charts are to be calculated, it is very useful as it saves time and labour.

Items 1-6 are essential if the charting is to be done properly, but item 7 can be dispensed with if a calculator is being used, as it is a simple matter to perform the necessary conversions with a machine.

A printed chart is useful if many charts are to be done, as they can be filed in an orderly manner. Initially, one can use scrap paper to practise with, thereby avoiding waste. Many tables are given in this book to enable the reader to calculate a natal chart, and details concerning the various reference works are listed under 'Recommended Reference Books and Materials'.

Calculating the Natal Chart: Time

Greenwich Mean Time at Birth
1. Birth time (Normally clock time) = Standard Time or Daylight Saving Time.
2. Daylight Saving Time, etc: Deduct from Clock Time Given =
3. Standard Time of Birth:
4. Zone Standard Time: Deduct for East Longitudes
                       Add for West Longitudes
5. Result = *Greenwich Mean Time at Birth*
            Planets calculated for this time

Local Sidereal Time at Birth
1. Sidereal Time at Noon Greenwich:
2. Interval of G.M.T. to/from Noon: Deduct a.m.: Add p.m.:
3. Correction Mean to Sidereal Time:
   9.86 secs. per hour (a.m. —, p.m. +)
4. Result = Sidereal Time at Greenwich at Birth:
5. Longitude Equivalent: Deduct West: Add East:
6. Result = *Local Sidereal Time at Birth*
            The Ascendant, M.C. and House Cusps for this time

Finding the G.M.T. at Birth

Example
Birth time 6.00 p.m. 10 January 1980, New York City.

		H	M	S	
1. Birth time		6	0	0	p.m.
2. No Daylight Saving Time		—	—	—	
3. Standard Time (Eastern Standard)		6	0	0	p.m.
4. Zone Standard (75° West)	add	5	0	0	
5. *Greenwich Mean Time at birth* *		11	0	0	p.m.

Planet's positions calculated for this time.

Finding the Local Sidereal Time at Birth

		H	M	S
1. Sidereal Time at noon at Greenwich		19	16	42
2. Interval of G.M.T. from noon	*add*	11	00	00
		30	16	42
3. Correction Mean to Sidereal Time	*add*		1	48
(9.86 secs. per hour × 11 hours)				
4. Sidereal Time at Greenwich at birth		30	18	30
5. Long. equivalent ($\frac{73° 57' West}{15}$)	*minus*	4	55	48
		25	22	42
	minus	24	00	00
6. *Local Sidereal Time at Birth* *		1	22	42

The Ascendant, M.C. and House Cusps calculated or extracted from the New York Tables of Houses for this Sidereal Time.

With the necessary equipment to hand, we can now commence to calculate a natal chart and as an illustration, we will start with a chart for London and then proceed to chart for various places abroad.

Example No. 1

	Time	Date	Place
Birth data:	7.15 p.m. G.M.T.	6 January 1980	London Lat. 51° 32'N Long. — —

We know that the time given is in Greenwich Mean Time because that is the Standard Time in operation at that date in England. Using the work sheet, we enter the appropriate data and the source from which we obtained the information:

	D	M	Y		Information from:
Birth date:	6.	1.	80		As given
Birth place:					
London: Lat.				51° 32' N	Gazetteer
Long.				— —	

	H	M	S		
Birth time:	7	15	00	p.m.	As given
G.M.T. at birth:	7	15	00	p.m.	As given— verified that G.M.T. was in operation

Time	H	M	S	Information from:
S.T. at noon:				
G.M.T.:	19	00	56	*Raphael's Ephemeris* 1980 6 January
Interval from noon:	+ 7	15	00 p.m.	As given
Result:	26	15	56	
Correction 9.86 secs.:	+	1	12	Table: Mean to Sidereal Time
S.T. at Greenwich at birth:	26	17	08	
Long. Equiv.:	—	—	—	
Deduct:	24	00	00	
Local S.T. at birth:	2	17	08	= Sidereal Time at London, 7.15 p.m.

From Tables of Houses for London, the Local Sidereal Time of birth (2.17.08) gives the following Zodiacal longitudes on the various house cusps.

10th	11th	12th	1st Ascendant	2nd	3rd
7 ♉	16 ♊	22 ♋	21 ♌	10 ♍	4 ♎

and therefore the opposite houses will have the same degrees but opposite signs.

4th	5th	6th	7th	8th	9th
7 ♏	16 ♐	22 ♑	21 ♒	10 ♓	4 ♈

On the blank chart form, we enter the signs and degrees as extracted from the Tables. As the time of birth was 7.15 p.m. G.M.T., we know that the Sun must have set some hours previously and therefore its position must be 'under the horizon' at the time of birth. Checking the signs on the cusps, we find Capricorn is on the 6th cusp and as the Sun is in this sign at about 15 degrees, this confirms that we have extracted the information from the London Tables correctly.

Example No. 1 Finding the Ascendant and M.C. from the Local Sidereal Time at birth.

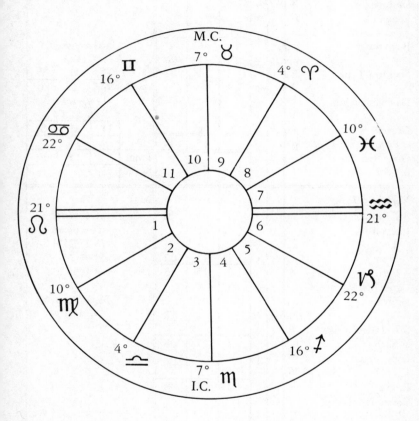

Birth data:
Time: 7.15 p.m. G.M.T.
Date: 6 January 1980
Place: London
Local Sidereal Time as per working sheet: 2 hrs 17 mins 08 secs

Local Sidereal Time Calculation

Form 'A' Worksheet			D	M	Y				
Birth date			6	1	1980				
Birth place:				London					
Latitude:	N	*S*	51 32	-	-				
Longitude:	*E*	*W*	- -	-	-				
			H	M	S				
Birth time:	a.m.						*Greenwich*		
	p.m.		7	15	00		*Date*		
Standard Time	E	—	-	-	-		D	M	Y
	W	+	-	-	-		6	1	80
Daylight Saving		—	-	-	-		*Interval of*		
							G.M.T.		
Greenwich Time	a.m.						H	M	S
at birth	p.m.		7	15	00	To	-	-	-
Greenwich Date						From	7	15	00
6.1.80						Noon			

Sidereal Time									
S.T. at noon G.M.T.			19	00	56		*Calculator*		
Interval							*Constant*		
To From Noon	a.m.	—	-	-	-		*INTERVAL*		
	p.m.	+	7	15	00		÷ 24		
Result			2	15	56		= 0.30208		
Correction 9.86 secs									
per hour	a.m.	—	-	-	-		*Log of Interval*		
	p.m.	+		1	12		= 0.5199		
S.T. at Greenwich									
at birth			2	17	08				
Long. Equiv.	E	+	-	-	-				
	W	—	-	-	-				
Result			2	17	08				
Correction (Long.)									
	E	—	-	-	-				
	W	+	-	-	-				
Local Sidereal Time									
at birth			2	17	08				
Add for South Lat.									
12 H			-	-	-				
From Tables of Houses			Asc. 21 ♌ M.C. 7 ♉						

Example No. 2   Inserting the planetary positions.

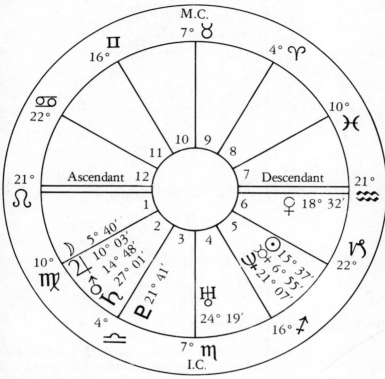

Placidus House System
Birth data:
Time: 7.15 p.m. G.M.T.
Date: 6 January 1980
Place: London

Planet	Symbol	Sign	House
Sun	☉	Capricorn	5
Moon	☽	Virgo	1
Mercury	☿	Capricorn	5
Venus	♀	Aquarius	6
Mars	♂	Virgo	2
Jupiter	♃	Virgo	2
Saturn	♄	Virgo	2
Uranus	♅	Scorpio	4
Neptune	♆	Sagittarius	5
Pluto	♇	Libra	3

Equal House System: 7.15 p.m. G.M.T., 6 January 1980, London.

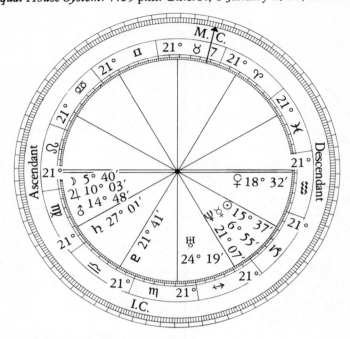

Finding the Planets' Positions

The first step in calculating the chart consists of finding the Local Sidereal Time of birth in order that we can determine the rising sign (Ascendant) and the signs and degrees on the various house cusps. Our next step is to calculate the positions of the planets for the *Greenwich Time* of birth. We are calculating for the Greenwich Time because the ephemeris is a Greenwich based ephemeris and the longitudes of the planets listed in the ephemeris are for noon G.M.T. Actually, the positions are for Ephemeris Time (+51 seconds) but, for our purpose, we can consider the listings as for Noon G.M.T.

There are two principal methods of calculating planetary positions: (1) by using proportional logarithms, (2) using a calculator. We will use both methods in order to illustrate the procedure of finding the planets' positions.

It may seem strange in this age of 'form filling' that, even with astrological calculations, we resort to completing forms of one kind or another, but experience has shown that, if we list all the relevant information in an orderly and methodical manner, the risk of errors and omissions is greatly reduced.

Work sheet (Form 'B') shows the entries that have been made in order to find the longitudes of the planets for the given time of birth (7.15 p.m. G.M.T.). An explanation of the various entries is as follows:

Form 'B'

Calculation of planets' longitudes using calculating machine.

7.15 p.m. G.M.T. 6 January 1980

$$Constant = (7.15)\frac{7.25}{24}$$

$$= \underline{0.30208}$$

	☉ ° '	☽ ° '	☿ ° '	♀ ° '	♂ ° '
Calculator 0.30208 Constant × daily motion = Motion required	0 18	3 35	0 28	0 22	0 02
Noon position Sign	♑	♍	♑	♒	♍
Longitude	15 19	2 05	6 27	18 10	14 46
Motion required a.m. —* Degs/Mins p.m. +*	0 18	3 35	0 28	0 22	0 02
= Planet's place at given time	15 37	5 40	6 55	18 32	14 48
*Reverse if planet is retrograde					

Planetary positions in numerical order

♈	♉	♊	♋	♌	♍	♎	♏	♐	♑	♒	♓
					☽ 5° 40'	♇ 21° 41'	♅ 24° 19'	♆ 21° 07'	☿ 6° 55'	♀ 18° 32'	
					♃ 10° 03'				☉ 15° 37'		
					♂ 14° 48'						
					♄ 27° 01'						

NATAL CHARTING

Form 'B' **WORKSHEET**

Calculation of planets' longitudes using proportional logarithms.

7.15 p.m. G.M.T. 6 January 1980

Planet	☉	☽	☿	♀	♂
	° ′	° ′	° ′	° ′	° ′
Motion in 24 hrs	1 01	11 52	1 33	1 14	0 07
Log of motion	1.3730	0.3059	1.1899	1.2891	2.3133
+ Log of interval	0.5199	0.5199	0.5199	0.5199	0.5199
= Log of motion required	1.8929	0.8258	1.7098	1.8090	2.8332
= Degrees/Mins	0 18	3 35	0 28	0 22	0 02
Noon position Sign	♑	♍	♑	♒	♍
Longitude	15 19	2 05	6 27	18 10	14 46
Motion during interval	—	—	—	—	—
Degrees/Mins p.m. + *	0 18	3 35	0 28	0 22	0 02
= Planet's place (Longitude) at given time	15 37	5 40	6 55	18 32	14 48

Reverse if planet is retrograde

© *J. Filbey*

1. Motion in 24 hours = distance planet has moved in 24 hours from noon on 6/7 January.
   Information from the daily motion table page 26 ephemeris.
2. Log of motion = log of 24 hours motion.
   Information from table of proportional logarithms.
3. Log of interval = G.M.T. interval from noon to birth time 7.15 and this log is the constant for all the calculations of planetary positions.
4. Log of motion required = the addition of the log of 24 hours motion and log of interval.
5. Degrees/minutes = the log of motion required expressed as degrees and minutes.
   Information from the table of proportional logs. (Note that we take the nearest entry in the tables to that required.)
6. The longitude of the planet and the sign it is in at noon as shown in the

ephemeris is listed, and to the noon position, we add the motion found. In this instance, the motion in 7 hours 15 minutes is added to the noon position and the result is the planet's longitude for the time given 7.15 p.m. If the planet had been retrograde, we would deduct the motion for the interval (p.m. birth, and added for an a.m. birth).

Note also that the log of 24 hours motion and the log of the interval are always added together irrespective of whether it is a.m. or p.m. birth. This part of the calculation is to determine the log of the motion required and a.m. or p.m. interval does not affect the result.

Inserting the Planets in the Chart

Having calculated the longitudes of the planets for the given time and having checked that our calculations are correct, we can proceed to insert them on the chart form. On the work sheet (calculation Form 'B') we have listed the planets in numerical order and according to their Zodiacal position. This enables us to make the necessary entries on the chart in a tidy and methodical manner. We have already determined the cusps of the houses and listed the signs on them, so we can now insert the planets in their appropriate positions, taking care that we place them in the correct house. For instance, the Sun is in 15° 37′ Capricorn, so its position will be in the 5th house, as this is the house which contains 0-22° of Capricorn. Likewise, with the rest of the planets which are inserted in their appropriate signs and houses. Example No. 2 (page 101) shows the planets in the signs and houses.

Form 'B'   **WORKSHEET**

Calculation of planets' longitudes for 6.30 a.m. G.M.T.
26 January 1980
(10.30 p.m. P.S.T. 25 January 1980 San Francisco)

Calculator

	☉ ° ′	☽ ° ′	☿ ° ′	♀ ° ′	♂ ° ′
Calculator 0.22916 Constant × daily motion = Motion required	0 14	3 06	0 24	0 17	0 02
Noon position Sign	♒	♉	♒	♓	♍ ℞
Longitude	5 41	29 53	9 12	12 36	14 40

Continued overleaf

Motion required a.m. —* Degrees/Minutes p.m. +*		0 14	3 06	0 24	0 17	0 02
Planet's place at given time		5 27	26 47	8 48	12 19	14 42
*Reverse if planet is retrograde						

Planetary positions in numerical order

♈	♉	♊	♋	♌	♍	♎	♏	♐	♑	♒	♓
	☽ 26° 47′				♃ 8° 46′	♇ 21° 47′	♅ 25° 03′	♆ 21° 46′		☉ 5° 27′	♀ 12° 19′
					♂ 14° 42′					☿ 8° 48′	
					♄ 26° 40′						

© *J. Filbey*

Form 'B'   **WORKSHEET**

Calculation of Planet's longitudes for 6.30 a.m. G.M.T.
26 January 1980
(10.30 p.m. P.S.T. 25 January 1980 San Francisco)

Logs

Planet	☉ ° ′	☽ ° ′	☿ ° ′	♀ ° ′	♂ ° ′
Motion in 24 hrs	1 01	13 31	1 44	1 13	0 08
Log of Motion	1.3730	0.2493	1.1413	1.2950	2.2553
+ Log of interval	0.6398	0.6398	0.6398	0.6398	0.6398
= Log of motion required	2.0128	0.8891	1.7811	1.9348	2.8951
= Degrees/Mins	0 14	3 06	0 24	0 17	0 02
Noon position Sign	♒	♉	♒	♓	♍ ℞
Longitude	5 41	29 53	9 12	12 36	14 40
Motion during interval a.m. —* Degrees/Mins p.m. +*	0 14	3 06	0 24	0 17	0 02
= Planet's place (Longitude) at given time	5 27	26 47	8 48	12 19	14 42
Reverse if planet is retrograde.					

Example No. 3   Finding the Ascendant and M.C. from the Local Sidereal
Time at birth.

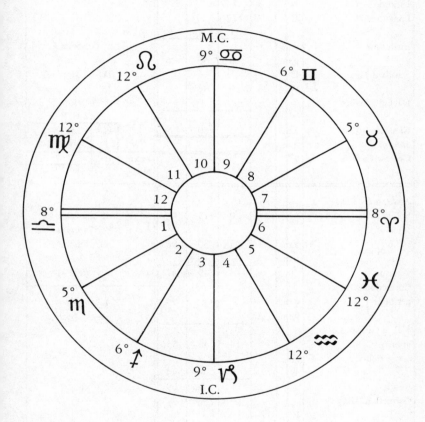

Birth data:
Time: 10.30 p.m. Pacific Standard Time
Date: 25 January 1980
Place: San Francisco
Local Sidereal Time as per working sheet: 6 hrs 40 mins 29 secs.

Local Sidereal Time Calculation

Form 'A' Worksheet			D	M	Y				
Birth date			25	1	1980				
Birth place:			San Francisco						
Latitude:	N	✗	3747	-	-				
Longitude:	✗	W	12226	-	-				
			H	M	S				
Birth time:	a.m.						*Greenwich*		
	p.m.		10	30	00		*Date*		
Standard Time	E	—	-	-	-		D	M	Y
	W	+	8	00	-		26	1	80
Daylight Saving		—	-	-	-		*Interval of*		
							G.M.T.		
Greenwich Time	a.m.		6	30	-		H	M	S
at birth	p.m.		-	-	-	To	5	30	-
Greenwich Date						From	-	-	-
26.1.80						Noon			

Sidereal Time

S.T. at noon G.M.T.			20	19	47		*Calculator*		
Interval							*Constant*		
To Noon	a.m.	—	5	30	00		*INTERVAL*		
From	p.m.	+	-	-	-		÷ 24		
Result			14	49	47		= 0.22916		
Correction 9.86 secs									
per hour	a.m.	—	-	-	54		*Log of Interval*		
	p.m.	+	-	-	-		= 0.6398		
S.T. at Greenwich									
at birth			14	48	53				
Long. Equiv.	E	+	-	-	-				
	W	—	8	09	44				
Result			6	39	09				
Correction (Long.)									
	E	—	-	-	-				
	W	+	-	01	20				
Local Sidereal Time									
at birth			6	40	29				
Add for South Lat.									
12 H			-	-	-				
From Tables of Houses			Asc. 8 ♎ M.C. 9 ♊						

Example No. 4 Inserting the planetary positions.

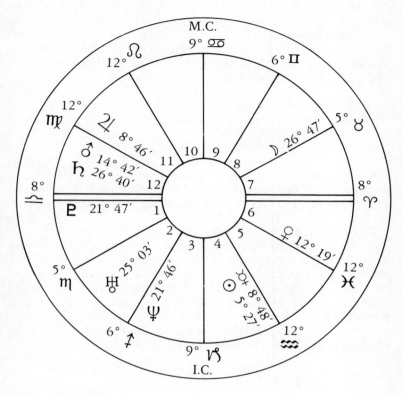

Birth data:
Time: 10.30 p.m. P.S.T.
Date: 25 January 1980
Place: San Francisco

Planet	Symbol	Sign	House
Sun	☉	Aquarius	4
Moon	☽	Taurus	8
Mercury	☿	Aquarius	4
Venus	♀	Pisces	6
Mars	♂	Virgo	12
Jupiter	♃	Virgo	11
Saturn	♄	Virgo	12
Uranus	♅	Scorpio	2
Neptune	♆	Sagittarius	3
Pluto	♇	Libra	1

Charting for Places Abroad (Northern Hemisphere)

In order to calculate a chart for places abroad, we have to convert the clock time given to the equivalent Greenwich Time of birth, and apply the longitude equivalent in time. We do this because we need to know the Greenwich Time in order to calculate the planets' places, and we apply the longitude equivalent because we need to know the Local Sidereal Time at birth in order to ascertain the rising sign and the house positions.

Example No. 3
Birth data: 10.30 p.m. Pacific Standard Time
                  25 January 1980, San Francisco
                  Lat. 37° 47' North, Long. 122° 26' West.

As the Standard Time is 8 hours slow on Greenwich, we add 8 hours to the time given (10.30 p.m.), which gives the Greenwich Time as 6.30 a.m. 26 January. Note that the date has changed. The planets' positions are calculated for 6.30 a.m. 26 January.

To find the Local Sidereal Time at birth we take the Sidereal Time at noon at Greenwich on 26 January, deduct the Greenwich Time interval to noon (5.30) less the correction for Mean to Sidereal Time (5.30 × 9.86 secs), which gives the Sidereal Time at Greenwich at birth. However, we are concerned with the Local Sidereal Time at birth, so from the Sidereal Time at Greenwich at birth (14.48.53) we deduct the longitude equivalent in time (122° 26' over 15) which is 8 hours 9 minutes 44 seconds, and if we wish to be precise, add the correction for longitude (1 min 20 secs), which gives us, 14.48.53 less 8.09.44 plus 1 min 20 secs:

14	48	53	
8	09	44	—
6	39	09	
	1	20	+
6	40	29	which is the Local Sidereal Time at birth.

From the Tables of Houses for Latitude 37° 58' (nearest) the Sidereal Time at birth (6.40.29) gives the Ascendant as 8° Libra and the M.C. as 9° Cancer. The workings and the completed chart are shown in Example 3 and 4.

Charting for Southern Latitudes

Introduction
The procedure for charting for places in the southern latitudes often causes confusion because the actual facts concerning the procedure are often

inadequately explained. There is no more difficulty in charting for a place in the South Pacific than there is in charting for London. The only difference is that there is an adjustment to make if using the Northern Latitude Table of Houses.

Many errors in southern latitude charting can be avoided if one thinks of how the heavens appear to a southern latitude observer. The horizon is a great circle and every horizon circle and plane for places in the northern hemisphere has a correspondence with its southern counterpart. The southern hemisphere observer looks at the same horizon from the opposite side along an axis. The points of intersection between the planes and circles of the horizon and Ecliptic are the points of the Ascendant and Descendant (1st and 7th cusps). The ascendant point in the northern hemisphere is the descendant or setting point in the southern hemisphere.

For example, places in New Zealand with a 12 hours time difference would have the Sun rising at about 6 a.m. and it would be setting at about 6 p.m. the previous day at a latitude in the northern hemisphere which was antipodal to the New Zealand latitude. Now, if we regard the Ecliptic (the Sun's path) from a southern hemisphere observer's viewpoint, we will see the Sun rise in the east, culminate in the north and set in the west. The northern hemisphere person sees the Sun rising in the east on his left hand if facing south, culminating in the south and setting in the west. The southern hemisphere person sees the Sun rising on his right hand and culminating in the north.

The rotation of the earth is from west to east and because the rising of the Sun, Moon and planets including the Zodiacal signs are determined by the earth's rotation, their rising is easterly for any latitude and longitude either north or south. Owing to the obliquity of the Ecliptic (23½°) certain signs of the Ecliptic are to the north and some to the south, and this inclination results in some signs rising more rapidly than others. Signs which rise quickly (short ascension) in one hemisphere will rise slowly (long ascension) in the opposite hemisphere. The southern hemisphere horizon in relation to the Ecliptic therefore acts obversely to the northern hemisphere horizon. Thus the number of degrees of a sign rising over a southern hemisphere horizon will not be the same as for a northern hemisphere horizon. Aries, for example, rises in one hemisphere in the same way that Libra rises in the opposite hemisphere. The midheaven is not affected and there is no alteration in numerical values.

The easiest way to understand southern latitude charting is to perform the necessary calculations bearing in mind that our reference tables (Tables of Houses) are for northern latitudes and that we must make an adjustment to the Local Sidereal Time. The calculation of a natal chart for southern latitudes can be summarized under 5 main headings.

Charting for Southern Latitudes. Example No. 1.
10.00 p.m. Standard Time, 6 January 1980, Melbourne,
Lat. 37° 50′ south, Long. 145° 00′ east.

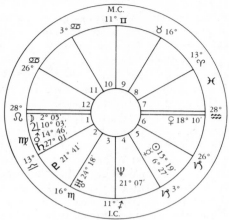

Placidus House System

Planet	Symbol	Sign	House
Sun	☉	Capricorn	5
Moon	☽	Virgo	1
Mercury	☿	Capricorn	5
Venus	♀	Aquarius	6
Mars	♂	Virgo	1
Jupiter	♃	Virgo	1
Saturn	♄	Virgo	1
Uranus	♅	Scorpio	3
Neptune	♆	Sagittarius	4
Pluto	♇	Libra	2

© *J. Filbey*

Southern Latitude

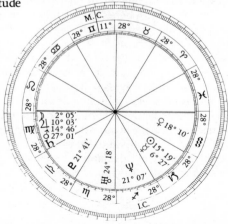

Equal House System: 10.00 p.m. Standard Time, 6 January 1980,
Melbourne, Lat. 37° 50′ south, Long. 145° east.

Local Sidereal Time Calculation

Form 'A' Worksheet			D	M	Y				
Birth date			6	1	1980				
Birth place:			Melbourne						
Latitude:	⋈	S	3750	-	-				
Longitude:	E	⋈	14500	-	-				
			H	M	S				
Birth time:	a.m.						*Greenwich*		
	p.m.		10	-	-		*Date*		
Standard Time	E	—	10	-	-		D	M	Y
	W	+	-	-	-		6	1	80
Daylight Saving	—		-	-	-		*Interval of*		
							G.M.T.		
Greenwich Time	a.m.		Noon	-	-		H	M	S
at birth	p.m.					To	-	-	-
Greenwich Date						From	-	-	-
6.1.80						Noon			

Sidereal Time									
S.T. at noon G.M.T.			19	00	56		*Calculator*		
Interval							*Constant*		
To Noon	a.m.	—	-	-	-		*INTERVAL*		
From	p.m.	+	-	-	-		*÷ 24*		
Result			19	00	56		-		
Correction 9.86 secs									
per hour	a.m.	—	-	-	-		*Log of Interval*		
	p.m.	+	-	-	-		-		
S.T. at Greenwich									
at birth			19	00	56				
Long. Equiv.	E	+	9	40	00				
	W	—	-	-	-				
Result			4	40	56				
Correction (Long.)									
	E	—	-	1	35				
	W	+	-	-	-				
Local Sidereal Time									
at birth			4	39	21				
Add for South Lat.									
12 H			12	-	-				
			16	39	21				
From Tables of Houses			Asc. 28 ♌ M.C. 11 ♊						

© *J. M. Filbey*

Procedure

1. Find the Local Sidereal Time of birth.
2. Add or subtract 12 hours from the time found in (1).
3. Take out the Sidereal Time found in (2) from a northern Table of Houses, e.g. Lat. 51° 32′ south, refer to the London tables.
4. Take the same degrees but reverse the signs as listed in the tables. e.g. if Leo is the 1st cusp, take Aquarius.
5. Insert the signs and planets in the chart in exactly the same manner as for a northern hemisphere birth. Do not reverse planetary positions. *The planets do not change signs, they are the same the world over.*

Chart Calculation: Southern Latitudes

Example No. 1
Birth data: 10.00 p.m. Standard Time 6 January 1980
                 Melbourne, Australia. Lat. 37° 50′ south,
                 Long. 145° east.

			H	M	S	
Birth time:			10	00	00	(assume no Daylight Saving Time)
Standard Time: east	—		10	00	00	
Greenwich Time:		Noon	12	00	00	
S.T. at noon Greenwich:			19	00	56	
Interval:			-	-	-	
Correction Mean to Sidereal:			-	-	-	
Long. Equiv. $\frac{145}{15}$	+	East	9	40	00	
Local Sidereal Time:			28	40	56	
12 hours adjustment southern lat.:	—		12	00	00	
			16	40	56	
Long. correction:	—			1	35	
Local Sidereal Time:			16	39	21	

Having made the adjustment of 12 hours, we refer to the tables for latitude 37° 50′ north or nearest thereto and extract the degree and sign for the Sidereal Time of 16 hours 39 minutes 21 seconds. This gives 28° Aquarius as the Ascendant and the M.C. as 11° Sagittarius. These signs have now to be reversed, giving 28° Leo as the Ascendant and 11° Gemini as the M.C. Likewise, with the other cusps.

Had we not reversed the signs, we would have the sign containing the Sun, Capricorn on the 11th cusp for a time of birth that was late evening (10.00 p.m. local time), which of course would be incorrect. The Sun is between the Descendant and the lower meridian at this time of day, and therefore the sign containing the Sun must also be 'under the horizon' at this time. The following chart shows the signs on the cusps with the planets listed in their correct positions for the time of birth. The planets are calculated for Greenwich Time which, in this particular instance, was noon G.M.T. so no calculation was involved, merely extracting the positions as listed in the ephemeris for noon on the 6 January.

Form 'B'   **WORKSHEET**

Calculation of planets' longitudes for 2.15 p.m. G.M.T.
27 January 1980
(2.15 a.m. Standard Time 28 January 1980
Hamilton, New Zealand)

Logs

Planet	☉	☽	☿	♀	♂
	° ′	° ′	° ′	° ′	° ′
Motion in 24 hrs	1 01	13 02	1 45	1 12	0 09
Log of Motion	1.3730	0.2652	1.1372	1.3010	2.2041
+ Log of interval	1.0280	1.0280	1.0280	1.0280	1.0280
= Log of motion required	2.4010	1.2932	2.1652	2.3290	3.2321
= Degrees/Mins	0 06	1 13	0 10	0 07	0 01
Noon position Sign	♒	♊	♒	♓	♍
Longitude	6 42	13 10	10 55	13 49	14 31 ℞
Motion during interval a.m. —*					
Degrees/Mins p.m. + *	0 06	1 13	0 10	0 07	0 01
= Planet's place (Longitude) at given time	6 48	14 23	11 05	13 56	14 30

Reverse if planet is retrograde.

© J. Filbey

Form 'B'   **WORKSHEET**

Calculation of planets' longitudes for 2.15 p.m. G.M.T.
27 January 1980
(2.15 a.m. Standard Time 28 January 1980,
Hamilton, New Zealand)

Calculator

	☉ ° ′	☽ ° ′	☿ ° ′	♀ ° ′	♂ ° ′
Calculator 0.09375 Constant × daily motion = Motion required	0 06	1 13	0 10	0 07	0 01
Noon position Sign	♒	♊	♒	♓	♍
Longitude	6 42	13 10	10 55	13 49	14 31
Motion required a.m. — * Degrees/Mins p.m. + *	0 06	1 13	0 10	0 07	0 01
Planet's place at given time	6 48	14 23	11 05	13 56	14 30

*Reverse if planet is retrograde

Planetary positions in numerical order

♈	♉	♊	♋	♌	♍	♎	♏	♐	♑	♒	♓
		☽ 14° 23′			♃ 8° 39′	♇ 21° 46′	♅ 25° 05′	♆ 21° 48′		☉ 6° 48′	♀ 13° 56′
					♂ 14° 30′					☿ 11° 05′	
					♄ 26° 38′						

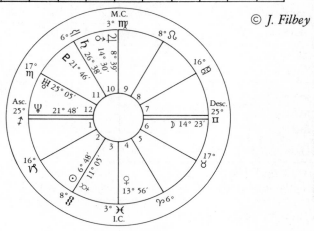

© J. Filbey

2.15 a.m. Standard Time 28 January 1980 Hamilton, Waipa, New Zealand, latitude 37° 48′ south, longitude 175° 17′ east (*see working papers*).

Planet	Symbol	Sign	House
Sun	☉	Aquarius	2
Moon	☽	Gemini	6
Mercury	☿	Aquarius	3
Venus	♀	Pisces	4
Mars	♂	Virgo	10
Jupiter	♃	Virgo	10
Saturn	♄	Virgo	10
Uranus	♅	Scorpio	12
Neptune	♆	Sagittarius	12
Pluto	♇	Libra	11

Local Sidereal Time Calculation

Form 'A' Worksheet			D	M	Y				
Birth date			28	1	1980				
Birth place:			Hamilton, Waipa,						
				N.Z.					
Latitude:	N	S	3748	-	-				
Longitude:	E	W	17517	-	-				
			H	M	S				
Birth time:	a.m.		2	15	-		*Greenwich*		
	p.m.		-	-	-		*Date*		
Standard Time	E	—	12	-	-		D	M	Y
	W	+	-	-	-		27	1	80
Daylight Saving	—		-	-	-		*Interval of*		
							G.M.T.		
Greenwich Time	a.m.						H	M	S
at birth	p.m.		2	15	-	To	-	-	-
Greenwich Date						From	2	15	-
27.1.80						Noon			
Sidereal Time									
S.T. at noon G.M.T.			20	23	44		*Calculator*		
Interval							*Constant*		
To Noon	a.m.	—	-	-	-		*INTERVAL*		
From	p.m.	+	2	15	-		÷ 24		
Result			22	38	44		= 0.09375		
Correction 9.86 secs									
per hour	a.m.	—	-	-	-		*Log of Interval*		
	p.m.	+	-	-	22		= 1.0280		

Continued overleaf

S.T. at Greenwich at birth			22	39	06	
Long. Equiv.	E	+	11	41	08	
	W	—	-	-	-	
Result			10	20	14	
Correction (Long.)						
	E	—	-	1	55	
	W	+	-	-	-	
Local Sidereal Time at birth			10	18	19	
Add for South Lat. 12 H			12	-	-	
			22	18	19	•
From Tables of Houses			Asc. 25 ♐		M.C. 3 ♍	

Southern Latitudes

New Zealand Chart: 2.15 a.m. Standard Time
                         28 January 1980
                         Hamilton, Waipa, N.Z.

The Standard Time of New Zealand is 12 hours in advance of Greenwich, and assuming no Daylight Saving Time was in operation (it is summer in January, south of the Equator), the corresponding Greenwich time will be 12 hours earlier, namely 2.15 p.m. on the previous day (27 January). This is the time for which the planets are calculated as we are using *Raphael's Ephemeris,* which is a Greenwich based ephemeris. The working papers show how the planets' positions are determined for this time.

   As the birth time was in the early morning in New Zealand, the Sun must be under the horizon at 2.15 a.m., so it will be somewhere between the lower meridian and the Ascendant. In this latitude at this time of the year, the Sun rises about 5 a.m. (page 40 *Raphael's Ephemeris*), so we know that the Sun's position in the chart is reasonably correct. If we calculated for 5 a.m. we would find Aquarius rising, because that is the sign containing the Sun.

   The Local Sidereal Time at birth (see working papers) is found by taking the Sidereal Time at noon at Greenwich on 27 January, adding the

G.M.T. interval (2.15 p.m.) plus the correction for Mean to Sidereal Time, which gives the Sidereal Time at Greenwich at birth. As New Zealand is east of Greenwich, in this case 175° 17′ east longitude, we convert this longitude into time at the rate of 15° to 1 hour, which gives 11 hours 41 minutes and 8 seconds, and because we are dealing with an east longitude place, we *add* this longitude equivalent, which gives the Local Sidereal Time at birth. The correction for longitude (1 minute 55 seconds) is shown on the working but, unless the birth data are precise, it can be ignored.

To the Local Sidereal at birth, we add 12 hours as we are dealing with a southern latitude birth, and from the Tables of Houses (37° 58′ north), which is the nearest table for the latitude of birth, we extract the degrees and signs as listed but *reverse* the signs. For this chart, we have a Local Sidereal Time of 10.18.19 to which we add 12 hours — 22.18.19.

The Tables of Houses (22.19.48 nearest Sidereal Time) give 25° Gemini as the Ascendant and 3° Pisces as the M.C. We know this cannot be correct for a 2.15 a.m. birth, as it would place the Sun in the 9th house. By *reversing* the signs that are listed for the Sidereal Time of 22.19.48, we obtain 25° Sagittarius for the Ascendant and 3° Virgo as the M.C. and this gives us the 'correct angles' for the time and place of birth.

Use of Calculator to Find Planets' Positions

The introduction of the electronic calculator has greatly simplified the various types of astrological calculations, reducing the time and labour connected with chart erection. For those who do the odd chart or so, the proportional logarithms as given in the ephemeris will be adequate for the calculations involved, but where many charts are calculated regularly, a calculator is an essential tool.

There are a wide variety of calculators available, but for astrological calculations, a machine which incorporates the sexagesimal function is very useful. There is little point in obtaining an expensive machine with all the various scientific functions unless one is going to make full use of it. Far better to purchase a machine which will do the work that is required, which, in the case of natal charting, only consists of simple proportion and conversion. Astrological arithmetic is really very simple, and it is only when one embarks on research programmes involving certain astronomical factors that the 'sums' become a little more complex.

In calculating the planetary positions for a given time, we can save much time and labour by firstly converting the interval of time before or after noon into a decimal of a day (24 hours). This decimal of a day will be the constant for that interval of time and, by multiplying the daily motion of the planet by this constant, we obtain the motion during that interval. This motion added to or deducted from the noon position of the planet will give its place for the time required. (See Tables—'Hours/minutes' as a decimal of a day.)

Example No. 1
Using a calculator find the Sun's position at 3.17 p.m. G.M.T.
2 January 1980.

Working
Sun's daily motion 2 January 1° 1′ 8″
        as a decimal: = 1.0188
   3.17 p.m. as a decimal: = 3.2833 divided by 24
                   = $\underline{0.1368}$ = constant.
Therefore 1.0188 × 0.1368
= 0.13937 = 8 minutes 22 seconds = Sun's motion in 3 hours 17
minutes, which added to the noon position on 2 January:

	°	′	″	
	11	14	33	Capricorn
	0	8	22	
	11	22	55	Capricorn

= *Sun's position at 3.17 p.m. G.M.T.*

Example No. 2
Find the Sun's position at 7.21 a.m. G.M.T. 2 January 1980.

Working
7.21 a.m. = 12.00
less 7.21 = 4.39 before noon: $\dfrac{4.39}{24}$

= $\dfrac{4.65}{24}$ = 0.1937
Sun's daily motion 1 January:
1° 1′ 8″ = 1.0188 × 0.1937 = 0.1974 = 11′ 51″, which deducted from
the noon position on 2 January

	°	′	″	
	11	14	33	
		11	51	
	11	2	42	Capricorn

= *Sun's position at 7.21 a.m. G.M.T.*

Example No. 3
Find the Moon's position at 9.19 p.m. G.M.T. 1 January 1980.

Working
9.19 p.m. = 9.19 after noon divided by 12 = $\dfrac{9.3166}{12}$
= 0.77638 (divided by 12 as we are working from noon to midnight).
Moon's motion from noon to midnight 1 January =

	°	′	″	
Midnight position 1/2 January:	6	14	44	Cancer
Noon position 1/2 January:	29	43	43	Gemini
Motion in 12 hours:	6	31	01	

6.31.01 = 6.5169 × 0.77638 = 5.0596 = 5° 3′ 35″
which added to the noon position:

29	43	43	
5	3	35	
4	47	18	Cancer

= *Moon's position* at 9.19 p.m. G.M.T. 1 January 1980

Example No. 4
Find the position of Mercury, Venus, Mars, Jupiter at 9.19 p.m. G.M.T. 1 January.

Working
9.19 p.m. = 9.19 divided by 24 = 0.3882 = constant

	Daily motion	*Decimal*
	° ′	
Mercury	1 32	1.5333 × constant 0.3882

= 0.5952 = 35′ 43″
which added to noon position

28°	43′	Sagittarius
	36′	(nearest)
29°	19′	Sagittarius

= *Mercury's position* at 9.19 p.m. 1 January

Venus

	H	M	
Constant	9	19	= 0.3882

Venus	*Daily motion*	*Decimal*
	1° 14′	1.2333 × 0.3882 = 0.4788

= 28′ 44″, which added to noon position

°	′	
12	01	Aquarius
	29	(nearest)
12	30	Aquarius

= *Position of Venus* at 9.19 p.m. 1 January

Mars	*Daily Motion*	*Decimal*
	0° 10′	0.1666 × 0.3882 = 0.0647

= 3′ 53″, which added to the noon position

	°	′	
	14	03	Virgo
		04	
	14	07	Virgo

= *Position of Mars* at 9.19 p.m. 1 January

Jupiter
This planet is moving so slowly that its position can be determined by inspection.

Example No. 5
Calculate the position of the Sun and Moon (using a calculator) for 7.15 p.m. G.M.T. 6 January 1980.

Working
$7.15 = \dfrac{7.25}{24} = 0.30208 = $ constant
Sun's daily motion 6 January = 61′ (ignore seconds)
Therefore 61 × 0.30208 = 18.42688 = 18′ 26″ nearest,
which added to the Sun's noon
position   15° 19′   Capricorn =
                                                                  18′

Sun's position at 7.15 p.m.   15° 37′   Capricorn

Moon's daily motion 6 January = 11° 52′ = 11.8666
Therefore 11.8666 × 0.30208 = 3.5847 = 3° 35′
which added to the Moon's noon
position   2°   5′   Virgo =
                                                                  3° 35′

Moon's position at 7.15 p.m.   5° 40′   Virgo

The daily motion multiplied by the constant (interval of time) gives the motion during that interval, and to convert the answer into minutes or seconds, multiply by 60.

Example: .42688′ × 60 = 25.61 (26″ nearest).
             .5847° × 60 = 35.08 (35′ nearest).

Calculation of Exact Ascendant and Midheaven

Introduction
When the time of birth is given to the nearest quarter of an hour or so, it is misleading and inaccurate to chart the Ascendant and M.C. by listing the

degree and *minute* as extracted from a Table of Houses. In all cases where there is uncertainty regarding the birth time it is sufficient to list the *degree* only, ignoring minutes. However, with precisely timed data, the chart should be calculated with precision and for the exact latitude. Errors involving the angles result in progressions and directions being 'off mark' insofar as the timing of events and conditions are concerned. In order to determine the exact degree rising and culminating, several methods of calculation are available and examples are given below.

In finding the exact degree and minute of the Ascendant and M.C. we use simple interpolation with the assistance of the proportional logarithm tables or with a calculator.

We can summarize the procedure under 3 headings:
1. *The M.C.* The degree and minute culminating is the same for all latitudes for a specified Sidereal Time. It is not affected by latitude, unlike the Ascending degree which varies according to latitude. Having found the exact M.C. for the stated Sidereal Time at birth, no further calculations are required—even if we have to interpolate between different latitudes, that is, to find the exact M.C. for a latitude not listed in the tables of houses.
2. *The Ascendant.* To find the exact Ascendant for a latitude not listed in the tables, we take the two latitudes nearest to the latitude required and work with the highest and lowest Sidereal Times nearest to the Sidereal Time at birth for both these latitudes. Examples will make this clear when we do the calculations.
3. Having found the exact Ascendant for the highest latitude and for the lowest latitude nearest to that of birth, we interpolate to find the exact Ascendant for the required latitude.

In using the log tables for these caluclations, we call the hours and minutes as tabulated *minutes and seconds.*

Calculations

For the M.C. we can either take the Sidereal Times and use logs or we can use the Right Ascension Table as Sidereal Time and Right Ascension are synonymous.

Example No. 1
Find the exact degree and minute of the M.C. for a Sidereal Time of 3 hours 16 minutes 00 seconds at London.

Working: Method 1

	H	M	S		°	′	
Right Ascension Table	3	16	00	=	49	00	
From R.A. tables 49° =					21	26	Taurus

which is the exact degree and minute culminating at this Sidereal Time. This is the easiest way to find the M.C.

Method 2: Finding Ascendant and M.C.
From London tables:

	(1) S.T.			(2) Asc.		(3) M.C.	(4) S.T.		
	H	M	S	°	'	°	H	M	S
Highest	3	18	19	1	36 ♍	22 ♉			
Required							3	16	00
Lowest	3	14	15	0	54	21	3	14	15
Difference		4	04	0	42	1		1	45

Proportional Logs.

			M	S			Log	
Col. 4	1.45 =		1	45	=		1.1372	
2	0.42 =		42	00	=		1.5351	*add*
							2.6723	
1	4.04 =		4	04	=		0.7710	*deduct*
			18	00	=		1.9013	

The lower Ascendant is 0° 54′ Virgo, to which we add 18 minutes as found above which gives 1° 12′ Virgo as the exact Ascendant at London for a Sidereal Time of 3 hours 16 minutes.

Method 3.
Using a calculator to prove that 3 hours 16 minutes Sidereal Time at London gives an Ascendant of 1° 12′ Virgo.

Working
Taking the highest and lowest Sidereal Times nearest to that required: 1.36 less 0.54 = 0.42′ and the difference between the required Sidereal Time 3.16.00 and the nearest lowest Sidereal Time 3.14.15 gives a difference of 1′ 45″, then

$$1.45 = \frac{1.75 \times 42}{4.066} = 18',$$

which confirms the calculation done with logs.

M.C.
The M.C. found from the Tables of Right Ascension is 21° 26′ Taurus. Check using logs.

Working

	M	S				
Difference in S.T.	1	45	=		1.1372	
(1°)	60	00	=		1.3802	*add*
					2.5174	
	4	04	=		0.7710	*deduct*
	26	00	=		1.7464	

M.C. Check using calculator

Working
1′ 45″ = 1.75 × 60′ divided by 4′ 04″

$$= \frac{1.75 \times 60}{4.066} = 25′ 49″ = 26′ \text{ nearest,}$$

which confirms the calculations done by logs and from the table of Right Ascension.

Normally, there is no need to calculate the angles exactly unless the birth time is precise, and these methods of finding the exact angles are given in order that should the need arise we are in a position to deal with the precise data.

Example No. 2
Find the exact Ascendant and M.C. for a Sidereal Time at London of 7 hours 54 minutes 10 seconds.

Calculator				*Sidereal Time*	H	M	S
From London tables							
	°	′					
Asc.	20	27	Libra	= Highest	7	56	12
Asc.	19	43		= Lowest	7	52	00
Diff.	0	44		= Difference		4	12
				Required	7	54	10
				Lowest	7	52	00
				Difference		2	10

Therefore if 4′ 12″ = 44′ over the Asc. 2′ 10″

$$= \frac{2.166 \times 44}{4.2}$$

= 23′ nearest which added to the lower Asc. 19° 43′ Libra = 20° 6′ = exact Ascendant.

Proportional Logs

M	S		Log	
2	10	=	1.0444	
44	00	=	1.5149	*add*
			2.5593	
4	12	=	0.7570	*deduct*
23	00	=	1.8023	

which confirms the result using the calculator.

Right Ascension tables to find M.C.
Convert the Sidereal Time required into R.A. (15° = 1 hour)

		°	′	″
7×15	=	105	00	00
$\dfrac{54'}{4}$	=	13	30	00
$\dfrac{10''}{4}$	=	0	2	30
		118	32	30

118° 32′ 30″

		°	′	°	′	
From R.A. tables		118	00	=	26	00	Cancer
		119	00	=	26	57	Cancer
Difference				=	0	57	

Therefore if 60′ = 57

$$32.5' = \frac{32.5 \times 57}{60} = 31'$$

which added to the M.C. (Sidereal Time 7.52.00) 26° Cancer gives 26° 31′ Cancer as the M.C. at the required Sidereal Time of 7.54.10.

Calculator
2′ 10″ = 2.166 × 60′ divided by 4′ 12″

$$= \frac{2.166 \times 60}{4.2} = 30' \, 56'' = 31' \text{ nearest}$$

which confirms previous calculations using Right Ascension tables.

Logs	M	S		Log	
Difference in S.T. =	2	10	=	1.0444	
	60	00	=	1.3802	*add*
				2.4246	
	4	12	=	0.7570	*deduct*
	31	00	=	1.6676	

By using at least two methods in calculations such as these the likelihood of error is reduced.

In example No. 2 we found the Ascendant to be 20° 6′ Libra (23′ was the amount to be added to the lower Asc. as listed in the Table of Houses 19° 43′ Libra). As an additional check on the M.C., we can say if 44′, which is the total difference between the lower and higher Ascendants, gives   60′   over   the   M.C.,   23   will   give

$$\frac{23 \times 60}{44} = 31',$$

which again confirms previous calculations.

Finding the Exact Ascendant for a Geographical Latitude Not Listed in the Tables of Houses

Introduction
Normally, it is sufficiently accurate to use a Table of Houses which is serviceable for places on or near to the latitude of birth. The London tables, for instance, can be used for places between 50-53° north latitude, but if the birth data are precise, then the angles should be calculated accurately. If there are no tables for the exact required latitude, then interpolation can be used to chart the exact Ascendant and M.C. The following examples show the procedure:

Example No. 1
Find the Ascendant and M.C. at latitude 54° 20′ north when the Sidereal Time of birth is 4.12.13.

Working	(1) Lat.		(2) Asc.			(3) Lat.	
	°	′	°	′		°	′
Highest	54	34	11	47	Virgo	-	-
Required	-	-	-	-		54	20
Lowest	53	58	11	38	Virgo	53	58
Difference	0	36	0	09		0	22

Using Proportional Logs

		Logs
Column 3	22′	1.8159
Column 2	09′	2.2041 *add*
		4.0200
Column 1	36′	1.6021 *deduct*
Result	5′ nearest	2.4179

To the lower Ascendant 11° 38′ add 5′ = 11° 43′ Virgo = exact Ascendant at 54° 20′ north.

Using Calculator
If 36′ = difference between higher and lower latitudes, 22′ (difference between lower latitude and latitude required) will equal, $\dfrac{22 \times 9}{36}$ (difference over Ascendant)
= 5.5′—say 5′ nearest.

The M.C. is the same for all latitudes for a specified Sidereal Time, therefore S.T. 4.12.13 will give the M.C. as follows:

	°	′				°	′	
From Tables Right	4	12	00	=	4	57	Gemini
Ascension	4	16	00	=	5	54	
Difference	0	4	00		0	57	

If $4' = 57'$ $13'' =$

$\dfrac{57 \times 0.216}{4} = 3'$ which added to the lesser M.C.

$4° 57'$ Gemini $= 5° 00'$ Gemini $=$ M.C. required.

Example No. 2
Find the exact Ascendant and M.C. at latitude 54° 10′ north when the Sidereal Time is 4.12.13.

Working	(1) Lat.		(2) Asc.		(3) M.C.	(4) Lat.	
	°	′	°	′	°	°	′
Highest (as found)	54	20	11	43	5		
Required						54	10
Lowest	53	58	11	38	5	53	58
Difference	0	22	0	05	-	0	12

Therefore, if 22′ (difference between highest and lowest latitudes) = 5′ over the Ascendant, 12′ difference in latitude equals $\dfrac{12 \times 5}{22} = 3'$ nearest,

which added to the lower ascendant = 11° 41′ Virgo = exact Ascendant at 54° 10′ north.

The M.C. is the same for all latitudes for a specified Sidereal Time and in this instance is 5° Gemini.

10.
CLASSIFICATION OF CHART FACTORS

The Astrological Aspects

Definition of Aspects
An aspect is the distance between two planets as measured along the Ecliptic in longitude. If for example the Sun is in 10° Scorpio and Saturn is in 10° Taurus, the distance apart is 180° and they are said to be in opposition.

Classification
Aspects are classified into two main categories, major and minor, although modern research is tending to confirm that many of the so-called minor aspects are more important than has hitherto been considered.

Major Aspects	Symbol	Degrees apart
Conjunction	☌	0
Semi-square	∠	45
Sextile	✶	60
Square	□	90
Trine	△	120
Opposition	☍	180

Minor Aspects

Semi-sextile	⊻	30
Semi-Quintile	⊥	36
Quintile	Q	72
Sesquiquadrate	⊡	135
Bi-Quintile	±	144
Quincunx	⊽	150

Nature of Aspects

Traditionally, aspects have been considered as either 'good' or 'bad', but this archaic classification has now been replaced by other descriptions such as harmonious or inharmonious, which is really a play on words. If two planets are in aspect, it is the nature of the planets which will determine how the aspect will operate. Mars square Saturn is a much more difficult contact than say Moon square Venus. In any case, all contacts have to be related to the chart as a whole: one cannot form judgement from a single contact.

Of the major aspects, the conjunction is probably the most powerful, and its effects are dependent on the two bodies involved. The square (90°) and the opposition (180°) are considered difficult and tension producing, while the sextile (60°) and the trine (120°) are thought to unconstrained and give ease of expression in various forms. Again, it depends on the planets forming the aspect as to how the contacts will operate, either physically or psychologically.

Even though the square and opposition aspect may cause tension, it can also give strength and initiative and the ability to face up to problems. Likewise, too many so-called good aspects such as the trine and sextile can lead to indolence and a placid acceptance of conditions. Of the minor aspects the quincunx (150°) is probably the most important and is often significant of some form of stress. The 'ideal chart' has a mixture of both 'easy' and 'difficult' aspects and the sign and house position of the planets in aspect will indicate how well the chart is integrated.

Planets which form no aspects, i.e. unaspected, and this does occur occasionally, are often thought to be a 'dumb note', but this need not be so—it depends on the sign and house containing the planet. Lack of contact can cause the planet to operate in its purest sense either actively or passively.

Aspects are one of the major factors in a chart, and it is from the study of the aspects in a chart, or what is just as important, lack of aspectual strength, that the personality of an individual can be assessed. Aspects to the angles (1st, 10th 7th, and 4th house cusps) generally give prominence in one way or another and such persons with angular contacts generally do not pass their days in obscurity.

Orbs of Aspects

In the ephemeris, the aspects are given when the contact is exact, but in listing aspects for a particular chart a certain orb is allowed either greater or lesser than the exact contact. For instance, a planet is within 'orb' of a conjunction or an opposition if it is within 8-9° of exactitude; a square or trine aspect if within 7-8° of exactitude. For the minor aspects, a very narrow orb is allowed, say 2-3. The amount allowed varies according to the strength of the aspect and the planets involved. A powerful contact can be allowed a wider orb than a weaker aspect.

Calculation of Aspects

All aspects need to be considered and entered in the aspect table after the chart has been calculated. The printed chart forms (see 'Recommended Requirements') have this aspect table in which the various aspects of a particular chart can be listed. As with all chart calculations, the approach must be methodical otherwise aspects may be overlooked. Basically, we are taking the distance between two planets, and this distance is arc in longitude.

For example in Chart No. 2, 6 January, 7.15 p.m. London, Venus is in Aquarius 18° 32′ and Pluto is in Libra 21° 41′. Counting from Libra to Aquarius, ignoring minutes, gives 9° Libra, 30° Scorpio, 30° Sagittarius, 30° Capricorn plus 18° Aquarius, making a total of 117°, which is within an orb of 120°. Venus is therefore trine Pluto. If the distance had been either 112° or 128° it would still be considered a trine aspect as we allow up to 7-8° from exactitude. With practice, the aspects can be noted by considering the signs and their classifications. This classification will be discussed in the chapter on Other Chart Factors.

Measuring aspects should always be done by noting the signs, not the houses. With the Placidean system of House division signs can be intercepted and one house may contain two signs or more which causes difficulties in measuring the distance that planets are apart.

PLANET		☉	☽	☿	♀	♂	♃	♄	♅	♆	♇
Sun	☉		△	☌	•		⚻	•	•	•	•
Moon	☽			△	□	□	□	•	•	☍	△
Mercury	☿				⚺	⚻	⚻	•	•	•	•
Venus	♀					☍	☍	•	•	□	
Mars	♂						☌	•	•	□	•
Jupiter	♃							•	•	•	•
Saturn	♄								✳	□	•
Uranus	♅									•	•
Neptune	♆										✳
Pluto	♇										
Asc.			•	•	•	•	•	□	⚺	☌	✳
M.C.			•	•	•	•	☌	•	•	•	•

Figure 18. Aspects in the chart for 2.15 a.m. Standard Time 28 January 1980, New Zealand.

Listing the Aspects

The aspect table on page 131 shows the aspects listed for the New Zealand chart (2.15 a.m. Standard Time, 28 January 1980, Hamilton, N.Z.). Astrology has its own 'shorthand and language', but the meanings of the various symbols and the different terms used are not difficult to understand. With a little practice, the various configurations formed by the planets one to another, and to the Ascendant and Midheaven can be recognized and tabulated.

In the New Zealand chart the following aspects are within orb:

1. Sun trine Moon, conjunction Mercury, quincunx Jupiter. The Sun is trine Moon because it is 128° distance from the Moon; it is conjunction Mercury as only 4° separate these two planets, and it is quincunx Jupiter because it is 148° from Jupiter. An exact trine would be 120°; an exact conjunction 0° and an exact quincunx 150°. However, as we have stated previously, an orb of so many degrees is allowable depending on the type of aspect and the planets involved.

2. The Moon has several major aspects being trine Mercury and Pluto, square Venus, Mars and Jupiter, and opposition Neptune. 123° separate the Moon from Mercury which is a close trine, and the square to Venus is exact within minutes, while the squares to Mars and Jupiter (exact for Mars and 6° for Jupiter are close enough to be powerful squares. This contact of the Moon with Mars/Jupiter and Venus is a 'T square' and is formed by planet(s) in opposition and planet(s) halfway between them forming a square. In this case Moon squares Venus/Mars/ Jupiter, with Venus opposition Mars/Jupiter. It is a powerful contact.

Ruling Planet: ♃		Ruler's House: 10	
Rising Planet: ♆		Positive: 5	
		Negative: 5	
Triplicities:			
Fire: Asc. 1		Own sign:	
Earth: M.C. 3		Exalted: ♀	
Air: 4		Detriment: ☉	
Water: 2		Fall: ♃	
Quadruplicities:			
Cardinal: 1		Angular: 4	
Fixed: 3		Succeedent: 2	
Mutable: 6		Cadent: 4	
Mutual Reception: ☿ - ♄			

Figure 19. Classification of other chart factors for New Zealand chart 2.15 a.m. Standard Time 28 January 1980. Lat. 37° 48′ south, Long. 175° 17′ east.

Other Chart Factors

Preparatory to chart analysis and assessment, a classification is made of certain factors associated with the planetary positions and the signs and houses in which the planets are placed. Many of these classifications are traditional and, although some are being confirmed by modern astrological research, others are not. However, as the student will sooner or later see various categories and terms mentioned in astrological works concerning groupings and divisions of planets, signs and houses, a brief explanation of these factors may prove useful.

The 12 signs of the Zodiac have from the earliest times been divided into several categories:

1. The four Elements, Fire, Earth, Air and Water (Triplicities).
2. Cardinal, Fixed and Mutable signs (Quadruplicities or Qualities).
3. Positive and Negative signs (Masculine and Feminine).

The following table shows how the signs are classified:

	Positive	Negative	Positive	Negative
	Fire	Earth	Air	Water
Cardinal	Aries	Capricorn	Libra	Cancer
Fixed	Leo	Taurus	Aquarius	Scorpio
Mutable	Sagittarius	Virgo	Gemini	Pisces

It is not the purpose of this book to deal with analysis and interpretation of charts, but in discussing the traditional divisions into which the signs are divided, we can comment on the 'expression' of the signs.

The positive signs are considered direct and outgoing; the negative signs receptive and passive. This, however, is a broad generalization and, as each chart is different according to the planetary groupings and house positions, so the expression of the signs will be either modified or accentuated. Fire signs may exhibit enthusiasm and initiative and be creative (particularly Leo), and Air may seek to communicate on a personal and impersonal level, but an unsympathetic combination of planet and sign will not be conducive to the natural expression of either sign or planet. Again, the complete chart has to be assessed and a synthesis made.

The Houses

The 12 houses of the chart are divided into three groups:

1. Angular (Houses) 1, 10, 7 and 4.
2. Succeedent (Houses) 2, 11, 8 and 5.
3. Cadent (Houses) 3, 12, 9 and 6.

The Angular houses are the important houses and planets in them, particularly if close to the Angles (cusps 1, 10, 7 and 4) exert maximum influence depending on the sign containing the planet and the aspects which the planet(s) receive. Although there is much nonsense and absurdity in astrological literature concerning planets, signs and houses, most astrologers do at least agree on the importance of angularity.

Traditionally, the houses are related to the signs, in that the first house is related to the first sign Aries, the second house to Taurus, the third to Gemini and so on. In other words, Angular houses have a correspondence with the Cardinal signs, the Succeedent houses with the Fixed signs, and the Cadent houses with the Mutable signs. There appears to be some justification for these correspondences, and experience shows that, although a planet will operate according to the sign it is in, it will also display certain facets, not only of the house where it is posited, but also some of the attributes connected with the natural sign of that house.

For example, many planets in the 9th house, say in Libra, may show a combination of the Libran and Sagittarian principles expressed through matters traditionally associated with the 9th house, such as mental and physical exploration, the administration of justice or in broader terms, anything which involves co-operative effort leading to the acquisition of knowledge and understanding.

Basically, the three divisions of the houses, Angular, Succeedent and Cadent represent the Qualities of the signs naturally associated with them.

1. Angular houses which are adjacent to the horizon and midheaven (1, 7, 10 and 4) correspond to the Cardinal signs (Aries, Libra, Capricorn and Cancer), and planets in these houses often operate not only via the signs in which they are actually placed, but also in a manner associated with the natural sign of that house. Mars in Aries is always Mars/Aries but, if it is in the 10th house, it is also Mars/Aries/Capricorn and its expression will be active and energetic as befits Mars/Aries, also practical and realistic, even a little cautious, due to the Capricorn house emplacement. The activity and expression of planets in signs and houses is of course, governed by the aspects they have, and the chart must be considered in its entirety.

2. Succeedent houses (2, 11, 8 and 5) are related to the Fixed signs (Taurus, Aquarius, Scorpio and Leo) and planets in these houses often show the qualities associated with these signs, fixity and stability. Mars, for example, in the second house may operate through the sign in which it is placed in a Taurean manner, that is, in a practical manner with a keen sense of economic values. It will be active and energetic but its energies are directed towards establishing sound foundations in order to achieve security.

   Planets in the 11th house (natural house of Aquarius) are often associated with a concern for humanity and their well-being. This concern, however, may be expressed in a detached autocratic manner, the objective being to accomplish the greatest good for the many. Aquarius and the 11th house represents that which is collective, as opposed to Leo and the 5th house which relates to the individual and personal involvement. All the Fixed signs are concerned with power, and planets in the Fixed houses often display an urge to acquire power for one reason or another.

3. Cadent houses (3, 12, 9 and 6) correspond to the Mutable signs (Gemini, Pisces, Sagittarius and Virgo). Adaptability and flexibility characterize these signs and their natural houses. The principal expression is communication at all levels; the acquisition and imparting of information. All the cadent houses have some connection with perception, learning, reasoning and intuition. Planets in these houses often act in a diffuse manner; Mars in the 3rd house can be very versatile and mentally agile, but its energies are liable to be scattered and not channelled in a constructive manner.

The Ruler

Traditionally, each sign has one and in some cases, two rulers, and these rulers have an affinity with the sign(s) with which they are associated. These rulers are the planets as shown below:

Planet	Sign	Natural House
Sun	Leo	5
Moon	Cancer	4
Mercury	Gemini	3
	Virgo	6
Venus	Taurus	2
	Libra	7
Mars	Aries	1
	Scorpio	8
Jupiter	Sagittarius	9
	Pisces	12
Saturn	Capricorn	10
	Aquarius	11
Uranus	Aquarius	11
Neptune	Pisces	12
Pluto	Scorpio	8

The modern planets, i.e. those discovered in modern times, Uranus, Neptune, and Pluto, are classified as co-rulers of the signs Aquarius, Pisces and Scorpio.

Ruling Planet

The Ascendant is referred to as the Ruling Sign, and the planet which rules the sign ascending is termed the ruling planet. If Libra was the Ascendant, then Venus would be the ruling planet. The position, both zodiacally and mundanely, of the ruling planet, and the aspects it receives, are very important factors of the chart. The ruler's house is the house containing the ruling planet and matters connected with that house are often very significant in the life. If the Ascendant was Gemini, and Mercury (the ruling planet) was in the third house, then the affairs of the third house, writing, teaching, travelling etc. would play an important part to a greater or lesser degree depending upon the sign that Mercury was in and the aspects it received.

Rising Planet

A planet is said to be rising if it is within about 8 degrees of the Ascendant, that is within a conjunction of the Ascendant, either 8° above or below. Conversely a planet near the Descendant (about 8 degrees) is setting and is important as it is close to an angle (7th).

Angular Planets

With the Placidus system of house division planets in the 1st, 10th, 7th and 4th houses are considered angular, although true angularity is really a conjunction within about 8 degrees of the actual angle. The Equal House System, which measures the houses from the Ascendant in 30-degree segments, does not use the term Succeedent and Cadent, and planets are only considered to be angular if within about 8 degrees of an angle. This is the correct interpretation of angularity. Planets angular are extremely important and operate very powerfully according to the sign they are in and the contacts they receive.

Sun/Moon Ruler

The ruling planet of the sign which contains the Sun or the Moon is the Sun/ruler or Moon/ruler. Sun in Scorpio and Moon in Taurus, the Sun ruler would be Mars and Pluto, and the Moon ruler would be Venus.

Own Sign

If a planet is in its own sign, e.g. Venus in Libra, it is said to be strong;

likewise if it is in a sign it rules, e.g. Venus in Taurus. If the planet is badly placed mundanely or if it lacks aspectual strength, being in a sign it rules or in its own sign will not be of much assistance.

Exalted, Detriment, Fall

Planets are exalted, in their detriment or fall if they are in certain signs. This is a traditional classification and although it may have some basis in fact, a planet well placed mundanely with strong aspects will always act in a prominent manner.

Planet	Exalted (Powerful)	Fall (Weak)	Detriment (Weak)
Sun	Aries	Libra	Aquarius
Moon	Taurus	Scorpio	Capricorn
Mercury	Virgo	Pisces	Sagittarius Pisces
Venus	Pisces	Virgo	Scorpio Aries
Mars	Capricorn	Cancer	Libra Taurus
Jupiter	Cancer	Capricorn	Gemini Virgo
Saturn	Libra	Aries	Cancer Leo

Uranus, Neptune and Pluto have no definite allocation in this scheme of exaltation, fall and detriment, but if the general classification is adopted then Uranus will be in its detriment in Leo (the opposite sign to which it rules), Neptune's sign of detriment will be Virgo, and Pluto's will be Taurus. Exaltation and fall regarding these planets is not known owing their comparatively recent discovery.

Mutual Reception

This is a term applied when two planets are each in a sign ruled by the other, e.g. Mercury in Scorpio, Mars in Virgo. It is considered to act like a conjunction but it is by no means certain that this is so.

Satellitium

When three or more planets are grouped together within about 8 degrees (a conjunction) either in one sign or at the end of a sign and the beginning of another, there is a strong concentration, and the signs and houses in which this satellitium occurs will be significant.

Dispositor

This is another traditional term that needs to be regarded with a certain amount of scepticism. The dispositor is that planet which rules a sign containing another planet. e.g. Mars in Leo, the dispositor is the Sun. Mars in Taurus, the dispositor is Venus.

Lack of Aspects

Planets which receive no aspects are always important for they may (a) indicate a lack of the quality associated with that planet, e.g. unaspected Mars, lack of initiative, or (b) they may act in the 'purest sense' unaffected by contacts with other planets, e.g. an over active Mars, rash and impetuous.

11.
SUBSIDIARY CHARTS

The Uncertain Birth-time

To calculate an accurate natal chart the time of birth is essential. However, when the time of birth is unknown or only known approximately, there are several methods by which a chart can be set up, even though the indications from that chart will not be as detailed as from an accurately timed chart. Various methods of rectification can be employed to try and arrive at a speculative time of birth, and this rectification consists of relating events and changes which have affected the life to the planetary progressions which were operating at a particular time in the life. From the progressions and their timing some idea of the birth-time can be obtained. Needless to say, the work involved is considerable and much time and labour plus a wide experience of astrological principles is essential.

A quicker way to deal with uncertain birth times is to set up simple charts based on either the Sun's noon position on the day of birth or true sunrise. An additional method is to list the twelve signs of the Zodiac on a chart form commencing with Aries and to insert the noon positions of the planets on the day of birth in the appropriate signs. Naturally, this will only give a very broad indication of character and no deductions can be made regarding house position because these will be unknown.

Chart 1: Solar Chart
Assuming birth occurred on 2 January, time unknown, we take the Sun's position at noon (11° Capricorn) and assume that this is the ascending sign and degree, (Capricorn 11°). In doing this we are setting up a speculative

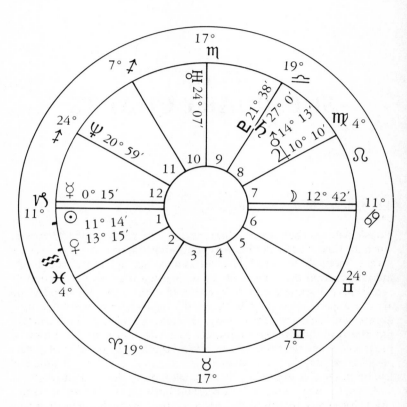

The Unknown Birth-time: Solar Chart (1). Birth date 2 January 1980;
Time unknown; London. Planetary positions as at noon G.M.T. Placidus
House System.

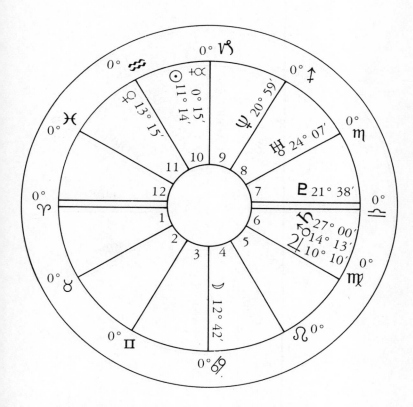

The Unknown Birth-time: Planets in the Natural Houses (2). Birth date 2 January 1980; Time unknown; London. Planetary positions as at noon G.M.T. Equal House System.

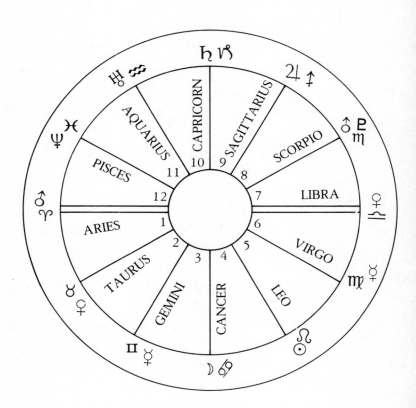

Signs, Rulers, Natural Houses.

chart for about sunrise. The planets' positions are taken as shown in the ephemeris for noon on that day (2 January).

We could of course, calculate the time of sunrise and then calculate the planets' positions for this time (about 8 a.m.) but there is no purpose in doing this as the difference in motion between 8 a.m. and noon will be slight except for the Moon. The house positions of the planets are not known because the time of birth is unknown, so no observations can be made regarding mundane position. If in fact birth had occurred at sunrise then the chart as shown would be the true natal chart with the planetary positions calculated for the time of birth (about 8 a.m.).

For a quick assessment of the zodiacal positions a chart form listing the signs commencing with the first sign (Aries) can be used and the planetary positions as at noon inserted in the appropriate signs. This is similar to the solar chart and only broad indications can be obtained from it. Nevertheless, these two kinds of chart listings will show the sign positions and give some indication of the planetary pattern operating on that particular day.

Subsidiary Charts

The Solar Return: Introduction

In addition to the natal chart which is, of course, valid from birth to death, other charts are sometimes used in conjunction with the natal chart, to assess the current trends which may be operating at a given time.

Of these subsidiary charts, one of the most valuable is the Solar Return, which is a 'revolution' chart cast for the exact time that the natal Sun returns to the longitude that it held at birth. This occurs each year on or about the birthday.

It is a personal chart as distinct from other types of return charts, such as the ingress, solstice or New Moon charts, which are mundane figures cast for the commencement of a new cycle. The Solar Return affords indications of the events and circumstances likely to be experienced during the year in which the return is operative. The year, of course, commencing from the date of the Solar Return.

Calculation

The usual method of calculating these returns is to ascertain the *exact* time when the Sun returns to the *exact* longitude that it held at birth. As the Sun moves one minute of arc in about 24 minutes of time, it is essential that its place is computed to the exact degree minute and second of longitude. Any uncertainty concerning the birth time will result in a corresponding error in the time of the Sun's return, and this will cause the cusps of the return chart to be inaccurate, particularly if a sign of short ascension is rising.

In determining the Sun's exact longitude several methods of calculation are available, but it should be noted that the four figure logarithms given in the ephemeris are not sufficiently accurate for this purpose. If logarithms are used, then Ternary proportional in conjunction with diurnal logarithms are required. The quickest way to find the exact longitude of the Sun is to use a calculating machine.

Although the Solar Return chart can be studied and analysed in isolation from other charts, its indications should be related to the natal chart, and also to any current progressions which may be operative during that time.

Planets angular in the return chart are always important, and if there are mutual aspects involving the natal chart, the year in question will be important. As a predictive instrument and technique, the Solar Return is extremely valuable. Its real value, however, lies in its progression, i.e. its movement from the commencement of the Solar Return year to the following year.

Lunar Returns

A Lunar Return is a chart cast for the exact time that the natal moon returns to the same longitude that it held at birth. This occurs every 27 days or so. These returns are computed to the nearest minute, odd seconds being ignored. As the Solar Return covers 12 months from the time of the Sun's return, so the Lunar Return covers 1 month from the time of the Moon's return to its natal longitude. The indications shown in the Lunar Return should be related to the natal chart and the current progressions. It may be that the Solar Return indicates the 'pattern of the year', and the Lunar Return the 'pattern of the month'. Only careful investigation with well-attested data will confirm this assumption. The method of calculating the Lunar return is similar to that used for the Solar Return.

Calculations
Solar Return
Assume that a person's natal Sun is 23° 40' 10" Capricorn, and the Solar Return is required for 1980/81.

Working
From the 1980 ephemeris: Sun's position:

		°	′	″
15 January:		24	29	23
14 January:		23	28	15
Daily motion:	=	1	01	08
Sun's natal position:		23	40	10
Sun's noon position 14 January 1980:		23	28	15
Difference:			11	55

Therefore if 61′ 8″ = 24 hours

11′ 55″ =

$$\frac{11.9166 \times 24}{61.1333} = 4.6782 = 4 \text{ hours } 41′$$

The Solar Return occurs at 4.41 p.m. G.M.T. 14 January 1980

A chart calculated for this time in the same manner as a natal chart will be the Solar Return chart for 1980/81.

Lunar Return
Assume that a person's natal Moon is 1° 55′ Scorpio, and that the Lunar Return is required for January 1980.

Working
From the 1980 ephemeris: Moon's position:

	°	′	″
Midnight 11/12 January:	7	41	49
Noon 11 January	1	33	27
Motion in 12 hours =	6	08	22
Moon's natal position:	1	55	00
Moon's noon position 11 January 1980:	1	33	27
Difference =		21	33

Therefore if 6° 8′ = 12 hours

21′ = (ignore seconds)

$$\frac{21 \times 12}{6.133} = 41.09 = 41′ \text{ nearest.}$$

The Lunar return occurs 41′ after noon on 11 January (12.41 p.m. G.M.T.).

A chart calculated for this time in the same manner as a natal chart will be the Lunar Return chart for January 1980.

12.
CHARTING EXERCISES

Questions

1. Find the Ascendant and M.C. for 9.15 a.m., 15 January 1980 London. Time given is G.M.T.
2. Find the Moon's position for 10.30 p.m. G.M.T., 10 January 1980. Take daily motion noon—noon.
3. Find the Sun's position for 11.55 p.m. G.M.T. 26 January 1980.
4. Find the Sun's position for 5.00 a.m. Eastern Standard Time, 6 January 1980, New York.
5. Find the Local Sidereal Time at 4.30 p.m. G.M.T., 6 January 1980 at London.
6. Find the Local Sidereal Time at 10.00 a.m. Pacific Standard Time, 6 January 1980, San Francisco.
7. Find the Local Sidereal Time, Asc. and M.C. for 5.00 p.m. Standard Time, 20 January 1980 at Melbourne, Australia.
8. Find the proportional logarithm of:
    (a) 10 hours 30′
    (b) 1° 1′
    (c) 13° 10′
9. What is the longitude equivalent of 115° 10′.
10. At what time of the day on 6 January 1980, at London, will 15° Virgo be the ascending sign and degree?

Answers

1. The Ascendant is 21° Aquarius and the M.C. is 14° Sagittarius.
2. The Moon's position is 24° 45′ Libra.
3. The Sun's position is 6° 11′ Aquarius.
4. The Sun's position is 15° 14′ Capricorn.
5. The Local Sidereal Time is 23 hours 31′ 40″.
6. The Local Sidereal Time is 16 hours 52′ 12″.
7. The Local Sidereal Time is 0 hours 35′ 19″ + 12 hours = Ascendant 20° Gemini, M.C. 10° Aries.
8. The proportional logarithms are:
   (a) 0.3590   (b) 1.3730   (c) 0.2607.
9. The longitude equivalent in time is 7 hours 40′ 40″.
10. 15° Virgo rises at London at 9.32 p.m. G.M.T.

GLOSSARY

Air: One of the four elements (Triplicities). The Zodiacal signs are Gemini, Libra and Aquarius.

Altitude: The elevation of a heavenly body above the horizon. A co-ordinate of the horizon system that measures a body's angular distance from the horizon from 0-90°.

Angles: The 1st, 10th, 7th and 4th houses of a natal chart; The Ascendant, Meridian, Descendant and nadir.

Aphelion: The point in a planet's orbit where a planet is at its greatest distance from the Sun.

Apogee: The point in the orbit where the Moon or a planet is at its greatest distance from the Earth.

Apparent Noon: The moment when the sun crosses the meridian.

Apparent Solar Time: The time interval between two successive transits of the sun across the meridian.

Aquarius: The 11th sign of the Zodiac. The Sun appears to enter this sign about 22 January each year.

Arctic: The polar area north of latitude 66° 33' north.

Aries: The 1st sign of the Zodiac. The Sun appears to enter this sign about 21 March each year (Vernal Equinox).

Ascendant: The eastern angle; the sign and degree of the Zodiac which is rising on the eastern horizon at the time and place of birth (*see* Angles).

Ascending: Planets between the 4th house and the M.C. rising eastward are said to be 'ascending'.

Aspect: The positions of two or more planets with respect to one another. The distance measured in Celestial Longitude that planets are apart. The conjunction, opposition, square and trine are the major aspects.

Astronomical Co-ordinates: Values in a reference system used to define a position of a body on the Celestial Sphere. The three principal systems are: 1. Horizon System; 2. Equatorial System; 3. Ecliptic System.

Autumnal Equinox: The September Equinox: The First Point of Libra: One of the points of intersection between the Celestial Equator and the Ecliptic that the Sun reaches when crossing from north to south on or about 23 September.

Birth Chart: A chart showing the positions of the Sun, Moon and planets for a given time and place. A chart for the birth time of any person, event or project.

Birth Time: The moment when an infant draws its first independent breath. The time that an event occurs, or a project is definitely commenced.

Cadent: The houses, 3rd, 6th, 9th and 12th.

Cancer: The 4th sign of the Zodiac. The Sun appears to enter this sign about 23 June each year.

Capricorn: The 10th sign of the Zodiac. The Sun appears to enter this sign about 21 December each year.

Cardinal Signs: The signs Aries, Cancer, Libra and Capricorn.

Celestial Equator: A great circle on the Celestial Sphere mid-way between the Celestial Poles.

Celestial Meridian: The great circle on the celestial Sphere which passes through the poles, zenith and nadir, and the north and south points of the horizon. The observer's meridian of longitude projected onto the celestial Sphere.

Celestial Poles: The points on the sky which are directly overhead at the terrestrial poles. The Earth's rotational axis extended into space.

Celestial Sphere: The apparent sphere, with the Earth at the centre, on which the celestial bodies appear to be projected.

Circumpolar Stars: Stars which are always seen above the horizon.

Civil Day: the 24 hour Mean Solar Day.

Common Signs: Another term for Mutuable signs. Gemini, Virgo, Sagittarius and Pisces.

Conjunction: When two bodies are within 8° of each other, as measured in Celestial Longitude.

Constellations: Star groupings. Those close to the Ecliptic have the same names as the signs of the Zodiac, but are in no way connected with the signs.

Culmination: The meridian passage of a celestial body.

Cusp: The point of division between either signs, or houses.

Day: The period of time equal to one rotation of the Earth. It can be measured as a Sidereal Day, a Solar Day or a Mean Solar Day.

Descendant: The point opposite to the Ascendant; the sign and degree setting on the western horizon at the time and place of birth.

Declination: The measurement of the angular distance of a body from the Celestial Equator.

Diurnal Circle: The apparent path of a celestial body across the sky during daylight hours.

Diurnal Motion: The apparent motion of celestial bodies across the sky from east to west.

Diurnal Arc: The measurement in degrees of a planet from its rising to its setting.

Earth: One of the triplicities: the zodiacal signs are Taurus, Virgo and Capricorn.

Eclipse: The total or partial obscuration when one celestial body is concealed by another.

Ecliptic: The great circle on the Celestial Sphere which is the Sun's apparent path.

Ecliptic System: Co-ordinate system, the fundamental plane of which, is the plane of the Ecliptic.

Elements: Fire, Air, Earth and Water, each of which consist of 3 signs of the Zodiac.

Elevation of the Pole: The latitude of the birth place.

Elongation: The angular distance of a celestial body from the Sun, either eastward or westward.

Ephemeris: A publication which lists astronomical/astrological data; essential for the calculation of astrological charts.

Equation of Time: The difference between Apparent Solar Time and Mean Solar Time.

Equator: A great circle on the surface of a celestial body whose plane passes through the centre of the body, and which is perpendicular to its axis of rotation.

Equator System: A co-ordinate system, whose fundamental plane is the plane of the Equator.

Equinoctial Signs: Aries and Libra.

Equinoxes: The two points of intersection between the Ecliptic and the Equator. When the sun reaches the equinoxes day and night are equal.

Fire: One of the Triplicities; the zodiacal signs are Aries, Leo and Sagittarius.

Fixed Signs: The signs Taurus, Leo, Scorpio and Aquarius.

Galaxy: A stellar system.

Gemini: Third sign of the Zodiac. The Sun appears to enter this sign on or about 22 May each year.

Greenwich: Suburb of London. Longitude is measured from the Greenwich meridian (0° meridian).

Gregorian Calendar: The New Style calendar which superseded the Old Style (Julian calendar).

Horizon: The great circle which marks the intersection of the horizontal plane with the celestial sphere.

Horizon System: A co-ordinate system with the horizon plane as the fundamental plane.

Hour Angle: The arc measured westward from the meridian. The angle between the hour circle of a body and the celestial meridian.

Houses: The 12 divisions of the birth chart numbered from the Ascendant in an anti-clockwise direction.

Imum Coeli: I.C. the lower meridian: the opposite point to the midheaven, M.C.

Inferior planets: Planets whose orbits are located within the orbit of the earth. Mercury and Venus.

International Date Line: The 180th meridian of longitude that passes across the Pacific Ocean.

Latitude Celestial: The angular distance of a body north or south of the Ecliptic. The Sun has no latitude.

Latitude Terrestrial: The distance of any place north or south of the Equator.

Leo: The fifth sign of the Zodiac. The Sun appears to enter this sign on or about 24 July each year.

Libra: The seventh sign of the Zodiac. The Sun appears to enter this sign on or about 24 September each year.

Libration: Irregularities of the Moon's motions about its axes.

Lights, The: Term used to denote the Sun and Moon.

Light Year: The distance that light travels in one year (186,000 miles per second).

Longitude Celestial: The distance of a body from the First Point of Aries, measured along the Ecliptic toward the east in either degrees and minutes or in signs degrees and minutes.

Longitude Terrestrial: The distance of any place east or west of Greenwich.

Luminaries: The Sun and Moon.

Lunation: The time from New Moon to New Moon; the sequence of phases of the Moon.

Lune: The portion of the surface of a sphere which is contained within two great semi-circles.

Magnitude: A measurement of a star's brightness.

Mean Solar Day: The interval of time between two successive culminations of the Sun.

Mean Solar Time: A measurement of time based on the motion of the Mean Sun.

Mean Sun: The fictitious Sun which is used as a timekeeper moving along the Equator as opposed to the true Sun which moves along the Ecliptic.

M.C. Medium Coeli (Midheaven): The highest point of the Ecliptic culminating.

Meridian: A great circle on the Celestial Sphere which passes through the poles, the zenith and the nadir, and corresponds to the terrestrial longitude.

Midnight Sun: Term used to describe the Sun when it is visible above the horizon at midnight and is circumpolar, north of the Arctic circle, or south of the Antarctic circle.

Movable Signs: Traditional term for the Cardinal signs, Aries, Cancer, Libra and Capricorn.

Mutable Signs: Term given to one of the Quadruplicities: the zodiacal signs are Gemini, Virgo, Sagittarius and Pisces.

Nadir: The point in the heavens that is directly opposite the zenith.

Negative Signs: Signs in the Earth or Water Triplicities.

Nodes: The points of intersection where a planet crosses the Ecliptic when moving from north to south latitude or vice versa.

Obliquity of the Ecliptic: The 23½° angle between the Celestial Equator and the Ecliptic.

Opposition: An aspect formed when two planets are 180 degrees apart.

Parallels: Normally refers to Parallels of Declination; circles parallel to the celestial Equator.

Perigee: The point in the orbit where the Moon or a planet is at its nearest distance to the Earth.

Perihelion: The point in a planet's orbit where a planet is at its nearest distance to the Sun.

Pisces: The twelfth sign of the Zodiac. The Sun appears to enter this sign on or about 20 February each year.

Planets: Celestial bodies such as the earth which revolve around the Sun as the centre and with it form the Solar System.

Polar Circle: A parallel circle on the celestial Sphere or on the Earth, 23½° from the pole. The 'midnight Sun' is observed from this latitude at the time of the solstice (Summer), and at the Winter solstice the sun is only at the horizon at noon.

Polarity: A zodiacal sign is said to have polarity with its opposite sign, e.g. Aries/Libra, Taurus/Scorpio, etc.

Pole/Polar Elevation: The height of the pole above the horizon as observed from any place is equal to the terrestrial latitude.

Positive Signs: The Fire and Air Triplicity signs, Aries, Leo, Sagittarius, Gemini, Libra and Aquarius.

Precession: The gradual advance of the equinoctial point (Vernal Equinox) westward at the rate of 50 seconds per year. Caused by the pole of the Equator revolving round the pole of the Ecliptic.

Prime Meridian: The Greenwich meridian which is the zero point for measurements of longitude on the Earth.

Prime Vertical: The great circle that intersects the horizon at the east and west points passing through the zenith at right angles to the meridian.

Quadrature: 90° distance; a square aspect.

Quadruplicities: The Cardinal, Fixed and Mutable qualities, which each contain four of the zodiacal signs.

Quincunx: An aspect of 150°.

Rectification: Method of ascertaining the true birth time through studying the planetary correspondences at the time of important events, etc.

Retrograde Motion: The apparent westward motion of a body which is contrary to the usual or direct motion.

Right Ascension: A co-ordinate of the equator system measured from the First Point of Aries eastward to the point which rises with a planet or part of the Ecliptic. The distance from 0° Aries along the equator.

Rising Sign/Planet: The sign on the Ascendant: a planet within 8° of the Ascendant either above or below.

Sagittarius: Ninth sign of the Zodiac. The Sun appears to enter this sign on or about 23 November each year.

Satellitium: A grouping of planets in one sign or house.

Scorpio: The eighth sign of the Zodiac. The Sun appears to enter this sign on or about 24 October each year.

Sextile: A 60° aspect.

Sidereal Time/Day/Year: Time based upon the rotation of the earth with respect to the stars; time between two successive culminations of the Vernal Equinox which denotes the commencement of the Sidereal Day: A Sidereal Year is the period of the Sun's revolution with respect to the stars and coincides with the Earth's revolution around the Sun.

Solar Time/Day/Year: The time used for civil purposes based upon the daily motion of the Sun: Solar Day is the time interval between two successive culminations of the apparent Sun; the average value of the Apparent Solar Day is termed the Mean Solar Day; the Solar Year is the Tropical Year (the year of the seasons).

Solstices: The time when the Sun has its greatest northern or southern Declination, which occurs about 22/23 June and December. The Sun is then farthest from the equator and appears to 'stand still'.

Standard Meridian: The meridian adopted for time zones.

Standard Time: The local civil time of a standard meridian, which is the time kept for all places within a particular zone; the difference between zones is normally 1 hour or 15 degrees of longitude reckoned from Greenwich.

Superior Planets: Those whose orbits lie outside that of the Earth: Mars, Jupiter, Saturn, Uranus, Neptune and Pluto.

Synastry: Term applied to the comparison of charts.

Synodic Month: The interval between two successive Full Moons; the length of the synodic month is 29.5306 days.

Taurus: The second sign of the Zodiac. The Sun appears to enter this sign on or about 21 April each year.

Transit: The passage of a body across the meridian; astrologically the current passage of a planet over a natal position.

Trine: 120° aspect.

Tropical Year: The year of the seasons; the time required for Sun to complete one revolution with respect to the Vernal Equinox (First Point of Aries).

Tropics: Two parallels of latitude which are equal to the inclination of the Ecliptic (23½°). The Tropic of Cancer is north of the Equator and the Tropic of Capricorn is south.

T-Square: Planets in opposition aspect with one or more planet(s) in square aspect.

Universal Time (U.T.): Mean Solar Time reckoned from mean midnight on the meridian of Greenwich.

Vernal Equinox (First Point of Aries): The point of intersection between the Ecliptic and the equator which the Sun crosses on or about 21 March each year. The point from which Right Ascension and Celestial Longitude are measured.

Virgo: Sixth sign of the Zodiac. The Sun appears to enter this sign on or about 24 August each year.

Water: One of the Triplicities; the zodiacal signs are Cancer, Scorpio and Pisces.

Zenith: The point on the Celestial Sphere directly above the observer, 90° distance from the horizon.

Zodiac: (Circle of Animals); a belt or band 8 degrees on either side of the Ecliptic. For astrological purposes, the Zodiac is divided into 12 signs of 30°.

RECOMMENDED READING AND REFERENCE MATERIALS

General Interest

J. A. West and J. G. Roonder. *The Case For Astrology*, Penguin (1973).
D. Parker. *The Question of Astrology*, Eyre and Spottiswoode (1970).
Michel Gauquelin. *Astrology and Science*, Mayflower (1972).
——. *The Cosmic Clocks*, Paladin (1973).
——. *Cosmic Influences on Human Behaviour*, Garnstone Press (1974).
John Addey. *Astrology Reborn*.

Astrological Analysis and Interpretation

D. and J. Parker. *The Compleat Astrologer*, Mitchell Beazley (1971).
M. E. Hone. *Modern Textbook of Astrology*, Fowler (1965).
——. *Applied Astrology*, Fowler (1962).
C. E. O. Carter. *The Foundations of Astrology*, Pythagorean Publications (1960).
——. *Astrological Aspects*, Fowler (1969).
Z. Dobyns. *The Astrologer's Casebook*, T.I.A. Publications, Los Angeles.
Linda Goodman. *Linda Goodman's Sun Signs*, Pan (1972).
Alan Oken. *As Above, So Below*, Bantam Books (1974).
Liz Greene. *Saturn*, Samuel Weiser (1976).
——. *Relating*, Coventure (1977).
Sheila Geddes. *The Art of Astrology*, Aquarian Press (1980).

Evaluating Future Trends

R. C. Davison. *The Technique of Prediction*, Fowler (1955).
Chester Kemp. *Progressions*, Astrological Association.

Technical

Dona Marie Lorenz. *Tools of Astrology: Houses*, Eomega Grove Press, Topanga, California.
R. Holden. *The Elements of House Division*, Fowler (1977).
Z. Dobyns. *Progressions, Directions and Rectification*, T.I.A. Publications.

Astronomy

J. B. Sidgwick. *Introducing Astronomy*, Faber and Faber (1957).
D. S. Evans. *Teach Yourself Astronomy*, English Universities Press (1973).
A. Rükl. *The Amateur Astronomer*, Octopus Books (1979).

Reference Materials

Raphael's Ephemerides
*Raphael's Tables of Houses
  for Northern Latitudes*
*Raphael's Tables of Houses
  for Great Britain*
*Raphael's Geocentric
  Longitudes and Declinations
  of Mars, Jupiter, Saturn,
  Uranus and Neptune*

W. Foulsham & Co. Ltd.
Yeovil Road,
Slough, England.

Pluto Ephemeris (E. Benjamin: 1840-1960)

The Aries Press

The American Book of Tables

Neil F. Michelson, Astro Computing Services, New York. Available from Thorsons Publishers Limited, Denington Estate, Wellingborough, Northamptonshire.

*The American Ephemeris for
for the 20th century
(1900-2000)* (includes Pluto)

Neil F. Michelson, Astro Computing Services.
Available from Thorsons Publishers Limited.

*Longitudes and Latitudes
  Throughout the World*
(excluding U.S.A.)

E. Dernay, American Federation of Astrologers.

*Longitudes and Latitudes in
  the U.S.A.*

E. Dernay

Time Changes in the U.S.A.
*Time Changes in Canada
  and Mexico*
Time Changes in the World
(excluding U.S.A., Canada
and Mexico)

Doris Chase Doane,
Professional Astrologers Incorporated, Hollywood.

Birth chart forms and sundry   Faculty of Astrological
  calculation materials   Studies.

Books and equipment available from stockists:

L. N. Fowler (Sales) Ltd.
1201 High Street
Chadwell Heath
Essex RM6 4DH

Zodiac
The Astrological Emporium
3 Kensington Mall
London W8

The Faculty of Astrological Studies
Hook Cottage
Vines Cross
Heathfield
Sussex

Compendium
240 Camden High Street NW1

Mercurius
80 Old Brompton Road SW7

Watkins
21 Cecil Court, Charing Cross Road WC2

Theosophical Bookshop
Great Russell Street WC1

Atlantis Bookshop
49a Museum Street WC1

ASTROLOGICAL
ORGANIZATIONS

More than thirty years ago, it was realized that astrologers, and particularly those that act as consultants, should be trained in sound techniques and practices.

As a teaching and examining body, *The Faculty of Astrological Studies* was founded in London in June 1948 by two forward-thinking men, E. Caselli and L. von Sommeruga of the Astrological Lodge. It was constituted as a non-profit making body for the purpose of training astrologers in sound techniques who would be able to contribute to the advancement of knowledge, and for setting examinations yearly to maintain a high standard which would command respect. Charles Carter and Margaret Hone were among the Founder Members, and since that time most leading astrologers in England have been proud to gain the Faculty's Diploma, and have signed its Code of Ethics as a mark of integrity and good faith.

The Faculty is now run by a democratically elected Council drawn from its Members, i.e. those who have become diploma holders. It has trained students from some one hundred countries, and its diploma is recognized internationally. Courses are constantly updated in the light of new developments in advanced astrological and psychological research.

Courses leading to the Certificate of the Faculty may be taken either by correspondence—with individual tuition—or by attending two terms of classes in London which commence each Autumn. Following this, the Diploma Course has a two year syllabus and may be taken also by correspondence or by classes in London. The three-year study completes the professional training programme. Examinations are held annually in May, but are not obligatory for students who do not wish to attain professional status.

The Faculty provides a lending library for U.K. students, runs Revision Weekends prior to the examinations, Summer Schools, and an Annual Open Day.

Diploma students who wish to work as consultants may subscribe to a list which is sent out by the Faculty to prospective clients. The rising demand for evening classes everywhere is increasing the need for suitably qualified teachers.

Further information can be obtained from:

> The Registrar
> Hook Cottage
> Vines Cross
> Heathfield
> Sussex TN21 9EN
> England

For those who do not necessarily wish to take examinations or gain a professional qualification, but require tuition suited to their personal requirements, Geddes Associates conduct courses by means of tape cassettes. S.A.E. for details to:

> Geddes (P.H.) Associates
> 89 Woodfield Road
> Thames Ditton
> Surrey KT7 0DS
> England

Two organizations which hold lectures and publish astrological journals are:

The Astrological Association, which holds regular meetings, an annual conference, and publishes a quarterly journal of a very high standard, *The Astrological Journal,* and numerous booklets. Details from The Astrological Association, 57 Woodside, Wimbledon, London SW19.

The Astrological Lodge of the Theosophical Society is an organization open to all those seriously interested in the study of astrology. It publishes a quarterly magazine *The Astrologer's Quarterly,* and has a library. It holds meetings every Monday in session with a beginners' class followed by a public lecture. Details from the Hon. Membership Secretary and Treasurer, 50 Gloucester Place, London W1.

CALCULATION TABLES

Table 1: Interval of Time to Noon

Many errors in natal charting originate initially, because the time interval to noon is incorrectly determined. It is very easy to make mistakes when subtracting the birth time from noon, and this table may assist in preventing errors.

Examples
What is the interval to noon for a birth time of:

		H	M			H	M
7.53 a.m.	=	4	7	1.17 a.m.	=	10	43
3.43 a.m.	=	8	17	6.19 a.m.	=	5	41
6.10 a.m.	=	5	50	9.24 a.m.	=	2	36

HOURS

MINS	0 H M	1 H M	2 H M	3 H M	4 H M	5 H M	6 H M
0	12 00	11 00	10 00	9 00	8 00	7 00	6 00
1	11 59	10 59	9 59	8 59	7 59	6 59	5 59
2	11 58	10 58	9 58	8 58	7 58	6 58	5 58
3	11 57	10 57	9 57	8 57	7 57	6 57	5 57
4	11 56	10 56	9 56	8 56	7 56	6 56	5 56
5	11 55	10 55	9 55	8 55	7 55	6 55	5 55
6	11 54	10 54	9 54	8 54	7 54	6 54	5 54
7	11 53	10 53	9 53	8 53	7 53	6 53	5 53
8	11 52	10 52	9 52	8 52	7 52	6 52	5 52
9	11 51	10 51	9 51	8 51	7 51	6 51	5 51
10	11 50	10 50	9 50	8 50	7 50	6 50	5 50
11	11 49	10 49	9 49	8 49	7 49	6 49	5 49
12	11 48	10 48	9 48	8 48	7 48	6 48	5 48
13	11 47	10 47	9 47	8 47	7 47	6 47	5 47
14	11 46	10 46	9 46	8 46	7 46	6 46	5 46
15	11 45	10 45	9 45	8 45	7 45	6 45	5 45
16	11 44	10 44	9 44	8 44	7 44	6 44	5 44
17	11 43	10 43	9 43	8 43	7 43	6 43	5 43
18	11 42	10 42	9 42	8 42	7 42	6 42	5 42
19	11 41	10 41	9 41	8 41	7 41	6 41	5 41
20	11 40	10 40	9 40	8 40	7 40	6 40	5 40
21	11 39	10 39	9 39	8 39	7 39	6 39	5 39
22	11 38	10 38	9 38	8 38	7 38	6 38	5 38
23	11 37	10 37	9 37	8 37	7 37	6 37	5 37
24	11 36	10 36	9 36	8 36	7 36	6 36	5 36
25	11 35	10 35	9 35	8 35	7 35	6 35	5 35
26	11 34	10 34	9 34	8 34	7 34	6 34	5 34
27	11 33	10 33	9 33	8 33	7 33	6 33	5 33
28	11 32	10 32	9 32	8 32	7 32	6 32	5 32
29	11 31	10 31	9 31	8 31	7 31	6 31	5 31
30	11 30	10 30	9 30	8 30	7 30	6 30	5 30

Table 1 (cont'd)

HOURS

MINS	0		1		2		3		4		5		6	
	H	M	H	M	H	M	H	M	H	M	H	M	H	M
31	11	29	10	29	9	29	8	29	7	29	6	29	5	29
32	11	28	10	28	9	28	8	28	7	28	6	28	5	28
33	11	27	10	27	9	27	8	27	7	27	6	27	5	27
34	11	26	10	26	9	26	8	26	7	26	6	26	5	26
35	11	25	10	25	9	25	8	25	7	25	6	25	5	25
36	11	24	10	24	9	24	8	24	7	24	6	24	5	24
37	11	23	10	23	9	23	8	23	7	23	6	23	5	23
38	11	22	10	22	9	22	8	22	7	22	6	22	5	22
39	11	21	10	21	9	21	8	21	7	21	6	21	5	21
40	11	20	10	20	9	20	8	20	7	20	6	20	5	20
41	11	19	10	19	9	19	8	19	7	19	6	19	5	19
42	11	18	10	18	9	18	8	18	7	18	6	18	5	18
43	11	17	10	17	9	17	8	17	7	17	6	17	5	17
44	11	16	10	16	9	16	8	16	7	16	6	16	5	16
45	11	15	10	15	9	15	8	15	7	15	6	15	5	15
46	11	14	10	14	9	14	8	14	7	14	6	14	5	14
47	11	13	10	13	9	13	8	13	7	13	6	13	5	13
48	11	12	10	12	9	12	8	12	7	12	6	12	5	12
49	11	11	10	11	9	11	8	11	7	11	6	11	5	11
50	11	10	10	10	9	10	8	10	7	10	6	10	5	10
51	11	09	10	09	9	09	8	09	7	09	6	09	5	09
52	11	08	10	08	9	08	8	08	7	08	6	08	5	08
53	11	07	10	07	9	07	8	07	7	07	6	07	5	07
54	11	06	10	06	9	06	8	06	7	06	6	06	5	06
55	11	05	10	05	9	05	8	05	7	05	6	05	5	05
56	11	04	10	04	9	04	8	04	7	04	6	04	5	04
57	11	03	10	03	9	03	8	03	7	03	6	03	5	03
58	11	02	10	02	9	02	8	02	7	02	6	02	5	02
59	11	01	10	01	9	01	8	01	7	01	6	01	5	01

Table 1 (cont'd)

HOURS

MINS	7		8		9		10		11	
	H	M	H	M	H	M	H	M	H	M
0	5	00	4	00	3	00	2	00	1	00
1	4	59	3	59	2	59	1	59	0	59
2	4	58	3	58	2	58	1	58	0	58
3	4	57	3	57	2	57	1	57	0	57
4	4	56	3	56	2	56	1	56	0	56
5	4	55	3	55	2	55	1	55	0	55
6	4	54	3	54	2	54	1	54	0	54
7	4	53	3	53	2	53	1	53	0	53
8	4	52	3	52	2	52	1	52	0	52
9	4	51	3	51	2	51	1	51	0	51
10	4	50	3	50	2	50	1	50	0	50
11	4	49	3	49	2	49	1	49	0	49
12	4	48	3	48	2	48	1	48	0	48
13	4	47	3	47	2	47	1	47	0	47
14	4	46	3	46	2	46	1	46	0	46
15	4	45	3	45	2	45	1	45	0	45
16	4	44	3	44	2	44	1	44	0	44
17	4	43	3	43	2	43	1	43	0	43
18	4	42	3	42	2	42	1	42	0	42
19	4	41	3	41	2	41	1	41	0	41
20	4	40	3	40	2	40	1	40	0	40
21	4	39	3	39	2	39	1	39	0	39
22	4	38	3	38	2	38	1	38	0	38
23	4	37	3	37	2	37	1	37	0	37
24	4	36	3	36	2	36	1	36	0	36
25	4	35	3	35	2	35	1	35	0	35
26	4	34	3	34	2	34	1	34	0	34
27	4	33	3	33	2	33	1	33	0	33
28	4	32	3	32	2	32	1	32	0	32
29	4	31	3	31	2	31	1	31	0	31
30	4	30	3	30	2	30	1	30	0	30

Table 1 (cont'd)

HOURS

MINS	7		8		9		10		11	
	H	M	H	M	H	M	H	M	H	M
31	4	29	3	29	2	29	1	29	0	29
32	4	28	3	28	2	28	1	28	0	28
33	4	27	3	27	2	27	1	27	0	27
34	4	26	3	26	2	26	1	26	0	26
35	4	25	3	25	2	25	1	25	0	25
36	4	24	3	24	2	24	1	24	0	24
37	4	23	3	23	2	23	1	23	0	23
38	4	22	3	22	2	22	1	22	0	22
39	4	21	3	21	2	21	1	21	0	21
40	4	20	3	20	2	20	1	20	0	20
41	4	19	3	19	2	19	1	19	0	19
42	4	18	3	18	2	18	1	18	0	18
43	4	17	3	17	2	17	1	17	0	17
44	4	16	3	16	2	16	1	16	0	16
45	4	15	3	15	2	15	1	15	0	15
46	4	14	3	14	2	14	1	14	0	14
47	4	13	3	13	2	13	1	13	0	13
48	4	12	3	12	2	12	1	12	0	12
49	4	11	3	11	2	11	1	11	0	11
50	4	10	3	10	2	10	1	10	0	10
51	4	09	3	09	2	09	1	09	0	09
52	4	08	3	08	2	08	1	08	0	08
53	4	07	3	07	2	07	1	07	0	07
54	4	06	3	06	2	06	1	06	0	06
55	4	05	3	05	2	05	1	05	0	05
56	4	04	3	04	2	04	1	04	0	04
57	4	03	3	03	2	03	1	03	0	03
58	4	02	3	02	2	02	1	02	0	02
59	4	01	3	01	2	01	1	01	0	01

Table 2: Conversion of Mean Solar into Mean Sidereal Time (9.86 seconds per hour)

Mean Time Hours	Amount '	Amount "	Mean Time '	Amount "	Mean Time '	Amount "
1	0	9.86	1	0.16	31	5.09
2	0	19.71	2	0.33	32	5.26
3	0	29.57	3	0.49	33	5.42
4	0	39.43	4	0.66	34	5.59
5	0	49.28	5	0.82	35	5.75
6	0	59.14	6	0.99	36	5.92
7	1	09.00	7	1.15	37	6.08
8	1	18.85	8	1.31	38	6.24
9	1	28.71	9	1.48	39	6.41
10	1	38.56	10	1.64	40	6.57
11	1	48.42	11	1.81	41	6.74
12	1	58.28	12	1.97	42	6.90
13	2	08.13	13	2.14	43	7.07
14	2	17.99	14	2.30	44	7.23
15	2	27.85	15	2.46	45	7.39
16	2	37.70	16	2.63	46	7.56
17	2	47.56	17	2.79	47	7.72
18	2	57.42	18	2.96	48	7.89
19	3	07.27	19	3.12	49	8.05
20	3	17.13	20	3.29	50	8.22
21	3	26.99	21	3.45	51	8.38
22	3	36.84	22	3.61	52	8.54
23	3	46.70	23	3.78	53	8.71
24	3	56.56	24	3.94	54	8.87
			25	4.11	55	9.04
			26	4.27	56	9.20
			27	4.44	57	9.37
			28	4.60	58	9.53
			29	4.76	59	9.69
			30	4.93		

Table 3: Longitude Equivalent in Time

Long. °	Equiv. Hours	Mins	Long. °	Equiv. Hours	Mins
1	0	04	39	2	36
2	0	08	40	2	40
3	0	12	41	2	44
4	0	16	42	2	48
5	0	20	43	2	52
6	0	24	44	2	56
7	0	28	45	3	00
8	0	32	46	3	04
9	0	36	47	3	08
10	0	40	48	3	12
11	0	44	49	3	16
12	0	48	50	3	20
13	0	52	51	3	24
14	0	56	52	3	28
15	1	00	53	3	32
16	1	04	54	3	36
17	1	08	55	3	40
18	1	12	56	3	44
19	1	16	57	3	48
20	1	20	58	3	52
21	1	24	59	3	56
22	1	28	60	4	00
23	1	32	61	4	04
24	1	36	62	4	08
25	1	40	63	4	12
26	1	44	64	4	16
27	1	48	65	4	20
28	1	52	66	4	24
29	1	56	67	4	28
30	2	00	68	4	32
31	2	04	69	4	36
32	2	08	70	4	40
33	2	12	71	4	44
34	2	16	72	4	48
35	2	20	73	4	52
36	2	24	74	4	56
37	2	28	75	5	00
38	2	32	76	5	04

Table 3 (cont'd)

Long. °	Equiv. Hours	Mins
77	5	08
78	5	12
79	5	16
80	5	20
81	5	24
82	5	28
83	5	32
84	5	36
85	5	40
86	5	44
87	5	48
88	5	52
89	5	56
90	6	00
91	6	04
92	6	08
93	6	12
94	6	16
95	6	20
96	6	24
97	6	28
98	6	32
99	6	36
100	6	40
101	6	44
102	6	48
103	6	52
104	6	56
105	7	00
106	7	04
107	7	08
108	7	12
109	7	16
110	7	20
111	7	24
112	7	28
113	7	32
114	7	36

Long. °	Equiv. Hours	Mins
115	7	40
116	7	44
117	7	48
118	7	52
119	7	56
120	8	00
121	8	04
122	8	08
123	8	12
124	8	16
125	8	20
126	8	24
127	8	28
128	8	32
129	8	36
130	8	40
131	8	44
132	8	48
133	8	52
134	8	56
135	9	00
136	9	04
137	9	08
138	9	12
139	9	16
140	9	20
141	9	24
142	9	28
143	9	32
144	9	36
145	9	40
146	9	44
147	9	48
148	9	52
149	9	56
150	10	00

Table 3 (cont'd)

Long. °	Equiv. Hours	Mins
151	10	04
152	10	08
153	10	12
154	10	16
155	10	20
156	10	24
157	10	28
158	10	32
159	10	36
160	10	40
161	10	44
162	10	48
163	10	52
164	10	56
165	11	00

Long. °	Equiv. Hours	Mins
166	11	04
167	11	08
168	11	12
169	11	16
170	11	20
171	11	24
172	11	28
173	11	32
174	11	36
175	11	40
176	11	44
177	11	48
178	11	52
179	11	56
180	12	00

Long. '	Equiv. '	"
1	0	04
2	0	08
3	0	12
4	0	16
5	0	20
6	0	24
7	0	28
8	0	32
9	0	36
10	0	40
11	0	44
12	0	48
13	0	52
14	0	56
15	1	00

Long. '	Equiv. '	"
16	1	04
17	1	08
18	1	12
19	1	16
20	1	20
21	1	24
22	1	28
23	1	32
24	1	36
25	1	40
26	1	44
27	1	48
28	1	52
29	1	56
30	2	00

Long. ′	Equiv. ′	″
31	2	04
32	2	08
33	2	12
34	2	16
35	2	20
36	2	24
37	2	28
38	2	32
39	2	36
40	2	40
41	2	44
42	2	48
43	2	52
44	2	56
45	3	00

Long. ′	Equiv. ′	″
46	3	04
47	3	08
48	3	12
49	3	16
50	3	20
51	3	24
52	3	28
53	3	32
54	3	36
55	3	40
56	3	44
57	3	48
58	3	52
59	3	56

Example:

What is the longitude equivalent in time of 145° 18′?

		H	M	S	
From Tables: 145°	=	9	40	00	
18′	=	0	01	12	+
		9	41	12	

Or using calculator:

$$145° \ 18′ = \frac{145.3}{15} = 9.6866 \qquad = \quad 9 \quad 41 \quad 12$$

Table 4: Right Ascension

Aries-Libra (For Libra add 12 hours S.T. 180° R.A.)						
Sidereal Time			R.A.		Long.	
H	M	S	°	′	°	′
0	00	00	0	00	0	00
0	04	00	1	00	1	05
0	08	00	2	00	2	11
0	12	00	3	00	3	16
0	16	00	4	00	4	21
0	20	00	5	00	5	27
0	24	00	6	00	6	32
0	28	00	7	00	7	37
0	32	00	8	00	8	42
0	36	00	9	00	9	48
0	40	00	10	00	10	53
0	44	00	11	00	11	58
0	48	00	12	00	13	03
0	52	00	13	00	14	07
0	56	00	14	00	15	12
1	00	00	15	00	16	17
1	04	00	16	00	17	21
1	08	00	17	00	18	26
1	12	00	18	00	19	30
1	16	00	19	00	20	34
1	20	00	20	00	21	38
1	24	00	21	00	22	42
1	28	00	22	00	23	46
1	32	00	23	00	24	50
1	36	00	24	00	25	53
1	40	00	25	00	26	56
1	44	00	26	00	28	00
1	48	00	27	00	29	03

Table 4: (cont'd)

Taurus-Scorpio (For Scorpio add 12 hours S.T. 180° R.A.)						
Sidereal Time			R.A.		Long.	
H	M	S	°	′	°	′
1	52	00	28	00	0	06
1	56	00	29	00	1	08
2	00	00	30	00	2	11
2	04	00	31	00	3	13
2	08	00	32	00	4	15
2	12	00	33	00	5	18
2	16	00	34	00	6	19
2	20	00	35	00	7	21
2	24	00	36	00	8	22
2	28	00	37	00	9	24
2	32	00	38	00	10	25
2	36	00	39	00	11	26
2	40	00	40	00	12	27
2	44	00	41	00	13	27
2	48	00	42	00	14	28
2	52	00	43	00	15	28
2	56	00	44	00	16	28
3	00	00	45	00	17	28
3	04	00	46	00	18	28
3	08	00	47	00	19	27
3	12	00	48	00	20	26
3	16	00	49	00	21	26
3	20	00	50	00	22	25
3	24	00	51	00	23	23
3	28	00	52	00	24	22
3	32	00	53	00	25	20
3	36	00	54	00	26	19
3	40	00	55	00	27	17
3	44	00	56	00	28	15
3	48	00	57	00	29	13

Table 4 (cont'd)

Gemini-Sagittarius (For Sagittarius add 12 hours S.T. 180° R.A.)						
Sidereal Time			R.A.		Long.	
H	M	S	°	'	°	'
3	52	00	58	00	0	10
3	56	00	59	00	1	08
4	00	00	60	00	2	05
4	04	00	61	00	3	03
4	08	00	62	00	4	00
4	12	00	63	00	4	57
4	16	00	64	00	5	54
4	20	00	65	00	6	50
4	24	00	66	00	7	47
4	28	00	67	00	8	43
4	32	00	68	00	9	40
4	36	00	69	00	10	36
4	40	00	70	00	11	32
4	44	00	71	00	12	28
4	48	00	72	00	13	24
4	52	00	73	00	14	20
4	56	00	74	00	15	16
5	00	00	75	00	16	11
5	04	00	76	00	17	07
5	08	00	77	00	18	02
5	12	00	78	00	18	58
5	16	00	79	00	19	53
5	20	00	80	00	20	49
5	24	00	81	00	21	44
5	28	00	82	00	22	39
5	32	00	83	00	23	34
5	36	00	84	00	24	29
5	40	00	85	00	25	25
5	44	00	86	00	26	20
5	48	00	87	00	27	15
5	52	00	88	00	28	10
5	56	00	89	00	29	05

Table 4 (cont'd)

Cancer-Capricorn (For Capricorn add 12 hours S.T. 180° R.A.)						
Sidereal Time			R.A.		Long.	
H	M	S	°	′	°	′
6	00	00	90	00	0	00
6	04	00	91	00	0	55
6	08	00	92	00	1	50
6	12	00	93	00	2	45
6	16	00	94	00	3	40
6	20	00	95	00	4	35
6	24	00	96	00	5	31
6	28	00	97	00	6	26
6	32	00	98	00	7	21
6	36	00	99	00	8	16
6	40	00	100	00	9	11
6	44	00	101	00	10	07
6	48	00	102	00	11	02
6	52	00	103	00	11	58
6	56	00	104	00	12	53
7	00	00	105	00	13	49
7	04	00	106	00	14	44
7	08	00	107	00	15	40
7	12	00	108	00	16	36
7	16	00	109	00	17	32
7	20	00	110	00	18	28
7	24	00	111	00	19	24
7	28	00	112	00	20	20
7	32	00	113	00	21	17
7	36	00	114	00	22	13
7	40	00	115	00	23	10
7	44	00	116	00	24	06
7	48	00	117	00	25	03
7	52	00	118	00	26	00
7	56	00	119	00	26	57
8	00	00	120	00	27	54
8	04	00	121	00	28	52
8	08	00	122	00	29	50

Table 4 (cont'd)

Leo-Aquarius (For Aquarius add 12 hours S.T. 180° R.A.)						
Sidereal Time			R.A.		Long.	
H	M	S	°	′	°	′
8	12	00	123	00	0	47
8	16	00	124	00	1	45
8	20	00	125	00	2	43
8	24	00	126	00	3	41
8	28	00	127	00	4	40
8	32	00	128	00	5	38
8	36	00	129	00	6	37
8	40	00	130	00	7	35
8	44	00	131	00	8	35
8	48	00	132	00	9	34
8	52	00	133	00	10	33
8	56	00	134	00	11	32
9	00	00	135	00	12	32
9	04	00	136	00	13	32
9	08	00	137	00	14	32
9	12	00	138	00	15	32
9	16	00	139	00	16	33
9	20	00	140	00	17	33
9	24	00	141	00	18	34
9	28	00	142	00	19	35
9	32	00	143	00	20	36
9	36	00	144	00	21	38
9	40	00	145	00	22	39
9	44	00	146	00	23	41
9	48	00	147	00	24	42
9	52	00	148	00	25	45
9	56	00	149	00	26	47
10	00	00	150	00	27	49
10	04	00	151	00	28	52
10	08	00	152	00	29	54

Table 4 (cont'd)

Virgo-Pisces (For Pisces add 12 hours S.T. 180° R.A.)						
Sidereal Time			R.A.		Long.	
H	M	S	°	′	°	′
10	12	00	153	00	0	57
10	16	00	154	00	2	00
10	20	00	155	00	3	04
10	24	00	156	00	4	07
10	28	00	157	00	5	10
10	32	00	158	00	6	14
10	36	00	159	00	7	18
10	40	00	160	00	8	22
10	44	00	161	00	9	26
10	48	00	162	00	10	30
10	52	00	163	00	11	34
10	56	00	164	00	12	39
11	00	00	165	00	13	43
11	04	00	166	00	14	48
11	08	00	167	00	15	53
11	12	00	168	00	16	57
11	16	00	169	00	18	02
11	20	00	170	00	19	07
11	24	00	171	00	20	12
11	28	00	172	00	21	18
11	32	00	173	00	22	23
11	36	00	174	00	23	28
11	40	00	175	00	24	33
11	44	00	176	00	25	39
11	48	00	177	00	26	44
11	52	00	178	00	27	49
11	56	00	179	00	28	55

Table 5(a): Hours and Minutes as a Decimal of a Day

M	HOURS					
	0	1	2	3	4	5
	Decimal of a Day					
0	0.000 000	0.041 667	0.083 333	0.125 000	0.166 667	0.208 333
1	.000 694	.042 361	.084 028	.125 694	.167 361	.209 028
2	.001 389	.043 056	.084 722	.126 389	.168 056	.209 722
3	.002 083	.043 750	.085 417	.127 083	.168 750	.210 417
4	.002 778	.044 444	.086 111	.127 778	.169 444	.211 111
5	0.003 472	0.045 139	0.086 806	0.128 472	0.170 139	0.211 806
6	.004 167	.045 833	.087 500	.129 167	.170 833	.212 500
7	.004 861	.046 528	.088 194	.129 861	.171 528	.213 194
8	.005 556	.047 222	.088 889	.130 556	.172 222	.213 889
9	.006 250	.047 917	.089 583	.131 250	.172 917	.214 583
10	0.006 944	0.048 611	0.090 278	0.131 944	0.173 611	0.215 278
11	.007 639	.049 306	.090 972	.132 639	.174 306	.215 972
12	.008 333	.050 000	.091 667	.133 333	.175 000	.216 667
13	.009 028	.050 694	.092 361	.134 028	.175 694	.217 361
14	.009 722	.051 389	.093 056	.134 722	.176 389	.218 056
15	0.010 417	0.052 083	0.093 750	0.135 417	0.177 083	0.218 750
16	.011 111	.052 778	.094 444	.136 111	.177 778	.219 444
17	.011 806	.053 472	.095 139	.136 806	.178 472	.220 139
18	.012 500	.054 167	.095 833	.137 500	.179 167	.220 833
19	.013 194	.054 861	.096 528	.138 194	.179 861	.221 528
20	0.013 889	0.055 556	0.097 222	0.138 889	0.180 556	0.222 222
21	.014 583	.056 250	.097 917	.139 583	.181 250	.222 917
22	.015 278	.056 944	.098 611	.140 278	.181 944	.223 611
23	.015 972	.057 639	.099 306	.140 972	.182 639	.224 306
24	.016 667	.058 333	.100 000	.141 667	.183 333	.225 000
25	0.017 361	0.059 028	0.100 694	0.142 361	0.184 028	0.225 694
26	.018 056	.059 722	.101 389	.143 056	.184 722	.226 389
27	.018 750	.060 417	.102 083	.143 750	.185 417	.227 083
28	.019 444	.061 111	.102 778	.144 444	.186 111	.227 778
29	.020 139	.061 806	.103 472	.145 139	.186 806	.228 472
30	0.020 833	0.062 500	0.104 167	0.145 833	0.187 500	0.229 167
31	.021 528	.063 194	.104 861	.146 528	.188 194	.229 861
32	.022 222	.063 889	.105 556	.147 222	.188 889	.230 556
33	.022 917	.064 583	.106 250	.147 917	.189 583	.231 250
34	.023 611	.065 278	.106 944	.148 611	.190 278	.231 944
35	0.024 306	0.065 972	0.107 639	0.149 306	0.190 972	0.232 639
36	.025 000	.066 667	.108 333	.150 000	.191 667	.233 333
37	.025 694	.067 361	.109 028	.150 694	.192 361	.234 028
38	.026 389	.068 056	.109 722	.151 389	.193 056	.234 722
39	.027 083	.068 750	.110 417	.152 083	.193 750	.235 417
40	0.027 778	0.069 444	0.111 111	0.152 778	0.194 444	0.236 111
41	.028 472	.070 139	.111 806	.153 472	.195 139	.236 806
42	.029 167	.070 833	.112 500	.154 167	.195 833	.237 500
43	.029 861	.071 528	.113 194	.154 861	.196 528	.238 194
44	.030 556	.072 222	.113 889	.155 556	.197 222	.238 889
45	0.031 250	0.072 917	0.114 583	0.156 250	0.197 917	0.239 583
46	.031 944	.073 611	.115 278	.156 944	.198 611	.240 278
47	.032 639	.074 306	.115 972	.157 639	.199 306	.240 972
48	.033 333	.075 000	.116 667	.158 333	.200 000	.241 667
49	.034 028	.075 694	.117 361	.159 028	.200 694	.242 361
50	0.034 722	0.076 389	0.118 056	0.159 722	0.201 389	0.243 056
51	.035 417	.077 083	.118 750	.160 417	.202 083	.243 750
52	.036 111	.077 778	.119 444	.161 111	.202 778	.244 444
53	.036 806	.078 472	.120 139	.161 806	.203 472	.245 139
54	.037 500	.079 167	.120 833	.162 500	.204 167	.245 833
55	0.038 194	0.079 861	0.121 528	0.163 194	0.204 861	0.246 528
56	.038 889	.080 556	.122 222	.163 889	.205 556	.247 222
57	.039 583	.081 250	.122 917	.164 583	.206 250	.247 917
58	.040 278	.081 944	.123 611	.165 278	.206 944	.248 611
59	0.040 972	0.082 639	0.124 306	0.165 972	0.207 639	0.249 306

Table 5(a) (cont'd)

M	HOURS					
	6	7	8	9	10	11
	Decimal of a Day					
0	0.250 000	0.291 667	0.333 333	0.375 000	0.416 667	0.458 333
1	.250 694	.292 361	.334 028	.375 694	.417 361	.459 028
2	.251 389	.293 056	.334 722	.376 389	.418 056	.459 722
3	.252 083	.293 750	.335 417	.377 083	.418 750	.460 417
4	.252 778	.294 444	.336 111	.377 778	.419 444	.461 111
5	0.253 472	0.295 139	0.336 806	0.378 472	0.420 139	0.461 806
6	.254 167	.295 833	.337 500	.379 167	.420 833	.462 500
7	.254 861	.296 528	.338 194	.379 861	.421 528	.463 194
8	.255 556	.297 222	.338 889	.380 556	.422 222	.463 889
9	.256 250	.297 917	.339 583	.381 250	.422 917	.464 583
10	0.256 944	0.298 611	0.340 278	0.381 944	0.423 611	0.465 278
11	.257 639	.299 306	.340 972	.382 639	.424 306	.465 972
12	.258 333	.300 000	.341 667	.383 333	.425 000	.466 667
13	.259 028	.300 694	.342 361	.384 028	.425 694	.467 361
14	.259 722	.301 389	.343 056	.384 722	.426 389	.468 056
15	0.260 417	0.302 083	0.343 750	0.385 417	0.427 083	0.468 750
16	.261 111	.302 778	.344 444	.386 111	.427 778	.469 444
17	.261 806	.303 472	.345 139	.386 806	.428 472	.470 139
18	.262 500	.304 167	.345 833	.387 500	.429 167	.470 833
19	.263 194	.304 861	.346 528	.388 194	.429 861	.471 528
20	0.263 889	0.305 556	0.347 222	0.388 889	0.430 556	0.472 222
21	.264 583	.306 250	.347 917	.389 583	.431 250	.472 917
22	.265 278	.306 944	.348 611	.390 278	.431 944	.473 611
23	.265 972	.307 639	.349 306	.390 972	.432 639	.474 306
24	.266 667	.308 333	.350 000	.391 667	.433 333	.475 000
25	0.267 361	0.309 028	0.350 694	0.392 361	0.434 028	0.475 694
26	.268 056	.309 722	.351 389	.393 056	.434 722	.476 389
27	.268 750	.310 417	.352 083	.393 750	.435 417	.477 083
28	.269 444	.311 111	.352 778	.394 444	.436 111	.477 778
29	.270 139	.311 806	.353 472	.395 139	.436 806	.478 472
30	0.270 833	0.312 500	0.354 167	0.395 833	0.437 500	0.479 167
31	.271 528	.313 194	.354 861	.396 528	.438 194	.479 861
32	.272 222	.313 889	.355 556	.397 222	.438 889	.480 556
33	.272 917	.314 583	.356 250	.397 917	.439 583	.481 250
34	.273 611	.315 278	.356 944	.398 611	.440 278	.481 944
35	0.274 306	0.315 972	0.357 639	0.399 306	0.440 972	0.482 639
36	.275 000	.316 667	.358 333	.400 000	.441 667	.483 333
37	.275 694	.317 361	.359 028	.400 694	.442 361	.484 028
38	.276 389	.318 056	.359 722	.401 389	.443 056	.484 722
39	.277 083	.318 750	.360 417	.402 083	.443 750	.485 417
40	0.277 778	0.319 444	0.361 111	0.402 778	0.444 444	0.486 111
41	.278 472	.320 139	.361 806	.403 472	.445 139	.486 806
42	.279 167	.320 833	.362 500	.404 167	.445 833	.487 500
43	.279 861	.321 528	.363 194	.404 861	.446 528	.488 194
44	.280 556	.322 222	.363 889	.405 556	.447 222	.488 889
45	0.281 250	0.322 917	0.364 583	0.406 250	0.447 917	0.489 583
46	.281 944	.323 611	.365 278	.406 944	.448 611	.490 278
47	.282 639	.324 306	.365 972	.407 639	.449 306	.490 972
48	.283 333	.325 000	.366 667	.408 333	.450 000	.491 667
49	.284 028	.325 694	.367 361	.409 028	.450 694	.492 361
50	0.284 722	0.326 389	0.368 056	0.409 722	0.451 389	0.493 056
51	.285 417	.327 083	.368 750	.410 417	.452 083	.493 750
52	.286 111	.327 778	.369 444	.411 111	.452 778	.494 444
53	.286 806	.328 472	.370 139	.411 806	.453 472	.495 139
54	.287 500	.329 167	.370 833	.412 500	.454 167	.495 833
55	0.288 194	0.329 861	0.371 528	0.413 194	0.454 861	0.496 528
56	.288 889	.330 556	.372 222	.413 889	.455 556	.497 222
57	.289 583	.331 250	.372 917	.414 583	.456 250	.497 917
58	.290 278	.331 944	.373 611	.415 278	.456 944	.498 611
59	0.290 972	0.332 639	0.374 306	0.415 972	0.457 639	0.499 306

Table 5(b): Minutes as a decimal of a Degree or Hour;
Seconds as a decimal of a Minute

' "	Decimal	' "	Decimal
1	0.0166	31	0.5166
2	.0333	32	.5333
3	.0500	33	.5500
4	.0666	34	.5666
5	.0833	35	.5833
6	.1000	36	.6000
7	.1166	37	.6166
8	.1333.	38	.6333
9	.1500	39	.6500
10	.1666	40	.6666
11	.1833	41	.6833
12	.2000	42	.7000
13	.2166	43	.7166
14	.2333	44	.7333
15	.2500	45	.7500
16	.2666	46	.7666
17	.2833	47	.7833
18	.3000	48	.8000
19	.3166	49	.8166
20	.3333	50	.8333
21	.3500	51	.8500
22	.3666	52	.8666
23	.3833	53	.8833
24	.4000	54	.9000
25	.4166	55	.9166
26	.4333	56	.9333
27	.4500	57	.9500
28	.4666	58	.9666
29	.4833	59	.9833
30	.5000		

Table 6: British Summer Time: All changes 2 a.m. G.M.T.

	Commenced					Ended					
	Jan	Feb	Mar	April	May	Jul	Aug	Sep	Oct	Nov	Dec
1916					21				1		
1917				8				17			
1918			24					30			
1919			30					29			
1920			28						25		
1921				3					3		
1922			26						8		
1923				22				16			
1924				13				21			
1925				19					4		
1926				18					3		
1927				10					2		
1928				22					7		
1929				21					6		
1930				13					5		
1931				19					4		
1932				17					2		
1933				9					8		
1934				22					7		
1935				14					6		
1936				19					4		
1937				18					3		
1938				10					2		
1939				16						19	
1940		25									31
*1941	1				*		*				31
*1942	1			*			*				31
*1943	1			*			*				31
*1944	1			*				*			31
*1945	1			*		*			7		
1946				14					6		
*1947			16	*			*			2	
1948			14						31		
1949				3					30		

* Denotes *Double* Summer Time in operation as listed below.

	April	May	Jul	Aug	Sep	
1941		4		10		
1942	5			9		
1943	4			15		
1944	2				17	
1945	2		15			
1946 Not observed						
1947	13			10		

* From 1941-1947 except 1946 *Double Summer Time* (+ 2 hours ahead of G.M.T.) from dates shown. Remainder of year 1 hour ahead from dates shown.

Example:
1941 from 1 January to 31 December 1 hour in advance of G.M.T. except for the period 4 May to 10 August + 2 (*Double Summer Time*).

Table 6 (cont'd)

	Commenced			Ended	
	Mar	April		Oct	
1950		16		22	
1951		15		21	
1952		20		26	
1953		19		4	
1954		11		3	
1955		17		2	
1956		22		7	
1957		14		6	
1958		20		5	
1959		19		4	
1960		10		2	
1961	26			29	
1962	25			28	
1963	31			27	
1964	22			25	
1965	21			24	
1966	20			23	
1967	19			29	

1968 from 18 February to 31 October 1971 British Standard Time in operation, 1 hour in advance of G.M.T.

Continued overleaf

	Mar			Oct	
1972	19			29	
1973	18			28	
1974	17			27	
1975	16			26	
1976	21			24	
1977	20			23	
1978	19			29	
1979	18			28	
1980	16			26	

Thereafter from 2 a.m. G.M.T. on the third Sunday in March until 2 a.m. G.M.T. on the fourth Sunday in October. This may be amended from 1981 in order that Great Britain and Europe observe the same periods of summer time.

Table 7: Standard Times (Corrected to September 1977)*

LIST I—PLACES FAST ON G.M.T. (mainly those EAST OF GREENWICH)

The times given ⎫ *added* to G.M.T. to give Standard Time.
below should be ⎭ *subtracted* from Standard Time to give G.M.T.

	h	m		h	m
Admiralty Islands	10		Egypt (United Arab Republic)	02	
Afghanistan	04	30	Equatorial Guinea, Republic of	01	
Albania*	01		Estonia	03	
Algeria‡*	01		Ethiopia	03	
Amirante Islands	04				
Andaman Islands	05	30	Fernando Póo‡	01	
Angola	01		Fiji	12	
Annobon Island‡	01		Finland	02	
Arabian Emirates, Federation of	04		France*	01	
Australia			Friendly Islands	13	
Australian Capital Territory*	10				
New South Wales¹*	10				
Northern Territory	09	30	Gabon	01	
Queensland	10		Germany	01	
South Australia*	09	30	Gibraltar‡	01	
Tasmania*	10		Gilbert Islands	12	
Victoria*	10		Greece*	02	
Western Australia	08		Guam*	10	
Austria*	01				
			Holland (The Netherlands)*	01	
Balearic Islands*	01		Hong Kong	08	
Bangladesh	06		Hungary	01	
Belgium*	01				
Benin (Dahomey)	01				
Botswana, Republic of	02		India	05	30
Brunei	08		Indonesia, Republic of		
Bulgaria	02		Bali, Bangka, Billiton, Java,		
Burma	06	30	Lombok, Madura, Sumatra	07	
Burundi	02		Borneo, Celebes, Flores, Sumba,		
			Sumbawa, Timor	08	
			Aru, Kei, Moluccas, Tanimbar,		
Cambodia (Democratic Kampuchea)	07		Irian Jaya	09	
Cameroun Republic	01		Iran*	03	30
Caroline Islands, east of long. E. 160°	12		Iraq	03	
west of long. E. 150°	10		Israel*	02	
Truk, Ponape	11		Italy*	01	
Central African Empire	01				
Chad	01				
Chagos Archipelago	05		Japan	09	
Chatham Islands‡	12	45	Jordan	02	
China²	08				
Christmas Island, Indian Ocean	07				
Cocos Keeling Islands	06	30	Kamchatka Peninsula	12	
Comoro Islands	03		Kenya	03	
Congo Republic	01		Korea	09	
Corsica‡*	01		Kuril Islands	11	
Crete*	02		Kuwait	03	
Cyprus, North*	02				
South*	02				
Czechoslovakia	01		Laccadive Islands	05	30
			Ladrone Islands	10	
			Laos	07	
Denmark	01		Latvia	03	
Djibouti	03		Lebanon	02	

* Summer time may be kept in these countries.
‡ The legal time may differ from that given here.
¹ Except Broken Hill Area which keeps 09ʰ 30ᵐ.
² All the coast, but some areas may keep summer time.

Table 7 (cont'd)

STANDARD TIMES (Corrected to September 1977)

LIST I—(continued)

	h	m		h	m
Lesotho ...	02		Schouten Islands	09	
Libya‡ ...	02		Seychelles	04	
Liechtenstein ...	01		Sicily* ...	01	
Lord Howe Island	10		Singapore	07	30
Luxembourg* ...	01		Socotra ...	03	
			Solomon Islands	11	
Macao ...	08		Somalia Republic	03	
Malagasy Republic	03		South Africa, Republic of	02	
Malawi ...	02		Southern Yemen	03	
Malaysia			South West Africa (Namibia)	02	
Malaya ...	07	30	Spain* ...	01	
Sabah, Sarawak	08		Spanish Morocco*	01	
Maldive Republic	05		Spitsbergen (Svalbard)	01	
Malta* ...	01		Sri Lanka ...	05	30
Manchuria ...	09		Sudan, Republic of	02	
Mariana Islands	10		Swaziland	02	
Marshall Islands[1]	12		Sweden ...	01	
Mauritius ...	04		Switzerland	01	
Monaco* ...	01		Syria* (Syrian Arab Republic)	02	
Mozambique ...	02				
			Taiwan ...	08	
Namibia (South West Africa)	02		Tanzania	03	
Nauru ...	11	30	Thailand	07	
Netherlands, The*	01		Tonga Islands ...	13	
New Caledonia	11		Truk ...	11	
New Hebrides ...	11		Tunisia*	01	
New Zealand* ...	12		Turkey*	02	
Nicobar Islands	05	30	Tuvalu Islands...	12	
Niger ...	01				
Nigeria, Republic of	01		Uganda ...	03	
Norfolk Island ...	11	30	Union of Soviet Socialist Republics[2]		
Norway ...	01		west of long. E. 40° ...	03	
Novaya Zemlya	05		long. E. 40° to E. 52° 30′ ...	04	
			long. E. 52° 30′ to E. 67° 30′	05	
Ocean Island ...	11	30	long. E. 67° 30′ to E. 82° 30′	06	
Okinawa ...	09		long. E. 82° 30′ to E. 97° 30′	07	
Oman ...	04		long. E. 97° 30′ to E. 112° 30′	08	
			long. E. 112° 30′ to E. 127° 30′	09	
Pakistan ...	05		long. E. 127° 30′ to E. 142° 30′	10	
Papua New Guinea	10		long. E. 142° 30′ to E. 157° 30′	11	
Pescadores Islands	08		long. E. 157° 30′ to E. 172° 30′	12	
Philippine Republic* ...	08		east of long. E. 172° 30′ ...	13	
Poland* ...	01				
			Vietnam, Northern	07	
Réunion ...	04		Southern‡ ...	07	
Rhodesia ...	02				
Romania ...	02		Wrangell Island	13	
Rwanda...	02				
Ryukyu Islands	09		Yugoslavia ...	01	
Sakhalin ...	11		Zaire		
Santa Cruz Islands	11		Kinshasa, Mbandaka	01	
Sardinia* ...	01		Haut-Zaire, Kivu, Kasai, Shaba ...	02	
Saudi Arabia ...	03		Zambia, Republic of ...	02	

* Summer time may be kept in these countries.
‡ The legal time may differ from that given here.
[1] Except the islands of Kwajalein and Eniwetok which keep a time 24ʰ slow on that of the rest of the islands.
[2] The boundaries between the zones are irregular; the longitudes given are approximate only.

Table 7 (cont'd)

STANDARD TIMES (Corrected to September 1977)

LIST II—PLACES NORMALLY KEEPING G.M.T.

Ascension Island	Great Britain[1]	Irish Republic*	Morocco	Senegal
Canary Islands*	Guinea Bissau	Ivory Coast	Portugal*	Sierra Leone
Channel Islands[1]	Guinea Republic	Liberia	Principe	Tangier
Faeroes, The	Iceland	Madeira	Rio de Oro[‡]	Togo Republic
Gambia	Ifni	Mali	St. Helena	Tristan da Cunha
Ghana	Ireland, Northern[1]	Mauritania (Dakhla)	São Tomé	Upper Volta

* Summer time may be kept in these countries.
‡ The legal time may differ from that given here.
[1] Summer time, one hour in advance of G.M.T., is kept from March 16[d] 02[h] to October 26[d] 02[h] G.M.T.

LIST III—PLACES SLOW ON G.M.T. (WEST OF GREENWICH)

The times given ⎱ subtracted from G.M.T. to give Standard Time.
below should be ⎰ added to Standard Time to give G.M.T.

	h	m			h	m
Argentina‡	03		Cape Verde Islands‡	01	
Austral Islands[1]	10		Cayman Islands	05	
Azores	01		Chile‡	03	
			Christmas Island, Pacific Ocean ...	10	
Bahamas*	05		Colombia	05	
Barbados	04		Cook Islands, except Niue ...	10	30
Belize*	06		Costa Rica	06	
Bermuda*	04		Cuba*	05	
Bolivia	04		Curaçao Island...	04	
Brazil, eastern[2]...	03				
Territory of Acre ...	05		Dominican Republic‡	04	
western	04				
British Antarctic Territory[3] ...	03		Easter Island (I. de Pascua)* ...	07	
			Ecuador	05	
Canada					
Alberta*	07		Falkland Islands[4]	04	
British Columbia*	08		Fanning Island	10	
Labrador*	04		Fernando de Noronha Island... ...	02	
Manitoba*	06		French Guiana‡	03	
New Brunswick*	04				
Newfoundland*	03	30	Galápagos Islands	06	
Northwest Territories*			Greenland, Scoresby Sound[5] ...	02	
east of long. W. 68° ...	04		Angmagssalik and west coast ...	03	
long. W. 68° to W. 85° ...	05		Thule area	04	
long. W. 85° to W. 102° ...	06		Grenada	04	
west of long. W. 102° ...	07		Guadeloupe	04	
Nova Scotia*	04		Guatemala	06	
Ontario*, east of long. W. 90° ...	05		Guiana, French‡	03	
west of long. W. 90° ...	06		Guyana, Republic of‡	03	
Prince Edward Island*	04				
Quebec*, east of long. W. 63° ...	04		Haiti	05	
west of long. W. 63° ...	05		Honduras	06	
Saskatchewan*					
east of long. W. 106° ...	06		Jamaica*	05	
west of long. W. 106° ...	07		Jan Mayen Island	01	
Yukon	08		Johnston Island	10	

* Summer time may be kept in these countries.
‡ The legal time may differ from that given here.
[1] This is the legal standard time, but local mean time is generally used.
[2] Including all the coast and Brasilia.
[3] Except South Georgia which keeps 02[h].
[4] Except Port Stanley which keeps 03[h]‡.
[5] Scoresby Sound may keep 03[h] in summer.

Table 7 (cont'd)

STANDARD TIMES (Corrected to September 1977)

LIST III—*(continued)*

				h	m
Juan Fernandez Islands	...	...	...	04	
Leeward Islands	...	...	...	04	
Low Archipelago	...	...	...	10	
Marquesas Islands[1]	...	...	...	09	30
Martinique	...	...	...	04	
Mexico‡*[2]	...	...	...	06	
Midway Islands	...	...	...	11	
Miquelon	...	...	...	03	
Nicaragua‡	...	...	...	06	
Niue Island	...	...	...	11	
Panama Canal Zone	...	...	...	05	
Panama, Republic of	...	...	...	05	
Paraguay*	...	...	...	04	
Peru	...	...	...	05	
Puerto Rico	...	...	...	04	
Rarotonga	...	...	...	10	30
St. Pierre and Miquelon	...	...	03	
Salvador, El	...	...	...	06	
Samoa	...	...	...	11	
Society Islands[1]	...	...	...	10	
South Georgia	...	...	...	02	
Surinam	...	...	...	03	30
Tobago	...	...	...	04	
Trindade Island, South Atlantic	...	02	
Trinidad	...	...	...	04	
Tuamotu Archipelago[1]	...	...	10	
Tubuai Islands[1]	...	...	...	10	
Turks and Caicos Islands*	...	...	05	
United States of America					
Alabama[3]	...	...	...	06	
Alaska[3], east of long. W. 137°	...	08	
long. W. 137° to W. 141°	...	09	
long. W. 141° to W. 161°	...	10	
long. W. 161° to W. 172° 30′	...	11	
Aleutian Islands	...	...	11	
Arizona	...	...	...	07	
Arkansas[3]	...	...	...	06	
California[3]	...	...	...	08	
Colorado[3]	...	...	...	07	
Connecticut[3]	...	...	...	05	
Delaware[3]	...	...	...	05	
District of Columbia[3]	...	...	05	
Florida[3, 4]	...	...	...	05	

				h
United States of America (*continued*)				
Georgia[3]	...	...	...	05
Hawaii	...	...	...	10
Idaho[3, 4]	...	...	...	07
Illinois[3]	...	...	...	06
Indiana[4]	...	...	...	05
Iowa[3]	...	...	...	06
Kansas[3, 4]	...	...	...	06
Kentucky[3, 4]	...	...	...	05
Louisiana[3]	...	...	...	06
Maine[3]	...	...	...	05
Maryland[3]	...	...	...	05
Massachusetts[3]	...	...	...	05
Michigan[3, 4]	...	...	...	05
Minnesota[3]	...	...	...	06
Mississippi[3]	...	...	...	06
Missouri[3]	...	...	...	06
Montana[3]	...	...	...	07
Nebraska[3, 4]	...	...	...	06
Nevada[3]	...	...	...	08
New Hampshire[3]	...	...	...	05
New Jersey[3]	...	...	...	05
New Mexico[3]	...	...	...	07
New York[3]	...	...	...	05
North Carolina[3]	...	...	...	05
North Dakota[3, 4]	...	...	...	06
Ohio[3]	...	...	...	05
Oklahoma[3]	...	...	...	06
Oregon[3, 4]	...	...	...	08
Pennsylvania[3]	...	...	...	05
Rhode Island[3]	...	...	...	05
South Carolina[3]	...	...	...	05
South Dakota[3], eastern part	...	06
western part	...	07
Tennessee[3, 4]	...	...	...	06
Texas[3]	...	...	...	06
Utah[3, 4]	...	...	...	07
Vermont[3]	...	...	...	05
Virginia[3]	...	...	...	05
Washington, D.C.[3]	...	...	...	05
Washington[3]	...	...	...	08
West Virginia[3]	...	...	...	05
Wisconsin[3]	...	...	...	06
Wyoming[3]	...	...	...	07
Uruguay	...	...	...	03
Venezuela‡	...	...	...	04
Virgin Islands	...	...	...	04
Windward Islands	...	...	...	04

* Summer time may be kept in these countries.
‡ The legal time may differ from that given here.
[1] This is the legal standard time, but local mean time is generally used.
[2] Except the states of Sonora, Sinaloa, Nayarit, and the Southern District of Lower California which keep 07ʰ, and the Northern District of Lower California which keeps 08ʰ.
[3] Summer (daylight-saving) time, one hour fast on the time given, is kept in these states from the last Sunday in April to the last Sunday in October, changing at 02ʰ 00ᵐ local clock time.
[4] This applies to the greater portion of the state.

*Reproduced from The Nautical Almanac 1980 with permission of the Director of Publishing Her Majesty's Stationery Office.

Table 8(a): Extract from *Raphael's Ephemeris*, January 1980

NEW MOON—January 17, 9h. 19m. p.m. (26° ♑ 55′)

2					JANUARY, 1980				[RAPHAEL'S	
D M	D W	Sidereal Time	☉ Long	☉ Dec	☽ Long	☽ Lat	☽ Dec	Node	MIDNIGHT ☽ Long	☽ Dec
		H. M. S.	° ′ ″	° ′	° ′ ″	° ′	° ′	° ′	° ′ ″	° ′
1	Tu	18 41 13	10♑13 25	23S 3	29♊43 43	4S28	18N59	1♍52	6♋14 44	19N 9
2	W	18 45 10	11 14 33	22 58	12♋41 54	3 47	19 4	1 49	19 5 8	18 44
3	Th	18 49 6	12 15 41	22 52	25 24 24	2 56	18 11	1 46	1♌39 47	17 24
4	F	18 53 3	13 16 50	22 47	7♌51 22	1 57	16 25	1 43	13 59 22	15 16
5	S	18 56 59	14 17 58	22 40	20 4 3	0S54	13 57	1 40	26 5 44	12 29
6	☉	19 0 56	15 19 6	22 34	2♍ 4 50	0N11	10 55	1 36	8♍ 1 48	9 14
7	M	19 4 52	16 20 15	22 26	13 57 8	1 15	7 28	1 33	19 51 23	5 38
8	Tu	19 8 49	17 21 23	22 19	25 45 9	2 15	3N46	1 30	1♎39 4	1N51
9	W	19 12 46	18 22 32	22 11	7♎33 45	3 10	0S 5	1 27	13 29 52	2S 2
10	Th	19 16 42	19 23 40	22 2	19 28 6	3 57	3 58	1 24	25 29 4	5 52
11	F	19 20 39	20 24 49	21 53	1♏33 27	4 34	7 44	1 20	7♏41 49	9 32
12	S	19 24 35	21 25 58	21 44	13 54 46	4 59	11 15	1 17	20 12 48	12 52
13	☉	19 28 32	22 27 6	21 34	26 36 20	5 11	14 21	1 14	3♐ 5 44	15 41
14	M	19 32 28	23 28 15	21 24	9♐41 12	5 7	16 51	1 11	16 22 53	17 47
15	Tu	19 36 25	24 29 23	21 13	23 10 45	4 46	18 30	1 8	0♑ 4 37	18 57
16	W	19 40 21	25 30 31	21 2	7♑ 4 11	4 8	19 7	1 5	14 9 0	19 0
17	Th	19 44 18	26 31 39	20 51	21 18 29	3 14	18 34	1 1	28 31 56	17 49
18	F	19 48 15	27 32 46	20 39	5♒48 34	2 6	16 47	0 58	13♒ 7 33	15 28
19	S	19 52 11	28 33 53	20 27	20 28 7	0N49	13 53	0 55	27 49 3	12 5
20	☉	19 56 8	29♑34 59	20 14	5♓ 9 53	0S31	10 6	0 52	12♓29 43	7 58
21	M	20 0 4	0♒36 4	20 1	19 47 53	1 49	5 43	0 49	27 3 46	3S24
22	Tu	20 4 1	1 37 8	19 48	4♈16 54	3 0	1S 3	0 46	11♈26 52	1N18
23	W	20 7 57	2 38 11	19 34	18 33 24	3 58	3N46	0 42	25 36 17	5 50
24	Th	20 11 54	3 39 13	19 20	2♉35 24	4 41	7 58	0 39	9♉30 40	9 59
25	F	20 15 50	4 40 14	19 6	16 22 5	5 7	11 50	0 36	23 9 41	13 31
26	S	20 19 47	5 41 14	18 51	29 53 30	5 15	15 0	0 33	6♊33 37	16 16
27	☉	20 23 44	6 42 13	18 36	13♊11 10	5 6	17 19	0 30	19 43 5	18 8
28	M	20 27 40	7 43 11	18 20	26 12 36	4 41	18 42	0 26	2♋38 45	19 1
29	Tu	20 31 37	8 44 7	18 5	9♋ 1 37	4 3	19 6	0 23	15 21 18	18 55
30	W	20 35 33	9 45 3	17 49	21 37 53	3 13	18 31	0 20	27 51 28	17 54
31	Th	20 39 30	10♒45 57	17S32	4♌ 2 11	2S15	17N 4	0♍17	10♌10 8	16N 2

D M	Mercury Lat	Mercury Dec		Venus Lat	Venus Dec		Mars Lat	Mars Dec		Jupiter Lat	Jupiter Dec
	° ′	° ′	° ′	° ′	° ′	° ′	° ′	° ′	° ′	° ′	° ′
1	0S38	24S 4	24S11	1S48	18S55	18S34	3N 9	9N11	9N 9	1N 8	8N48
3	0 51	24 16	24 21	1 47	18 17	17 50	3 13	9 7	9 5	1 8	8 49
5	1 3	24 24	24 25	1 46	17 27	17 4	3 16	9 4	9 3	1 9	8 51
7	1 14	24 25	24 24	1 45	16 40	16 16	3 20	9 2	9 1	1 9	8 53
9	1 24	24 22	24 18	1 44	15 52	15 27	3 24	9 1	9 1	1 10	8 55
11	1 33	24 13	24 6	1 42	15 1	14 36	3 28	9 2	9 2	1 10	8 58
13	1 42	23 58	23 49	1 40	14 10	13 43	3 32	9 3	9 4	1 11	9 1
15	1 49	23 38	23 25	1 37	13 16	12 49	3 36	9 6	9 8	1 11	9 4
17	1 55	23 11	22 56	1 34	12 21	11 54	3 40	9 10	9 12	1 12	9 8
19	2 0	22 39	22 21	1 31	11 26	10 59	3 44	9 14	9 18	1 12	9 11
21	2 3	22 1	21 39	1 28	10 28	9 59	3 48	9 21	9 24	1 13	9 15
23	2 5	21 16	20 51	1 24	9 30	9 1	3 52	9 28	9 32	1 13	9 19
25	2 5	20 25	19 57	1 19	8 31	8 1	3 55	9 36	9 41	1 14	9 24
27	2 3	19 28	18 57	1 15	7 31		3 59	9 46	9 51	1 14	9 28
29	2 0	18 25	17S52	1 10	6 31	6S 0	4 2	9 56	10N 2	1 15	9 33
31	1S54	17S16		1S 5	5S29		4N 5	10N 8		1N15	9N38

FIRST QUARTER—January 24, 1h. 58m. p.m. (3°♉ 44′)

FULL MOON—January 2, 9*h.* 2*m.* *a.m.* (11° ♋ 7 ′)

EPHEMERIS] **JANUARY, 1980** 3

D M	☿ Long.	♀ Long.	♂ Long.	♃ Long.	♄ Long.	♅ Long.	♆ Long.	♇ Long.	☉	☿	♀	♂	♃	♄	♅	♆	♇
	° ′	° ′	° ′	° ′	° ′	° ′	° ′	° ′									
1	28 ♐ 43	12 ♒ 1	14 ♍ 3	10 ♍ 11	27 ♍ 0	24 ♏ 4	20 ♐ 57	21 ♎ 37		☍	⚼			□			
2	0 ♑ 15	13 15	14 13	10 ℞ 10	27 0	24 7	20 59	21 38	☍			✱	✱		⚼		
3	1 47	14 29	14 22	10 9	27 1	24 10	21 1	21 39				∠	∠	✱	△		□
4	3 20	15 43	14 31	10 7	27 1	24 13	21 3	21 39					⊻	∠		⚼	
5	4 53	16 56	14 39	10 5	27 1	24 15	21 5	21 40		⚼	☍	⊻			□	△	✱
☼	6 27	18 10	14 46	10 3	27 1	24 18	21 7	21 41	⚼	△				⊻			∠
7	8 0	19 24	14 53	10 1	27 ℞ 1	24 21	21 9	21 41	△			☌	●				
8	9 35	20 38	14 59	9 59	27 1	24 23	21 11	21 42						●	✱	□	⊻
9	11 9	21 51	15 4	9 56	27 1	24 26	21 14	21 42		□	⚼		⊻		∠		
10	12 44	23 5	15 8	9 53	27 0	24 28	21 16	21 43	□		△	⊻	∠		⊻	✱	☌
11	14 20	24 18	15 12	9 50	27 0	24 31	21 18	21 43				∠		⊻		∠	
12	15 55	25 32	15 15	9 47	26 59	24 34	21 20	21 44		✱		✱	✱	∠			
☼	17 32	26 45	15 18	9 44	26 59	24 36	21 22	21 44	✱		□			✱	☌	⊻	⊻
14	19 9	27 59	15 20	9 40	26 58	24 38	21 24	21 45	∠	∠		□	□				∠
15	20 46	29 ♒ 12	15 21	9 37	26 57	24 41	21 26	21 45	⊻	⊻	✱			□	⊻	☌	✱
16	22 24	0 ♓ 26	15 ℞ 21	9 33	26 56	24 43	21 28	21 45					△		∠		
17	24 2	1 39	15 20	9 29	26 55	24 45	21 30	21 46	☌	☌	∠	△	⚼	△	✱	⊻	□
18	25 41	2 52	15 19	9 25	26 54	24 47	21 32	21 46			⊻	⚼		⚼		∠	
19	27 20	4 5	15 17	9 20	26 53	24 50	21 33	21 46							□	✱	△
☼	29 ♑ 0	5 18	15 14	9 16	26 51	24 52	21 35	21 46	⊻	⊻	●		☍				⚼
21	0 ♒ 41	6 32	15 10	9 11	26 50	24 54	21 37	21 46	∠	∠		☍		☍	△	□	
22	2 22	7 45	15 6	9 6	26 48	24 56	21 39	21 46	✱	✱	⊻				⚼		
23	4 3	8 58	15 0	9 1	26 46	24 58	21 41	21 47			∠		⚼			△	☍
24	5 45	10 10	14 54	8 56	26 44	25 0	21 43	21 47	□	□		⚼	△			⚼	
25	7 28	11 23	14 48	8 51	26 42	25 2	21 44	21 ℞ 47			✱	△		⚼			
26	9 12	12 36	14 40	8 45	26 40	25 3	21 46	21 47	△					△	☍		
☼	10 55	13 49	14 31	8 39	26 38	25 5	21 48	21 46		△	□	□	□				⚼
28	12 40	15 1	14 22	8 34	26 36	25 7	21 50	21 46	⚼	⚼				□		☍	△
29	14 25	16 14	14 12	8 27	26 34	25 8	21 51	21 46				✱	✱		⚼		
30	16 10	17 26	14 1	8 21	26 31	25 10	21 53	21 46			△		∠	✱	△		□
31	17 ♒ 55	18 ♓ 38	13 ♍ 50	8 ♍ 15	26 ♍ 29	25 ♏ 12	21 ♐ 55	21 ♎ 46			⚼	∠	⊻			⚼	

D M	Saturn. Lat.	Saturn. Dec.	Uranus. Lat.	Uranus. Dec.	Neptune. Lat.	Neptune. Dec.	Pluto. Lat.	Pluto. Dec.
	° ′	° ′	° ′	° ′	° ′	° ′	° ′	° ′
1	2 N 10	3 N 11	0 N 17	18 S 31	1 N 21	21 S 48	17 N 2	7 N 24
3	2 10	3 11	0 17	18 32	1 21	21 48	17 3	7 24
5	2 11	3 11	0 17	18 34	1 21	21 48	17 4	7 25
7	2 12	3 12	0 17	18 35	1 21	21 48	17 6	7 25
9	2 12	3 12	0 17	18 36	1 21	21 49	17 7	7 26
11	2 13	3 13	0 17	18 38	1 21	21 49	17 8	7 27
13	2 13	3 14	0 17	18 39	1 21	21 49	17 9	7 27
15	2 14	3 15	0 17	18 40	1 21	21 49	17 10	7 28
17	2 14	3 17	0 17	18 41	1 21	21 49	17 11	7 29
19	2 15	3 18	0 17	18 42	1 21	21 50	17 13	7 30
21	2 15	3 20	0 17	18 43	1 21	21 50	17 14	7 31
23	2 16	3 22	0 17	18 44	1 21	21 50	17 15	7 32
25	2 16	3 24	0 17	18 45	1 21	21 50	17 16	7 33
27	2 17	3 26	0 17	18 46	1 21	21 50	17 18	7 34
29	2 17	3 28	0 17	18 47	1 21	21 51	17 19	7 35
31	2 N 18	3 N 31	0 N 17	18 S 47	1 N 21	21 S 51	17 N 20	7 N 37

Mutual Aspects.

1. ☉ △ ♃. ♀ ⚼ ♄.
2. ☿ ⊥ ♅. ♀ P ♅.
3. ♀ ∇ ♂. 4. ☿ Q ♇.
5. ☉ △ ♂. 6. ♄ Stat.
8. ☿ △ ♃, ∠ ♅. ♀ ± ♄, ✱ ♆.
9. ☿ △ ♇.
11. ☉ P ♆. ♀ □ ♅.
12. ☉ ⊻ ♆, □ ♇. ☿ △ ♂.
13. ☿ ∇ ♄.
15. ☉ ⚼ ♃, ✱ ♅. ☿ ⊻ ♆.
16. ☿ □ ♇. ♂ Stat.
17. ☉ △ ♄. ☿ ⚼ ♃, ✱ ♅.
18. ☉ ⊥ ♆.
19. ☿ △ ♄, ⊥ ♆. ♀ Q ♆.
21. ☉ ☌ ☿, ⊥ ♀, ⚼ ♂. ☿ ⊥ ♀, ⚼ ♂, P ♆. ♀ ⚼ ♇.
22. ☿ ± ♃.
23. ☉ ± ♃. ♀ P ♂, ☍ ♃, P ♃.
24. ♇ Stat.
25. ☿ Q ♅, ∠ ♆, ✱ ♇.
26. ☉ P ♅. ☿ ± ♂, ∇ ♃. ♆
27. ☉ Q ♅, ∠ ♆. ☿ ⚼ ♄. ☿ P ♇.
28. ☿ P ♅. ☿ ☍ ♂.
29. ☉ ± ♂, ∇ ♃. ☿ ∇ ♂. ♀ ± ♇.
30. ☉ P ☿.

LAST QUARTER—January 10, 11*h.* 49*m.* *a.m.* (19° ♎ 23 ′)

Reproduced with permission from Raphael's Ephemeris 1980, available from the copyright holders. © W. Foulsham & Co., Slough, England.

Table 8(b): Proportional Logarithms

PROPORTIONAL LOGARITHMS FOR FINDING THE PLANETS' PLACES

Min.	0	1	2	3	4	5	6	7	8	9	10	11	12	13	14	15	Min.
0	3.1584	1.3802	1.0792	.9031	7781	6812	6021	5351	4771	4260	3802	3388	3010	2663	2341	2041	0
1	3.1584	1.3730	1.0756	9007	7763	6798	6009	5341	4762	4252	3795	3382	3004	2657	2336	2036	1
2	2.8573	1.3660	1.0720	8983	7745	6784	5997	5330	4753	4244	3788	3375	2998	2652	2330	2032	2
3	2.6812	1.3590	1.0685	8959	7728	6769	5985	5320	4744	4236	3780	3368	2992	2646	2325	2027	3
4	2.5563	1.3522	1.0649	8935	7710	6755	5973	5310	4735	4228	3773	3362	2986	2640	2320	2022	4
5	2.4594	1.3454	1.0614	8912	7692	6741	5961	5300	4726	4220	3766	3355	2980	2635	2315	2017	5
6	2.3802	1.3388	1.0580	8888	7674	6726	5949	5289	4717	4212	3759	3349	2974	2629	2310	2012	6
7	2.3133	1.3323	1.0546	8865	7657	6712	5937	5279	4708	4204	3752	3342	2968	2624	2305	2008	7
8	2.2553	1.3258	1.0511	8842	7639	6698	5925	5269	4699	4196	3745	3336	2962	2618	2300	2003	8
9	2.2041	1.3195	1.0478	8819	7622	6684	5913	5259	4690	4188	3737	3329	2956	2613	2295	1998	9
10	2.1584	1.3133	1.0444	8796	7604	6670	5902	5249	4682	4180	3730	3323	2950	2607	2289	1993	10
11	2.1170	1.3071	1.0411	8773	7587	6656	5890	5239	4673	4172	3723	3316	2944	2602	2284	1988	11
12	2.0792	1.3010	1.0378	8751	7570	6642	5878	5229	4664	4164	3716	3310	2938	2596	2279	1984	12
13	2.0444	1.2950	1.0345	8728	7552	6628	5866	5219	4655	4156	3709	3303	2933	2591	2274	1979	13
14	2.0122	1.2891	1.0313	8706	7535	6614	5855	5209	4646	4148	3702	3297	2927	2585	2269	1974	14
15	1.9823	1.2833	1.0280	8683	7518	6600	5843	5199	4638	4141	3695	3291	2921	2580	2264	1969	15
16	1.9542	1.2775	1.0248	8661	7501	6587	5832	5189	4629	4133	3688	3284	2915	2574	2259	1965	16
17	1.9279	1.2719	1.0216	8639	7484	6573	5820	5179	4620	4125	3681	3278	2909	2569	2254	1960	17
18	1.9031	1.2663	1.0185	8617	7467	6559	5809	5169	4611	4117	3674	3271	2903	2564	2249	1955	18
19	1.8796	1.2607	1.0153	8595	7451	6546	5797	5159	4603	4109	3667	3265	2897	2558	2244	1950	19
20	1.8573	1.2553	1.0122	8573	7434	6532	5786	5149	4594	4102	3660	3258	2891	2553	2239	1946	20
21	1.8361	1.2499	1.0091	8552	7417	6519	5774	5139	4585	4094	3653	3252	2885	2547	2234	1941	21
22	1.8159	1.2445	1.0061	8530	7401	6505	5763	5129	4577	4086	3646	3246	2880	2542	2229	1936	22
23	1.7966	1.2393	1.0030	8509	7384	6492	5752	5120	4568	4079	3639	3239	2874	2536	2223	1932	23
24	1.7781	1.2341	1.0000	8487	7368	6478	5740	5110	4559	4071	3632	3233	2868	2531	2218	1927	24
25	1.7604	1.2289	0.9970	8466	7351	6465	5729	5100	4551	4063	3625	3227	2862	2526	2213	1922	25
26	1.7434	1.2239	0.9940	8445	7335	6451	5718	5090	4542	4055	3618	3220	2856	2520	2208	1917	26
27	1.7270	1.2188	0.9910	8424	7318	6438	5706	5081	4534	4048	3611	3214	2850	2515	2203	1913	27
28	1.7112	1.2139	0.9881	8403	7302	6425	5695	5071	4525	4040	3604	3208	2845	2509	2198	1908	28
29	1.6960	1.2090	0.9852	8382	7286	6412	5684	5061	4516	4032	3597	3201	2839	2504	2193	1903	29
30	1.6812	1.2041	0.9823	8361	7270	6398	5673	5051	4508	4025	3590	3195	2833	2499	2188	1899	30
31	1.6670	1.1993	0.9794	8341	7254	6385	5662	5042	4499	4017	3583	3189	2827	2493	2183	1894	31
32	1.6532	1.1946	0.9765	8320	7238	6372	5651	5032	4491	4010	3576	3183	2821	2488	2178	1889	32
33	1.6398	1.1899	0.9737	8300	7222	6359	5640	5023	4482	4002	3570	3176	2816	2483	2173	1885	33
34	1.6269	1.1852	0.9708	8279	7206	6346	5629	5013	4474	3994	3563	3170	2810	2477	2168	1880	34
35	1.6143	1.1806	0.9680	8259	7190	6333	5618	5003	4466	3987	3556	3164	2804	2472	2164	1875	35
36	1.6021	1.1761	0.9652	8239	7174	6320	5607	4994	4457	3979	3549	3157	2798	2467	2159	1871	36
37	1.5902	1.1716	0.9625	8219	7159	6307	5596	4984	4449	3972	3542	3151	2793	2461	2154	1866	37
38	1.5786	1.1671	0.9597	8199	7143	6294	5585	4975	4440	3964	3535	3145	2787	2456	2149	1862	38
39	1.5673	1.1627	0.9570	8179	7128	6282	5574	4965	4432	3957	3529	3139	2781	2451	2144	1857	39
40	1.5563	1.1584	0.9542	8159	7112	6269	5563	4956	4424	3949	3522	3133	2775	2445	2139	1852	40
41	1.5456	1.1540	0.9515	8140	7097	6256	5552	4947	4415	3942	3515	3126	2770	2440	2134	1848	41
42	1.5351	1.1498	0.9488	8120	7081	6243	5541	4937	4407	3934	3508	3120	2764	2435	2129	1843	42
43	1.5249	1.1455	0.9462	8101	7066	6231	5531	4928	4399	3927	3501	3114	2758	2430	2124	1838	43
44	1.5149	1.1413	0.9435	8081	7050	6218	5520	4918	4390	3919	3495	3108	2753	2424	2119	1834	44
45	1.5051	1.1372	0.9409	8062	7035	6205	5509	4909	4382	3912	3488	3102	2747	2419	2114	1829	45
46	1.4956	1.1331	0.9383	8043	7020	6193	5498	4900	4374	3905	3481	3096	2741	2414	2109	1825	46
47	1.4863	1.1290	0.9356	8023	7005	6180	5488	4890	4365	3897	3475	3089	2736	2409	2104	1820	47
48	1.4771	1.1249	0.9330	8004	6990	6168	5477	4881	4357	3890	3468	3083	2730	2403	2099	1816	48
49	1.4682	1.1209	0.9305	7985	6875	6155	5466	4872	4349	3882	3461	3077	2724	2398	2095	1811	49
50	1.4594	1.1170	0.9279	7966	6960	6143	5456	4863	4341	3875	3454	3071	2719	2393	2090	1806	50
51	1.4508	1.1130	0.9254	7947	6945	6131	5445	4853	4333	3868	3448	3065	2713	2388	2085	1802	51
52	1.4424	1.1091	0.9228	7929	6930	6118	5435	4844	4324	3860	3441	3059	2707	2382	2080	1797	52
53	1.4341	1.1053	0.9203	7910	6915	6106	5424	4835	4316	3853	3434	3053	2702	2377	2075	1793	53
54	1.4260	1.1015	0.9178	7891	6900	6094	5414	4826	4308	3846	3428	3047	2696	2372	2070	1788	54
55	1.4180	1.0977	0.9153	7873	6885	6081	5403	4817	4300	3838	3421	3041	2691	2367	2065	1784	55
56	1.4102	1.0939	0.9128	7854	6871	6069	5393	4808	4292	3831	3415	3034	2685	2362	2061	1779	56
57	1.4025	1.0902	0.9104	7836	6856	6057	5382	4798	4284	3823	3408	3028	2679	2356	2056	1774	57
58	1.3949	1.0865	0.9079	7818	6841	6045	5372	4789	4276	3817	3401	3022	2674	2351	2051	1770	58
59	1.3875	1.0828	0.9055	7800	6827	6033	5361	4780	4268	3809	3395	3016	2668	2346	2046	1765	59
	0	1	2	3	4	5	6	7	8	9	10	11	12	13	14	15	

RULE:—Add proportional log. of planet's daily motion to log. of time from noon, and the sum will be the log. of the motion required. Add this to planet's place at noon, if time be p.m., but subtract if a.m. and the sum will be planet's true place. If Retrograde, subtract for p.m., but add for a.m.

What is the Long. of ☽ Mar. 11th, 1980 at 2.15 p.m.?

☽'s daily motion—13° 42'	
Prop. Log. of 13° 42'	.2435
Prop. Log. of 2h. 15m.	1.0280
☽'s motion in 2h. 15m. = 1° 17' or Log.	1.2715

☽'s Long. on Mar. 11th. = 9°♓25' + 1° 17' =

10°♓42'

The Daily Motions of the Sun, Moon, Mars, Venus and Mercury will be found on pages 26 to 28.

Table 8(c): Table of Houses for London

TABLES OF HOUSES FOR LONDON, Latitude 51° 32′ N.

Block 1

Sidereal Time (H. M. S.)	10 ♈	11 ♉	12 ♊	Ascen ♋	2 ♌	3 ♍
0 0 0	0	9	22	26 36	12	3
0 3 40	1	10	23	27 17	13	3
0 7 20	2	11	24	27 56	14	4
0 11 0	3	12	25	28 42	15	5
0 14 41	4	13	25	29 17	15	6
0 18 21	5	14	26	29 55	16	7
0 22 2	6	15	27	0♌34	17	8
0 25 42	7	16	28	1 14	18	8
0 29 23	8	17	29	1 55	18	9
0 33 4	9	18	♋	2 33	19	10
0 36 45	10	19	1	3 14	20	11
0 40 26	11	20	1	3 54	20	12
0 44 8	12	21	2	4 33	21	13
0 47 50	13	22	3	5 12	22	14
0 51 32	14	23	4	5 52	23	15
0 55 14	15	24	5	6 30	23	16
0 58 57	16	25	6	7 9	24	16
1 2 40	17	26	6	7 50	25	17
1 6 23	18	27	7	8 30	26	18
1 10 7	19	28	8	9 9	26	19
1 13 51	20	29	9	9 48	27	19
1 17 35	21	♊	10	10 28	28	20
1 21 20	22	1	10	11 8	28	21
1 25 6	23	2	11	11 48	29	22
1 28 52	24	3	12	12 28	♍	23
1 32 38	25	4	13	13 8	1	24
1 36 25	26	5	14	13 48	1	25
1 40 12	27	6	14	14 28	2	25
1 44 0	28	7	15	15 8	3	26
1 47 48	29	8	16	15 48	4	27
1 51 37	30	9	17	16 28	4	28

Block 2

Sidereal Time (H. M. S.)	10 ♉	11 ♊	12 ♋	Ascen ♌	2 ♍	3 ♎
1 51 37	0	9	17	16 28	4	28
1 55 27	1	10	18	17 8	5	29
1 59 17	2	11	19	17 48	6	♎
2 3 8	3	12	19	18 28	7	1
2 6 59	4	13	20	19 9	8	2
2 10 51	5	14	21	19 49	9	2
2 14 44	6	15	22	20 29	9	3
2 18 37	7	16	22	21 10	10	4
2 22 31	8	17	23	21 51	11	5
2 26 25	9	18	24	22 32	11	6
2 30 20	10	19	25	23 14	12	7
2 34 16	11	20	25	23 55	13	8
2 38 13	12	21	26	24 36	14	9
2 42 10	13	22	27	25 17	15	10
2 46 8	14	23	28	25 58	15	11
2 50 7	15	24	29	26 40	16	12
2 54 7	16	25	29	27 22	17	12
2 58 7	17	26	♌	28 4	18	13
3 2 8	18	27	1	28 46	18	14
3 6 9	19	27	2	29 28	19	15
3 10 12	20	28	3	0♍10	20	16
3 14 15	21	29	3	0 54	21	17
3 18 19	22	♋	4	1 36	22	18
3 22 23	23	1	5	2 20	22	19
3 26 29	24	2	6	3 2	23	20
3 30 35	25	3	7	3 45	24	21
3 34 41	26	4	7	4 28	25	22
3 38 49	27	5	8	5 11	26	23
3 42 57	28	6	9	5 54	27	24
3 47 6	29	7	10	6 38	27	25
3 51 15	30	8	11	7 21	28	25

Block 3

Sidereal Time (H. M. S.)	10 ♊	11 ♋	12 ♌	Ascen ♍	2 ♎	3 ♏
3 51 15	0	8	11	7 21	28	25
3 55 25	1	9	12	8 5	29	26
3 59 36	2	10	12	8 49	♎	27
4 3 48	3	10	13	9 33	1	28
4 8 0	4	11	14	10 17	2	29
4 12 13	5	12	15	11 2	2	♏
4 16 26	6	13	16	11 46	3	1
4 20 40	7	14	17	12 30	4	2
4 24 55	8	15	17	13 15	5	3
4 29 10	9	16	18	14 0	6	4
4 33 26	10	17	19	14 45	7	5
4 37 42	11	18	20	15 30	8	6
4 41 59	12	19	21	16 15	8	7
4 46 16	13	20	21	17 0	9	8
4 50 34	14	21	22	17 45	10	9
4 54 52	15	22	23	18 30	11	10
4 59 10	16	23	24	19 16	12	11
5 3 29	17	24	25	20 3	13	12
5 7 49	18	25	26	20 49	14	13
5 12 9	19	25	27	21 35	14	14
5 16 29	20	26	28	22 20	15	14
5 20 49	21	27	28	23 6	16	15
5 25 9	22	28	29	23 51	17	16
5 29 30	23	29	♍	24 37	18	17
5 33 51	24	♌	1	25 23	19	18
5 38 12	25	1	2	26 9	20	19
5 42 34	26	2	3	26 55	21	20
5 46 55	27	3	4	27 41	21	21
5 51 17	28	4	4	28 27	22	22
5 55 38	29	5	5	29 13	23	23
6 0 0	30	6	6	30 0	24	24

Block 4

Sidereal Time (H. M. S.)	10 ♋	11 ♌	12 ♍	Ascen ♎	2 ♎	3 ♏
6 0 0	0	6	6	0♎0	24	24
6 4 22	1	7	7	0 47	25	25
6 8 43	2	8	8	1 33	26	26
6 13 5	3	9	9	2 19	27	27
6 17 26	4	10	10	3 5	28	28
6 21 48	5	11	10	3 51	28	29
6 26 9	6	12	11	4 37	29	♐
6 30 30	7	13	12	5 23	♏	1
6 34 51	8	14	13	6 9	1	2
6 39 11	9	15	14	6 55	2	3
6 43 31	10	16	15	7 40	2	4
6 47 51	11	16	16	8 26	3	4
6 52 11	12	17	16	9 12	4	5
6 56 31	13	18	17	9 58	5	6
7 0 50	14	19	18	10 43	6	7
7 5 8	15	20	19	11 28	7	8
7 9 26	16	21	20	12 14	8	9
7 13 44	17	22	21	12 59	8	10
7 18 1	18	23	22	13 45	9	11
7 22 18	19	24	23	14 30	10	12
7 26 34	20	25	24	15 15	11	13
7 30 50	21	26	25	16 0	12	14
7 35 5	22	27	25	16 45	13	15
7 39 20	23	28	26	17 30	13	16
7 43 34	24	29	27	18 15	14	17
7 47 47	25	♍	28	18 59	15	18
7 52 0	26	1	29	19 43	16	19
7 56 12	27	2	29	20 27	17	20
8 0 24	28	3	♎	21 11	18	20
8 4 35	29	4	1	21 56	18	21
8 8 45	30	5	2	22 40	19	22

Block 5

Sidereal Time (H. M. S.)	10 ♌	11 ♍	12 ♎	Ascen ♎	2 ♏	3 ♐
8 8 45	0	5	2	22 40	19	22
8 12 54	1	5	3	23 24	20	23
8 17 3	2	6	3	24 7	21	24
8 21 11	3	7	4	24 50	22	25
8 25 19	4	8	5	25 34	23	26
8 29 26	5	9	6	26 18	23	27
8 33 31	6	10	7	27 1	24	28
8 37 37	7	11	8	27 44	25	29
8 41 41	8	12	8	28 26	26	♑
8 45 45	9	13	9	29 8	27	1
8 49 48	10	14	10	29 50	27	2
8 53 51	11	15	11	0♏32	28	3
8 57 52	12	16	12	1 15	29	4
9 1 53	13	17	12	1 58	♐	4
9 5 53	14	18	13	2 39	1	5
9 9 53	15	18	14	3 21	1	6
9 13 52	16	19	15	4 3	2	7
9 17 50	17	20	16	4 44	3	8
9 21 47	18	21	16	5 26	3	9
9 25 44	19	22	17	6 7	4	10
9 29 40	20	23	18	6 48	5	11
9 33 35	21	24	18	7 29	5	12
9 37 29	22	25	19	8 9	6	13
9 41 23	23	26	20	8 50	7	14
9 45 16	24	27	21	9 31	8	15
9 49 9	25	28	22	10 11	9	16
9 53 1	26	28	23	10 51	9	17
9 56 52	27	29	23	11 32	10	18
10 0 43	28	♎	24	12 11	11	19
10 4 33	29	1	25	12 53	12	20
10 8 25	30	2	26	13 33	13	21

Block 6

Sidereal Time (H. M. S.)	10 ♍	11 ♎	12 ♏	Ascen ♏	2 ♐	3 ♑
10 8 23	0	2	26	13 33	13	20
10 12 12	1	3	26	14 13	14	21
10 16 0	2	4	27	14 53	15	22
10 19 48	3	5	28	15 33	15	23
10 23 35	4	5	29	16 13	16	24
10 27 22	5	6	29	16 52	17	25
10 31 8	6	7	♏	17 32	18	26
10 34 54	7	8	1	18 12	19	27
10 38 40	8	9	2	18 52	20	28
10 42 25	9	10	2	19 31	20	29
10 46 9	10	11	3	20 11	21	♒
10 49 53	11	11	4	20 50	22	1
10 53 37	12	12	4	21 30	23	2
10 57 20	13	13	5	22 9	24	3
11 1 3	14	14	6	22 49	24	4
11 4 46	15	15	7	23 28	25	5
11 8 28	16	16	7	24 6	26	6
11 12 10	17	17	8	24 47	27	8
11 15 52	18	17	9	25 27	28	9
11 19 34	19	18	10	26 6	29	10
11 23 15	20	19	10	26 45	♑	11
11 26 56	21	20	11	27 25	1	12
11 30 37	22	21	12	28 5	1	13
11 34 18	23	22	13	28 44	2	14
11 37 58	24	23	13	29 24	3	15
11 41 39	25	23	14	0♐3	4	16
11 45 19	26	24	15	0 43	5	17
11 49 0	27	25	15	1 23	6	18
11 52 40	28	26	16	2 3	6	19
11 56 20	29	27	17	2 43	7	20
12 0 0	30	27	17	3 23	8	21

TABLES OF HOUSES FOR LONDON, Latitude 51° 32′ N.

Upper table — Panel 1

Sidereal Time (H. M. S.)	10 ♎	11 ♎	12 ♏	Ascen ♐	2 ♑	3 ♒
12 0 0	0	27	17	3 23	8	21
12 3 40	1	28	18	4 4	9	23
12 7 20	2	29	19	4 45	10	24
12 11 0	3	♏	20	5 26	11	25
12 14 41	4	1	20	6 7	12	26
12 18 21	5	1	21	6 48	13	27
12 22 2	6	2	22	7 29	14	28
12 25 42	7	3	23	8 10	15	29
12 29 23	8	4	23	8 51	16	♓
12 33 4	9	5	24	9 33	17	2
12 36 45	10	6	25	10 15	18	3
12 40 26	11	6	25	10 57	19	4
12 44 8	12	7	26	11 40	20	5
12 47 50	13	8	27	12 22	21	6
12 51 32	14	9	28	13 4	22	7
12 55 14	15	10	28	13 47	23	9
12 58 57	16	11	29	14 30	24	10
13 2 40	17	11	♐	15 13	25	11
13 6 23	18	12	1	15 56	26	12
13 10 7	19	13	2	16 44	27	13
13 13 51	20	14	2	17 29	28	14
13 17 35	21	15	3	18 14	29	16
13 21 20	22	16	4	0 ♒	♒	17
13 25 6	23	17	5	1 18	1	18
13 28 52	24	17	5	2 31	2	20
13 32 38	25	18	6	21 18	4	21
13 36 25	26	19	7	22 6	5	22
13 40 12	27	20	7	22 54	6	23
13 44 0	28	21	8	23 42	7	25
13 47 48	29	22	9	24 31	8	26
13 51 37	♏	22	10	25 20	10	27

Upper table — Panel 2

Sidereal Time (H. M. S.)	10 ♏	11 ♏	12 ♐	Ascen ♐	2 ♒	3 ♓
13 51 37	0	22	10	25 20	10	27
13 55 27	1	23	11	26 10	11	28
13 59 17	2	24	11	27 2	12	♈
14 3 8	3	25	12	27 53	14	1
14 6 59	4	26	13	28 45	15	2
14 10 51	5	26	14	29 36	16	4
14 14 44	6	27	15	0 ♑ 29	18	5
14 18 37	7	28	15	1 23	19	6
14 22 31	8	29	16	2 18	20	8
14 26 25	9	♐	17	3 14	22	9
14 30 20	10	1	18	4 11	23	10
14 34 16	11	2	19	5 9	25	11
14 38 13	12	2	20	6 7	26	13
14 42 10	13	3	20	7 6	28	14
14 46 8	14	4	21	8 6	29	15
14 50 7	15	5	22	9 8	♓	17
14 54 7	16	6	23	10 11	2	18
14 58 7	17	7	24	11 14	4	19
15 2 8	18	8	25	12 17	5	20
15 6 9	19	10	26	13 20	6	21
15 10 12	20	11	27	14 35	9	23
15 14 15	21	12	27	15 43	11	24
15 18 19	22	13	28	16 52	12	26
15 22 23	23	14	29	18 1	13	27
15 26 29	24	15	♑	19 16	16	28
15 30 35	25	16	1	20 32	17	29
15 34 41	26	18	2	21 48	19	♉
15 38 47	27	19	3	23 3	21	1
15 42 53	28	20	5	24 19	23	2
15 46 59	29	21	6	25 27	24	3
15 51 5	♐	23	7	26 54	26	5

Upper table — Panel 3

Sidereal Time (H. M. S.)	10 ♐	11 ♐	12 ♑	Ascen ♑	2 ♓	3 ♉
15 51 15	0	18	6	27 15	26	6
15 55 25	1	19	7	28 42	28	7
15 59 36	2	20	8	0 ♒ 11	♈	9
16 3 48	3	21	9	1 42	2	10
16 8 0	4	22	10	3 16	3	11
16 12 13	5	23	11	4 53	5	12
16 16 26	6	24	12	6 32	7	14
16 20 40	7	25	13	8 13	9	15
16 24 55	8	26	14	9 57	11	16
16 29 10	9	27	16	11 44	12	17
16 33 26	10	28	17	13 34	14	18
16 37 42	11	29	18	15 26	16	20
16 41 59	12	♑	19	17 20	18	21
16 46 16	13	1	20	19 18	20	22
16 50 34	14	2	21	21 21	22	23
16 54 52	15	3	22	23 29	23	25
16 59 10	16	4	24	25 36	25	26
17 3 29	17	5	25	27 46	27	27
17 7 49	18	6	26	0 ♈ 28	28	28
17 12 9	19	7	27	2 19	♉	29
17 16 29	20	8	29	4 40	2	♊
17 20 49	21	9	♒	7 2	3	1
17 25 9	22	10	1	9 26	5	2
17 29 30	23	11	3	11 54	7	3
17 33 51	24	12	4	14 24	8	5
17 38 12	25	13	6	16 57	10	6
17 42 34	26	14	7	19 33	11	7
17 46 55	27	15	8	22 13	13	8
17 51 17	28	16	10	24 40	14	9
17 55 38	29	17	11	27 16	16	10
18 0 0	0	18	13	0 0	17	11

Lower table — Panel 1

Sidereal Time (H. M. S.)	10 ♑	11 ♑	12 ♒	Ascen ♈	2 ♉	3 ♊
18 0 0	0	18	13	0 0	17	11
18 4 22	1	20	14	2 39	19	13
18 8 43	2	21	16	5 19	20	14
18 13 5	3	22	17	7 55	22	15
18 17 26	4	23	19	10 29	23	16
18 21 48	5	24	20	13 2	25	17
18 26 9	6	25	22	15 36	26	18
18 30 30	7	26	23	18 6	28	19
18 34 51	8	27	25	20 34	29	20
18 39 11	9	29	27	22 59	♊	21
18 43 31	10	♈	28	25 22	1	22
18 47 51	11	1	♈	27 42	2	23
18 52 11	12	2	2	29 58	4	24
18 56 31	13	3	3	2 ♉ 13	5	25
19 0 0	14	4	4	4 24	6	26
19 5 8	15	6	6	6 30	8	27
19 9 26	16	7	8	8 36	9	28
19 13 44	17	8	10	10 40	10	29
19 18 1	18	9	12	12 39	11	♋
19 22 18	19	10	14	14 35	12	1
19 26 34	20	12	16	16 28	13	2
19 30 50	21	13	18	17 14	14	3
19 35 5	22	14	19	18 3	16	4
19 39 20	23	15	21	18 48	17	5
19 43 34	24	16	23	19 28	18	6
19 47 47	25	18	25	20 9	19	7
19 52 0	26	19	27	20 45	20	8
19 56 12	27	20	28	21 18	21	9
20 0 24	28	21	♈	21 49	22	10
20 4 35	29	23	2	1 ♊ 19	23	11
20 8 45	30	24	4	2 45	24	12

Lower table — Panel 2

Sidereal Time (H. M. S.)	10 ♒	11 ♒	12 ♈	Ascen ♊	2 ♊	3 ♋
20 8 45	0	24	4	2 45	24	12
20 12 54	1	25	6	4 9	25	12
20 17 3	2	27	7	5 32	26	13
20 21 11	3	28	9	6 53	27	14
20 25 19	4	29	11	8 12	28	15
20 29 26	5	♓	13	9 27	29	16
20 33 31	6	2	14	10 43	♋	17
20 37 37	7	3	16	11 58	1	18
20 41 41	8	4	18	13 9	2	19
20 45 45	9	6	19	14 18	3	20
20 49 48	10	7	21	15 25	5	21
20 53 51	11	8	23	16 32	6	21
20 57 52	12	9	24	17 39	8	22
21 1 53	13	11	26	18 44	9	23
21 5 53	14	12	28	19 48	9	24
21 9 53	15	13	29	20 52	11	25
21 13 13	16	15	♈	21 53	12	26
21 17 50	17	16	1	22 53	13	27
21 21 47	18	17	2	23 52	14	28
21 25 55	19	18	4	24 51	15	29
21 29 40	20	20	7	25 48	12	♌
21 33 35	21	22	8	26 44	13	♌
21 37 29	22	23	10	27 40	14	1
21 41 23	23	24	11	28 34	15	2
21 45 45	24	26	13	29 29	15	3
21 49 9	25	26	14	0 ♋ 22	16	4
21 53 1	26	28	15	1 15	17	4
21 56 52	27	29	16	2 7	18	5
22 0 43	28	♈	18	2 57	19	6
22 4 33	29	2	19	3 48	19	7
22 8 30	30	3	20	4 38	20	8

Lower table — Panel 3

Sidereal Time (H. M. S.)	10 ♓	11 ♈	12 ♉	Ascen ♋	2 ♋	3 ♌
22 8 23	0	3	20	4 38	20	8
22 12 12	1	4	21	5 28	21	8
22 16 0	2	6	23	6 17	22	9
22 19 48	3	7	24	7 5	23	10
22 23 35	4	8	25	7 53	23	11
22 27 22	5	9	26	8 42	24	12
22 31 8	6	10	28	9 29	25	13
22 34 54	7	12	29	10 16	26	14
22 38 40	8	13	♋	11 2	26	14
22 42 25	9	14	1	11 47	27	15
22 46 9	10	15	2	12 31	28	16
22 49 53	11	17	3	13 16	29	17
22 53 37	12	18	4	14 1	29	18
22 57 20	13	19	5	14 45	♌	19
23 1 3	14	20	6	15 28	1	19
23 4 46	15	21	7	16 11	2	20
23 8 28	16	23	8	16 54	2	21
23 12 10	17	24	9	17 37	3	22
23 15 52	18	25	10	18 20	4	23
23 19 26	19	27	11	19 3	5	24
23 23 15	20	27	12	19 45	5	24
23 26 56	21	29	13	20 26	6	25
23 30 37	22	♉	14	21 8	7	26
23 34 18	23	1	15	21 50	7	27
23 38 0	24	2	16	22 31	8	28
23 41 39	25	3	17	23 12	9	28
23 45 19	26	4	18	23 53	9	29
23 49 0	27	5	19	24 32	10	♍
23 52 40	28	6	20	25 15	11	1
23 56 20	29	6	21	25 56	12	2
24 0 0	30	9	22	26 36	13	3

Table 8(d): Table of Houses for Northern Latitudes

TABLES OF HOUSES FOR ATHENS, *Latitude* 37° 58' N.

Sidereal Time H. M. S.	10 ♈	11 ♉	12 ♊	Ascen ♋	2 ♌	3 ♍
0 0 0	0	6	16	17 15	8	1
0 3 40	1	7	15	18 1	9	2
0 7 20	2	8	16	18 67	9	3
0 11 0	3	9	17	19 33	10	4
0 14 41	4	10	18	20 19	11	4
0 18 21	5	11	18	21 4	12	5
0 22 2	6	12	19	21 50	12	6
0 25 42	7	13	20	22 35	13	7
0 29 23	8	14	21	23 20	14	8
0 33 4	9	15	22	24 6	15	9
0 36 45	10	16	23	24 51	15	10
0 40 26	11	17	24	25 36	16	11
0 44 8	12	18	25	26 21	17	11
0 47 50	13	19	25	27 6	18	12
0 51 32	14	20	26	27 51	19	13
0 55 14	15	21	27	28 36	19	14
0 58 57	16	22	28	29 22	20	15
1 2 40	17	23	29	0♋ 6	21	16
1 6 23	18	24	♋	0 52	22	17
1 10 7	19	25	1	1 37	23	18
1 13 51	20	26	1	2 22	23	19
1 17 35	21	27	2	3 7	24	20
1 21 20	22	28	3	3 52	25	21
1 25 6	23	29	4	4 37	26	21
1 28 52	24	♋	5	5 23	27	22
1 32 38	25	1	6	6 8	28	23
1 36 25	26	2	7	6 54	28	24
1 40 12	27	3	7	7 39	29	25
1 44 0	28	4	8	8 25	♍	26
1 47 48	29	5	9	9 11	1	27
1 51 37	30	6	10	9 56	2	28

Sidereal Time H. M. S.	10 ♉	11 ♊	12 ♋	Ascen ♌	2 ♍	3 ♎
1 51 37	0	6	10	9 56	2	28
1 55 27	1	7	11	10 42	3	29
1 59 17	2	8	12	11 28	3	♎
2 3 8	3	9	13	12 13	5	2
2 6 59	4	10	13	13 1	5	2
2 10 51	5	10	14	13 47	6	3
2 14 44	6	11	15	14 33	7	4
2 18 37	7	12	16	15 20	7	5
2 22 31	8	13	17	16 7	8	5
2 26 25	9	14	18	16 54	9	6
2 30 20	10	15	18	17 40	10	7
2 34 16	11	16	19	18 28	11	8
2 38 13	12	17	20	19 15	12	9
2 42 10	13	18	21	20 2	13	10
2 46 8	14	19	22	20 50	13	11
2 50 7	15	20	23	21 37	14	12
2 54 7	16	21	24	22 25	15	13
2 58 7	17	22	24	23 13	16	14
3 2 8	18	23	25	24 2	17	15
3 6 9	19	24	26	24 50	18	16
3 10 12	20	25	27	25 38	19	17
3 14 15	21	25	28	26 27	20	18
3 18 19	22	26	29	27 16	21	19
3 22 23	23	27	29	28 7	22	20
3 26 29	24	28	♌	28 54	22	21
3 30 35	25	29	1	29 44	23	22
3 34 41	26	♏	2	0♍ 34	24	23
3 38 49	27	1	3	1 24	25	24
3 42 57	28	2	4	2 14	26	25
3 47 6	29	3	5	3 4	27	26
3 51 15	30	4	6	3 54	28	27

Sidereal Time H. M. S.	10 ♊	11 ♋	12 ♌	Ascen ♍	2 ♎	3 ♏
3 51 15	0	4	6	3 54	28	27
3 55 25	1	5	7	4 44	28	28
3 59 36	2	6	7	5 35	♎	29
4 3 48	3	7	8	6 26	1	♏
4 8 0	4	8	9	7 17	2	1
4 12 13	5	9	10	8 8	3	2
4 16 26	6	10	11	8 59	4	3
4 20 40	7	11	12	9 50	5	4
4 24 55	8	12	13	10 42	5	5
4 29 10	9	13	14	11 33	6	6
4 33 26	10	14	15	12 25	7	7
4 37 42	11	14	16	13 17	8	8
4 41 59	12	15	17	14 9	9	9
4 46 16	13	16	17	15 1	10	10
4 50 34	14	17	18	15 53	11	11
4 54 52	15	18	19	16 45	12	12
4 59 10	16	19	20	17 38	12	13
5 3 29	17	20	21	18 30	13	14
5 7 49	18	21	22	19 23	14	15
5 12 9	19	22	23	20 16	16	16
5 16 29	20	23	24	21 9	17	17
5 20 49	21	24	25	22 2	18	18
5 25 9	22	25	26	22 55	19	19
5 29 30	23	26	27	23 48	20	20
5 33 51	24	27	28	24 41	21	21
5 38 12	25	28	29	25 34	22	22
5 42 34	26	29	♍	26 27	23	23
5 46 55	27	♍	1	27 20	24	24
5 51 17	28	1	1	28 13	25	25
5 55 38	29	2	2	29 7	26	26
6 0 0	30	3	3	30 0	27	27

Sidereal Time H. M. S.	10 ♌	11 ♍	12 ♎	Ascen ♎	2 ♏	3 ♐
6 0 0	0	3	3	0 0	27	27
6 4 22	1	4	4	0 53	28	28
6 8 43	2	5	5	1 47	29	29
6 13 5	3	6	6	2 40	29	♐
6 17 26	4	7	7	3 33	♏	1
6 21 48	5	8	8	4 20	1	2
6 26 9	6	9	9	5 19	2	3
6 30 30	7	10	10	6 12	3	4
6 34 51	8	11	11	7 5	4	5
6 39 11	9	12	12	7 58	5	6
6 43 31	10	13	13	8 51	6	7
6 47 51	11	14	14	9 44	7	8
6 52 11	12	15	15	10 37	8	9
6 56 31	13	16	16	11 30	9	10
7 0 5	14	17	17	12 22	10	11
7 5 8	15	18	18	13 15	11	12
7 9 26	16	19	19	14 7	12	13
7 13 44	17	20	20	14 59	13	14
7 18 1	18	21	21	15 51	13	15
7 22 18	19	22	22	16 43	14	16
7 26 34	20	23	23	17 35	15	16
7 30 50	21	24	24	18 27	16	17
7 35 5	22	25	25	19 18	17	1b
7 39 20	23	26	25	20 10	18	19
7 43 34	24	27	26	21 1	19	20
7 47 47	25	28	27	21 52	20	21
7 52 0	26	29	28	22 43	21	22
7 56 12	27	♏	29	23 34	22	23
8 0 24	28	1	♎	24 25	23	24
8 4 35	29	2	1	25 16	23	25
8 8 46	30	3	2	26 6	24	26

Sidereal Time H. M. S.	10 ♍	11 ♎	12 ♎	Ascen ♏	2 ♏	3 ♐
8 8 46	0	3	2	26 6	24	26
8 12 54	1	4	3	26 56	25	27
8 17 3	2	5	4	27 46	26	28
8 21 11	3	6	5	28 36	27	29
8 25 19	4	7	6	29 26	28	♐
8 29 26	5	8	7	0♏ 16	29	1
8 33 31	6	9	8	1 6	♐	2
8 37 37	7	10	8	1 55	1	3
8 41 41	8	11	9	2 44	1	4
8 45 45	9	12	10	3 33	2	5
8 49 48	10	13	11	4 22	3	5
8 53 51	11	14	12	5 10	4	6
8 57 52	12	15	13	5 58	5	7
9 1 53	13	16	14	6 47	6	8
9 5 53	14	17	15	7 35	6	9
9 9 53	15	18	16	8 23	7	10
9 13 52	16	19	16	9 10	8	11
9 17 50	17	20	17	9 58	9	12
9 21 47	18	21	18	10 45	10	13
9 25 44	19	22	19	11 32	11	14
9 29 40	20	23	20	12 20	12	15
9 33 35	21	24	21	13 6	12	16
9 37 29	22	25	22	13 53	13	17
9 41 23	23	26	22	14 40	14	18
9 45 16	24	26	23	15 27	15	19
9 49 9	25	27	24	16 13	16	20
9 53 1	26	28	25	16 59	17	20
9 56 52	27	29	26	17 46	18	21
10 0 42	28	♎	27	18 32	18	22
10 4 33	29	1	28	19 18	19	23
10 8 23	30	2	28	20 4	20	24

Sidereal Time H. M. S.	10 ♎	11 ♎	12 ♏	Ascen ♐	2 ♐	3 ♑
10 8 23	0	2	28	20 4	20	24
10 12 12	1	3	29	20 49	21	25
10 16 0	2	4	♏	21 35	22	26
10 19 48	3	5	1	22 21	23	27
10 23 35	4	6	2	23 6	23	28
10 27 22	5	7	2	23 52	24	29
10 31 8	6	8	3	24 37	25	♑
10 34 54	7	9	4	25 23	26	1
10 38 40	8	9	5	26 8	26	2
10 42 25	9	10	6	26 53	27	3
10 46 9	10	11	7	27 38	28	4
10 49 53	11	12	7	28 23	29	5
10 53 37	12	13	8	29 7	♑	6
10 57 20	13	14	9	29 54	1	7
11 1 3	14	15	10	0♐ 38	2	8
11 4 46	15	16	11	1 24	3	8
11 8 28	16	17	11	2 9	4	10
11 12 10	17	18	12	2 54	5	12
11 15 52	18	19	13	3 39	5	12
11 19 34	19	19	14	4 24	6	13
11 23 15	20	20	15	5 9	7	14
11 26 56	21	21	15	5 54	8	15
11 30 37	22	22	16	6 40	9	16
11 34 18	23	23	17	7 25	10	17
11 37 58	24	24	18	8 10	11	18
11 41 39	25	25	18	8 56	12	19
11 45 19	26	26	19	9 41	12	20
11 49 0	27	26	20	10 27	13	21
11 52 40	28	27	21	11 13	14	22
11 56 20	29	28	22	11 59	15	23
12 0 0	30	29	22	12 45	16	24

TABLES OF HOUSES FOR ATHENS, *Latitude 37° 58' N.*

Sidereal Time H. M. S.	10 ≙	11 ≙	12 m	Ascen ♐ °	'	2 ♑	3 ≈
12 0 0	0	29	22	13	45	16	24
12 3 40	1	m	23	13	31	17	25
12 7 20	2	1	24	14	17	18	26
12 11 0	3	2	25	15	3	19	27
12 14 41	4	3	26	15	50	20	28
12 18 21	5	3	26	16	37	21	29
12 22 2	6	4	27	17	24	22	X
12 25 42	7	5	28	18	11	23	2
12 29 23	8	6	29	18	58	24	3
12 33 4	9	7	30	19	46	25	4
12 36 45	10	8	♐	20	33	26	5
12 40 26	11	9	1	21	21	27	6
12 44 8	12	10	2	22	10	28	7
12 47 50	13	10	3	23	0	≈	8
12 51 32	14	11	3	23	47	m	9
12 55 14	15	12	4	24	36	1	10
12 58 57	16	13	5	25	25	2	11
13 2 40	17	14	6	26	16	3	12
13 6 23	18	15	7	27	5	4	14
13 10 7	19	16	7	27	56	5	15
13 13 51	20	16	8	28	47	6	16
13 17 35	21	17	9	29	38	7	17
13 21 20	22	18	10	0 vf	30	8	18
13 25 6	23	19	11	1	22	9	19
13 28 52	24	20	11	2	14	10	20
13 32 38	25	21	12	3	7	11	22
13 36 25	26	22	13	4	1	12	23
13 40 12	27	22	14	4	55	13	24
13 44 0	28	23	15	5	49	15	25
13 47 48	29	24	16	6	44	16	26
13 51 37	30	25	16	7	39	17	27

Sidereal Time H. M. S.	10 m	11 m	12 ♐	Ascen vf °	'	2 ≈	3 X
13 51 37	0	25	16	7	39	17	27
13 55 27	1	26	17	8	35	18	29
13 59 17	2	27	18	9	32	19	T
14 3 8	3	28	19	10	29	20	1
14 6 59	4	29	20	11	26	22	2
14 10 51	5	29	21	12	24	23	3
14 14 44	6	♐	21	13	23	24	4
14 18 37	7	1	22	14	23	25	6
14 22 31	8	2	23	15	23	27	7
14 26 25	9	3	24	16	24	28	8
14 30 20	10	4	25	17	26	29	10
14 34 16	11	5	26	18	29	X	11
14 38 13	12	6	27	19	32	2	12
14 42 10	13	6	28	20	36	3	13
14 46 8	14	7	29	21	41	4	14
14 50 7	15	8	29	22	47	6	15
14 54 7	16	9	vf	23	53	7	17
14 58 7	17	10	1	25	1	8	18
15 2 8	18	11	2	26	9	10	19
15 6 9	19	12	3	27	18	11	20
15 10 12	20	13	4	28	29	13	21
15 14 15	21	14	5	29	41	14	23
15 18 19	22	15	6	0 ≈	53	15	24
15 22 23	23	16	7	2	6	17	25
15 26 29	24	18	8	3	18	18	26
15 30 35	25	17	9	4	36	20	27
15 34 41	26	18	10	5	53	21	29
15 38 49	27	19	11	7	11	23	♉
15 42 57	28	20	12	8	29	24	1
15 47 6	29	21	13	9	49	25	2
15 51 15	30	22	14	11	10	27	3

Sidereal Time H. M. S.	10 ♐	11 ♐	12 vf	Ascen m °	'	2 X	3 ♉
15 51 15	0	22	14	11	10	27	3
15 55 25	1	23	15	12	32	28	5
15 59 36	2	24	16	13	56	T	6
16 3 48	3	25	17	15	20	1	7
16 8 0	4	26	18	16	46	3	8
16 12 13	5	27	19	18	13	4	9
16 16 26	6	28	20	19	41	6	11
16 20 40	7	29	21	21	11	7	12
16 24 55	8	vf	22	22	42	9	13
16 29 10	9	1	24	24	13	10	14
16 33 26	10	2	25	25	46	12	15
16 37 42	11	3	26	27	21	13	16
16 41 59	12	4	27	28	56	15	18
16 46 16	13	5	28	0 X	33	16	19
16 50 34	14	6	29	2	9	18	20
16 54 52	15	7	≈	3	49	19	21
16 59 10	16	8	2	5	28	21	22
17 3 29	17	9	3	7	9	22	23
17 7 49	18	10	4	8	51	24	24
17 12 9	19	11	5	10	33	25	26
17 16 26	20	12	7	12	16	26	27
17 20 40	21	13	8	14	0	28	28
17 25 9	22	14	9	15	44	29	29
17 29 30	23	15	10	17	30	♉	Π
17 33 51	24	16	12	19	16	2	1
17 38 12	25	17	13	21	2	4	2
17 42 34	26	18	14	22	49	5	3
17 46 55	27	19	16	24	37	6	4
17 51 17	28	20	17	26	24	8	5
17 55 38	29	21	18	28	12	9	7
18 0 0	0	22	20	0	0	10	8

Sidereal Time H. M. S.	10 vf	11 vf	12 ≈	Ascen T °	'	2 ♉	3 Π
18 0 0	0	22	20	0	0	10	8
18 4 22	1	23	21	1	48	12	9
18 8 43	2	24	22	3	36	13	10
18 13 5	3	26	24	5	23	14	11
18 17 26	4	27	25	7	11	16	12
18 21 48	5	28	26	8	58	17	13
18 26 9	6	29	28	10	44	18	14
18 30 30	7	≈	X	12	30	20	15
18 34 51	8	1	1	14	16	21	16
18 39 11	9	2	2	16	2	22	17
18 43 31	10	3	4	17	44	23	18
18 47 51	11	4	5	19	27	25	19
18 52 11	12	6	6	21	9	26	20
18 56 31	13	7	8	22	51	27	21
19 0 50	14	8	9	24	32	28	22
19 5 8	15	9	11	26	11	29	23
19 9 26	16	10	12	27	50	1	24
19 13 44	17	11	14	29	27	2	25
19 18 1	18	12	15	1 ♂	4	3	26
19 22 18	19	14	17	2	39	4	27
19 26 34	20	15	18	4	14	5	28
19 30 50	21	16	20	5	47	6	29
19 35 5	22	17	21	7	19	8	♋
19 39 20	23	18	23	8	49	9	1
19 43 34	24	19	24	10	19	10	2
19 47 47	25	21	26	11	47	11	3
19 52 0	26	22	27	13	14	12	4
19 56 12	27	23	28	14	40	13	5
20 0 24	28	24	T	16	4	14	6
20 4 35	29	25	2	17	28	15	7
20 8 45	30	27	3	18	50	16	8

Sidereal Time H. M. S.	10 ≈	11 ≈	12 T	Ascen ♉ °	'	2 Π	3 ♋
20 8 45	0	27	3	18	50	16	8
20 12 54	1	28	5	20	11	17	9
20 17 3	2	29	6	21	31	19	10
20 21 11	3	X	7	22	49	19	11
20 25 19	4	1	9	24	7	20	12
20 29 26	5	3	10	25	24	21	13
20 33 31	6	4	12	26	39	22	14
20 37 37	7	5	13	27	54	23	14
20 41 41	8	6	15	29	7	24	15
20 45 45	9	8	16	0 Π	19	25	16
20 49 48	10	9	17	1	31	26	17
20 53 51	11	10	19	2	44	27	18
20 57 52	12	11	20	3	51	28	19
21 1 53	13	12	22	4	59	29	20
21 5 53	14	13	23	6	7	♋	21
21 9 53	15	15	24	7	13	1	22
21 13 52	16	16	26	8	19	1	23
21 17 50	17	17	27	9	24	2	23
21 21 47	18	18	28	10	28	3	24
21 25 44	19	20	♉	11	31	4	25
21 29 40	20	21	1	12	34	5	26
21 33 31	21	22	2	13	37	6	27
21 37 29	22	23	3	14	37	7	28
21 41 23	23	24	5	15	37	9	Ω
21 45 16	24	26	6	16	37	9	1
21 49 9	25	27	7	17	36	10	1
21 53 1	26	28	8	18	34	11	2
21 56 52	27	29	10	19	31	11	3
22 0 43	28	T	11	20	28	12	4
22 4 33	29	1	12	21	25	13	4
22 8 23	0	3	13	22	21	14	5

Sidereal Time H. M. S.	10 X	11 T	12 ♉	Ascen Π °	'	2 ♋	3 Ω
22 8 23	0	3	13	22	21	14	5
22 12 12	1	4	14	23	16	14	6
22 16 0	2	5	15	24	11	15	7
22 19 48	3	6	17	25	5	16	8
22 23 35	4	7	18	25	59	17	8
22 27 22	5	8	19	26	53	18	9
22 31 8	6	10	20	27	46	19	10
22 34 54	7	11	21	28	38	20	12
22 38 40	8	12	22	29	30	20	12
22 42 25	9	13	23	0 ♋	22	21	13
22 46 9	10	14	24	1	13	22	14
22 49 56	11	15	25	2	4	23	14
22 53 37	12	16	26	2	55	23	15
22 57 20	13	18	27	3	44	24	16
23 1 3	14	19	28	4	35	24	17
23 4 46	15	20	29	5	24	26	18
23 8 28	16	21	Π	6	13	27	19
23 12 10	17	22	1	7	2	27	20
23 15 52	18	23	2	7	50	28	21
23 19 34	19	24	3	8	39	29	21
23 23 15	20	25	4	9	27	30	22
23 26 56	21	26	5	10	14	Ω	23
23 30 37	22	27	6	11	1	1	24
23 34 18	23	28	7	11	49	2	25
23 37 58	24	♉	8	12	36	3	26
23 41 39	25	1	9	13	23	4	27
23 45 19	26	2	10	14	10	4	27
23 49 0	27	3	11	14	57	5	28
23 52 40	28	4	12	15	43	6	29
23 56 20	29	5	13	16	29	7	m
24 0 0	30	6	14	17	15	8	1

INDEX